Special Admission

The American Campus

Founded by Harold S. Wechsler

The books in the American Campus series explore recent developments and public policy issues in higher education in the United States. Topics of interest include access to college, and college affordability; college retention, tenure and academic freedom; campus labor; the expansion and evolution of administrative posts and salaries; the crisis in the humanities and the arts; the corporate university and for-profit colleges; online education; controversy in sport programs; and gender, ethnic, racial, religious, and class dynamics and diversity. Books feature scholarship from a variety of disciplines in the humanities and social sciences.

For a list of all the titles in the series, please see the last page of the book.

Special Admission

How College Sports Recruitment
Favors White Suburban Athletes

KIRSTEN HEXTRUM

Rutgers University Press

New Brunswick, Camden, and Newark, New Jersey, and London

Library of Congress Cataloging-in-Publication Data
Names: Hextrum, Kirsten, author.
Title: Special admission : how college sports recruitment favors white suburban
    athletes / Kirsten Hextrum.
Description: New Brunswick, New Jersey : Rutgers University Press, 2021. |
    Series: The American campus | Includes bibliographical references and index.
Identifiers: LCCN 2020053770 | ISBN 9781978821200 (paperback) |
    ISBN 9781978821217 (hardcover) | ISBN 9781978821224 (epub) |
    ISBN 9781978821231 (mobi) | ISBN 9781978821248 (pdf)
Subjects: LCSH: College athletes—Recruiting—United States. | College sports—
    Corrupt practices—United States. | Discrimination in higher education—United States. |
    Universities and colleges—United States—Admission—Corrupt practices.
Classification: LCC GV350.5 .H48 2021 | DDC 796.04/3092—dc23
LC record available at https://lccn.loc.gov/2020053770

A British Cataloging-in-Publication record for this book is available from the British Library.

♾ The paper used in this publication meets the requirements of the American National
Standard for Information Sciences—Permanence of Paper for Printed Library Materials,
ANSI Z39.48-1992.

www.rutgersuniversitypress.org

Manufactured in the United States of America

For Shannon and Robin, my first and forever teammates

Contents

Preface

In March 2019 fifty individuals were indicted in Operation Varsity Blues (OVB), a college admission conspiracy led by Rick Singer (Rosen et al., 2019a). Eight years prior, Singer created a "side door" admission scheme in which he leveraged college coaches' and administrators' power to recommend someone for admission. Singer paid these contacts to "designate certain applicants as recruited athletes or as other favored candidates," securing their spot at their preferred university (Smith, 2019, p. 2). Rates varied by institution. Singer charged clients $250,000 for admission to University of Southern California (USC), whereas admission to Georgetown University cost $400,000 (Smith, 2019). Between 2011 and 2018, Singer accepted $25 million from families in exchange for admission (Smith, 2019). While twenty-two parents were indicted, Singer admitted his scheme supported over eight hundred parents (Smith, 2019). The parents were celebrities, wealthy bankers, and chief executives, which drew public and press attention to the scandal.

FBI Agent Laura Smith, lead investigator into Singer's crimes, submitted a 204-page affidavit summarizing the evidence against Singer. In conjunction with federal prosecutors, Smith compiled a case arguing that OVB violated three federal laws: mail fraud, bribery, and racketeering (Rosen et al., 2019a). The court filings against Singer contrast his side-door scheme to the legal process of athletic admission. Smith (2019) writes that athletic admissions permit coaches to recruit athletes who may not otherwise be admitted through the general admission process. Athletic recruitment and admission are positioned as "important assets of the University" that contribute to a "composition of undergraduate classes" (Smith, 2019, p. 9). Furthermore, throughout the affidavit, Smith (2019) presents Singer's clients as illegitimate athletes, whereas the legal process supports the admission of *legitimate* athletes.

As one of the few scholars who study college athletic admissions (other notable studies include Eckstein, 2017; Shulman and Bowen, 2001), reporters contacted me for comment pertaining to the OVB indictments. Most asked if I had found instances of fraud or bribery in my studies of athletic admissions. I said no and instead described the similarities between my findings and Singer's actions. I directed reporters' attention to how Singer's scheme does not deviate from but instead parallels legal athletic admission.

Viewing Singer's actions as deviant assumes that the current athletic admissions process operates in a fair, transparent, and/or equitable fashion. Contrasting frames such as deviant versus fair and fake versus real entrench dichotomous and oppositional thinking. If Singer's actions are wrong, then legal athletic admissions cannot use his strategies. If Singer used his knowledge, connections, and clients' money to penetrate athletic admissions, then athletic admissions never use one's knowledge, connections, and money. I suggested that we should reject such frames and instead see the parallels and similarities between Singer's actions and the actions taken by successfully recruited athletes. Singer is not a deviant; Singer is a well-informed insider who knew how the athletic admission process works.

Singer acted criminally because he used *direct* capital exchanges, also known as bribery. Current federal law disallows public officials to receive money in exchange for goods—in this case college admission (Smith, 2019). No laws prohibit *indirect* capital exchanges in college admissions. Families can invest an unlimited amount in a child to prepare them for college admission.[1] Researchers have continuously shown that college admissions reward and favor those who can invest monies into a youth over their life span to improve their odds for university acceptance (e.g., Davies and Guppy, 1997; Espenshade and Radford, 2009; Guinier, 2015; Khan, 2012; Lareau, 2015; McDonough, 1997; Rivera, 2016; Shamash, 2018; Stevens, 2009; Weis et al., 2014). Families paying for-profit college advising companies to help their children gain an edge in admission is one such investment. Companies like Ivy Coach charge families up to $1.5 million total or $300 per hour for private sessions to train children in all areas of college preparation including course selection and completion, standardized test-taking strategies, and admission essays (Goldstein and Healy, 2019). Singer ran one such legal for-profit advising company, where he developed the knowledge, skills, and connections to create a successful and illegal bribery scheme.

Throughout this book I argue that college athletic admissions require and reward families who can make indirect capital investments in their children. Developing the athletic talent required for admission requires individual, familial, and community investments. These investments are legal and advantage those who can afford them—white suburban athletes.

In following the details of OVB, I thought Singer's plot was redundant. Universities have constructed an admission system that grants coaches unilateral discretion to evaluate athletic merit. Famed designer Mossimo Giannulli and his wife, actress Lori Loughlin, pled guilty to paying Singer and USC $500,000 to admit their daughters as rowers. Their daughters' applications falsely claimed they rowed for an exclusive private club located in the expensive housing area of western Los Angeles (Rosen et al., 2019b). Such illegal efforts are unnecessary for athletic admission. In *Special Admission* I share insights from successfully recruited college athletes who lacked athletic merit and had little or no experience in their college sport prior to admission. These athletes and their families did not directly pay for admission but instead indirectly purchased access over their lifetime by living in exclusive suburbs, attending well-funded schools, and forging social connections. In this way, Singer helped celebrities look down the social rung and use their wealth to expediate the practices and investments done daily across U.S. suburbs. OVB and the findings I portray here showcase the outsized influence white suburbia has on American institutions.

Prosecuting celebrities for conspiring and corrupting a fair athletic admission system makes for a good story. Placing Singer and his clients on trial presents athletic admission as a meritocratic system that prohibits individuals from using their wealth and status to gain special access. Yet criminalizing the actions in OVB is a sleight of hand. Our attention is drawn to the shuffling cards, and we miss that the game was rigged from the start. Parents can purchase admission for athletes, it just occurs over a life span.

Special Admission

Introduction

In December 2016 I completed my forty-seventh interview with a college athlete for this book. My initial analysis indicated that college sport recruitment and admission favored white, middle-class athletes.[1] That same month news feeds were saturated with a more familiar college sports story. Caylin Moore, a football player at Texas Christian University, had received the 2017 Rhodes scholarship. News reports used his biography to highlight the common-sense story that college sports is an upward mobility vehicle for low-income Black men.

Moore, a Black man from a Los Angeles "hood" (Rittenberg, 2016, para. 22), survived physical abuse, economic instability, and life in a "gang-riddled" neighborhood (Osborne, 2016, para. 14) to become first a college football player, then a Fulbright and Rhodes scholar, then a professional athlete. Dogged reporters uncovered how Moore's mother raised him on her own while surviving sexual and physical abuse, working multiple jobs, attending night school, and coaching a youth football team (Buck, 2017; Martin, 2017; Osborne, 2016; Rittenberg, 2016).

The conditions of Moore's life narrated in media accounts inform the public's understanding of how society operates. In an ABC News article, one reporter explained what Moore endured to become a college athlete:

> Moore's family struggled financially. Dinner often came from the Dollar Menu at McDonald's or Carl's Jr. There were times when Moore's mother didn't have enough money to feed all three of her kids. [Moore explains how he dealt with hunger.] "I would just do pushups to take the pain from my stomach to the pain in my arms." [Moore] spent most of his childhood sharing a bed with his mother and two siblings, living in a house without hot water on the

1

crime-ridden border of Compton and Carson, south of Los Angeles. He collected cans and bottles to buy football cleats, blossomed in Snoop Dogg's youth league and went on to play in high school and college. He has been a Fulbright scholar and, yes, a campus custodian. At TCU he majors in economics, minors in math and sociology, and carries a GPA of 3.934. (Rittenberg, 2016, paras. 3, 12)

In December 2016 the public first learned about Caylin Moore, but it was not the first time the public heard a story like Moore's. The details recounted reflect an American society that easily accepts the extreme suffering of certain populations. In these two paragraphs we learn how Moore's family endured violence, under- and unemployment, and food and housing insecurity. The realities Moore survived arise from centuries-long U.S. state policies and practices encompassing all facets of social life—education, housing, transportation, and employment—that have created, exploited, and maintained segregated and chronically deprived Black communities (Crenshaw, 1988; Fields, 2001; Harris, 1993; Kurashige, 2008; Ladson-Billings, 1994, 2003; Lassiter, 2012; Leonardo, 2004, 2009; Massey and Denton, 1998; Mills, 2003; Roediger, 2017; Rothstein, 2017; Vaught, 2011, 2017).

This narrative laden with suffering becomes digestible because Moore's family, by virtue of their race, gender, and class positions, is constructed as deserving their fate. As Joy James (1996) explains, the state enables "the plague of criminality, deviancy, immortality, and corruption" to become "embodied in the black [body]" as "both sexual and social pathology are branded by skin color (as well as by gender and sexual orientation)" (p. 26). Since the United States became a formalized government, the state has perpetuated the notion that those who are born into poverty and/or born into bodies not seen as white and as male are inherently corrupt, deficient, and suspect, and therefore deserve their lower social position (Crenshaw, 1988; Du Bois, 1935; Harris, 1993; James, 1996; McClintock, 1995; Mills, 1997, 2003). By creating and supporting such narratives, the state bears no responsibility for ameliorating the chronic and historic conditions of race, gender, and economic inequality.

Moore's story also presents the acceptable ways he—and those like him—can challenge and later cure his suffering. James (1996) writes that the concerted effort to link poverty and skin color legitimates the expansion of state intervention: "The dreams and desires of a society and state will be centered on the control of the black body" (pp. 26–27). Stories of gang violence, poverty, and hunger justify expanded state surveillance and control of Black communities. We know from scholars of the white supremacist carceral state (e.g., James, 1996; Shabazz, 2015; Vaught, 2017) that if Moore challenged his conditions by stealing bread from a local grocery store to feed his family, he would become ensnared in a profit-seeking state prison system and labeled as a justifiably imprisoned social deviant. By virtue of his subject position, Moore is presented with a narrow, improbable (but not impossible) pathway to avoid imprisonment and leave his community: pursue the state-sponsored sports path to college.

Locating the State in College Sports

The pathway to college via sport is "state-sponsored" because the athletic merit universities desire requires access to spaces shaped by state actions. I refer to *the* state as a singular object to distill what political philosopher Wendy Brown (1992) describes as the "unbounded terrain of power and techniques . . . capable of tremendous economic, political, and ecological effects" that characterize how we encounter political repression and social control (p. 12). Theorizing the state, and the effects of state power on society, goes beyond the visible expressions of state control such as the U.S. Constitution. These formal, rigid, and visible forms of state power (e.g., the U.S. military) emerge in times of obvious public threats like international conflict and more easily gain public consent to their presence and occupation (Brown, 1992, 1995, 2019).

More perplexing is how the state secures and maintains public consent to its continued and constant intrusion into the private lives of individuals during times of peace. The contemporary form of state power relies upon an "ensemble of discourses, rules, and practices, cohabiting in limited, tension-ridden, [and] often contradictory relation with one another" (Brown, 1992, p. 12). This more insidious and expansive articulation of the state requires coordination with other institutions that may not immediately appear as state-run, sanctioned, or propagated, but still partially or completely achieve the goals of the state (Brown, 1992, 1995, 2019; Crenshaw, 1988; Gramsci, 1971; Harris, 1993). Cultural institutions like sports, schools, and families build collective agreement to the existing social order and further the state's presence in our daily lives (Brown, 1992).

Locating the presence and goals of the state exposes the breadth and depth of social control and domination in American institutions. The state coordinates across and entwines various forms of power including race, class, gender, sexuality, nationality, and religion. Distilling state power to one mode (the military) or one form (class) inaccurately portrays the workings of inequity. Tracing the presence of the state and inequity in college sports requires dialectical and dialogical approaches across varied scholarly traditions. Throughout the book I interlace insights from scholars who have documented the colonial, white supremacist, patriarchal, capitalist, and neoliberal aims of the state to broadly understand what social, cultural, political, and economic conditions facilitate the unequal conditions under which athletes ascend to college. I contextualize each theoretical tradition when it first arises. Another quick look at Moore's route to college shows why such a varied and layered approach to the state is needed.

Moore's story illustrates the *formal, relational,* and *removal* techniques of state power. Moore's community, South-Central Los Angeles, is the product of *formal* state legislative action. The prerogative power to pass and enforce laws reflects that which makes a state a state (Brown, 1992). In the mid-twentieth century, California passed redlining laws that prohibited racial minorities from living in white suburban communities. There were no corollary prohibitions on where white people could live. For these laws to achieve their intended effect—racially segregated housing—the state relied upon white citizens to choose to live in white areas over more racially integrated ones. Here, the state used its *relational* powers or partnering with elite or privileged groups to enact its will (Brown, 1995; Crenshaw, 1988; Gramsci, 1971). One way white people were convinced to move to the suburbs was through the *removal* of the state. The suburbs' lack of visible policing—a *formal* state presence that circumscribes Black and Brown neighborhoods—signaled to white people that these areas were safe (Shabazz, 2015).

Moore accessed football through the interrelationship of *formal, relational,* and *removal* modes of state power. The state's *removal* of safe and accessible community and educational opportunities for Moore forced him to pursue another pathway. Despite the media's overemphasis on Moore's individual will-power, even the slightest knowledge of football should give a shrewd reader the impression that Moore cannot become a college-level football player by doing push-ups in his room at night. The skills, expertise, and knowledge required to learn a technical game like football necessitate coaches, facilities, equipment, and teammates. In Moore's case, he received said benefits not through a public school team but instead through philanthropy. Rapper and reality television star Snoop Dogg started a nonprofit football program in Moore's area. This program reflects the *formal* and *relational* aspects of the state as the state legally grants wealthy individuals, like Snoop Dogg, tax benefits for starting charitable organizations. Partnering with elites once again frees the state from addressing inequality. Instead, the state can point to noblesse oblige as the solution. The success of someone like Moore emerging from South-Central solidifies the state's position that even those from state-neglected areas can achieve upward mobility. We also learn that sports create college access. The nonprofit organization gave Moore the skills desired by college football coaches—coaches whom the state authorizes to offer university admission. We learn that someone with the right work ethic, stamina, and commitment can use this chance to improve their social standing by attending college. These details are further reduced into a commonsense idea that college sports provide a pathway of opportunity for low-income, racially marginalized men.

The Common Sense of Mobility

Despite its claim to be otherwise, the U.S. state is an ideological engine (Apple, 2004; Crenshaw, 1988; Du Bois, 1935; Giroux, 1981, 2014). In partnership with digital and analog media platforms, the state has marketed the narrative that America is an open and upwardly mobile society (Apple, 2004; Collins, 2005; Johnson, 2014; Leonard, 2017; Messner, 2002). This is why Moore's story of ascendance is believable—we have heard it before. The details of his narrative are confirmed and amplified across other "true" accounts of sport and mobility. Sport, and American football in particular, is portrayed in films like *The Blind Side* and television shows like *Last Chance U* as a setting where individuals with the right grit, work ethic, and physicality can improve their social standing.

Antonio Gramsci's (1971) notion of the social "common sense" explains how social narratives bolster state power and control. The "common sense" results from the coalescing of disparate narratives disseminated across diverse institutions into "self-evident truths" that explain how society operates (Crehan, 2016, p. 1). Capitalist democracies like the United States can use overt force, like the military, to control the public, but this tactic risks public dissent and uprising. To control through consent building, the state extends its reach into other institutions that shape public opinion such as education, sports, media, religion, and families. Consent is achieved as individuals interact with institutions. These interactions are as innocuous as a white suburban man sharing an article about Moore with his fantasy football league or as contrived as that same man sending his children to public schools that teach youth that America is a fair and free society where anyone can excel. A "common sense" emerges through these interactions uniting sports fans and elementary school students under a shared sense of how society operates. Gramsci termed this process *achieving cultural hegemony*.

Importantly, common sense lives beyond the ephemeral realm of beliefs and ideas. Scholars have tracked how institutions and groups that support and propagate the common sense are rewarded with greater state benefits (Apple, 2004; Brown, 2005, 2019; Crenshaw, 1988; Fabricant and Fine, 2015; Giroux, 2014; Harvey, 2005; McLaren, 2014; Vaught, 2011, 2017; Weis and Fine, 2012, 2013). In this way, the common sense adopts material and structural dimensions, and motivates others to similarly adhere. As chapter 1 discusses, the largest and most powerful governing body of college sports, the National Collegiate Athletic Association (NCAA), is one such organization that receives state benefits in exchange for supporting the common sense.

No other nation uses state support to integrate elite athletics into educational institutions. The NCAA, a nonprofit organization, oversees the relationship between school and sport. Their mission is to "support learning through sports by integrating athletics and higher education to enrich the college experience of student-athletes" (NCAA, 2015, para. 2). Like other arms of the state (e.g., military or taxes), the NCAA is not a singular thing but a collection of member institutions and individuals. Through its diffuse organizational membership (discussed in forthcoming chapters), the NCAA's reach and the state's power expand.

The NCAA's nonprofit status emanates from their mission and objective to provide educational opportunities through athletic participation (Smith, 2011; Southall and Staurowsky, 2013). In March 2018, the NCAA issued a press release titled "NCAA Recruiting Facts: College Sports Create a Pathway to Opportunity for Student-Athletes." The document used aggregate numbers such as the number of college athletes (492,000), the total financial support given to college athletes ($3 billion in athletic scholarships available), and the academic successes of college athletes (87 percent graduation rate) to portray the NCAA as an upward mobility avenue (NCAA, 2018). This press release shapes the commonsense notion that sports are upward mobility vehicles. The public statements do not say who truly benefits from college athletics: white, middle-class athletes.

The "common sense" also disguises, minimizes, and erases alternative views of how society functions. Celebrating sports as a pathway to opportunity disguises two social realities. First, we do not see how pursuing sports for mobility harms Black communities. Harry Edwards, a sociologist and organizer of the 1968 Black athlete Olympic revolt, authored the foremost critique of the premise that college sports function as a mobility engine for Black Americans. Edwards, and a legion of later scholars (e.g., Beamon, 2008, 2010; Coakley, 2015; Cooper, 2012; Eitzen, 2016; Harrison, 2000; Hawkins, 2013; Sack and Staurowsky, 1998), demonstrated the "infinitesimal" odds of someone making it to college and later professional sports by comparing the numbers of athletes at each level of sport: youth to high school to college to professional. In 2019, a boy's high school basketball player had at 1 percent chance and a boy's high school football player had a 2.8 percent chance of transitioning to a Division I team (NCAA, 2019). Of those who became college athletes, 1.2 percent of men's basketball and 1.6 percent of men's football players were drafted to the professional leagues (NCAA, 2019). The miniscule odds for athletic advancement indicate that professional sports remains an elusive pathway for mobility. Edwards argued that sport success requires a unilateral focus on athletics to the detriment of developing more viable skills. Thus, the 99 percent of youth who focused on sport and did not become a college or professional athlete are left with skills undervalued and unrecognized in employment.

Edwards's critique lives on in today's research on college athlete exploitation. This scholarship reveals how athletic departments recruit students who are academically underprepared for college coursework, provide students few meaningful opportunities to explore their educational interests, steer students into majors in which they have little interest, offer few to no opportunities for professional development outside of athletics, and isolate students in athlete-only environments (Beamon, 2008, 2010; Eitzen, 2016; Hawkins, 2013; Jayakumar and Comeaux, 2016; Sack and Staurowsky, 1998). The culminating effects leave few chances for a college athlete to access and activate the educational opportunities promised in exchange for their athletic labor. When we celebrate Moore's story, we disguise the harm done to those who pursued the same path but never became Rhodes scholars or professional athletes.

The notion of sports as a mobility engine conceals another truth about intercollegiate athletics. The focus on the few Black men who do use sports for mobility obscures how the majority of college athletes are white and middle-class. This reality receives scarce research attention and is *Special Admission*'s central focus. College sports do offer mobility—lateral, not upward.

The State's Pathway to College

The commonsense narrative regarding sports and upward mobility assumes athletics are accessible in ways other institutions, like politics, are not. The uniquely American phenomenon of college sports—the combination of elite sports and elite education—provides double the mobility opportunity. An athlete without the required academic merits can use her athletic merits for college admission. While competing for her college team, she can develop the athletic skills to pursue post-college professional or Olympic sports and develop the academic skills to pursue white-collar employment. College sports thus provide an alternative educational path—a way in which athletes can trade their athletic merit to upgrade their academic credentials.

Special Admission offers the counternarrative to the notion that college sports provide mobility. The reason most college athletes are white and middle-class is because athletic merit is not objective. Measures of merit undergird the belief that the United States is organized as a meritocracy. Meritocracy—"the greatest American lie" (Vaught, 2017, p. 13)—cements the notion that success is individually earned and the resulting social hierarchies are just. In truth, athletic merit is a cultural construct that varies across time, place, and sport. To develop the athletic competencies sporting institutions value, someone must access familial, communal, and economic resources. These resources all flow through the state directly or indirectly.

State Institutions: Reproduction at the Junction

Positioning college sport as a state institution permits inquiry into larger questions about power reproduction or the role social and cultural sites play in maintaining the structural divides that define the nation. Bowles and Gintis

(1976) produced a well-cited yet controversial study of the relationship between capitalism, the state, and schools. In *Schooling in Capitalist America*, they argued that the goal of state-sponsored schools is to ensure the maintenance and expansion of capitalism. Schools do so by providing the technological know-how to produce capitalist innovation and by producing a fragmented and amendable labor base. Their correspondence theory of schooling linked one's incoming class status to one's educational and employment outcomes. Schools, they argued, take working-class kids and prepare them for working-class jobs. They concluded only limited mobility exists in our schools, despite American narratives selling the contrary.

Bowles and Gintis's analysis missed the opportunity to link capitalist reproduction and racial inequality. They positioned unequal race-based schooling and social outcomes as *products of* capitalism. They concluded that since people of color are more often working-class, they will encounter a school system that trains them for working-class jobs. Bowles and Gintis also did not answer questions like *why* people of color are more often working-class or *why* working-class people would continue to attend schools if they are so misaligned with their social interests.

Forty-years prior, W.E.B. Du Bois (1935) addressed these questions ignored by Bowles and Gintis. In *Black Reconstruction* Du Bois documented how the state secures support for capitalism by offering material and psychological rewards to poor and working-class white people by elevating their racial position. Du Bois's insights have carried on in current studies of how state-run schools achieve unique forms of racism that cannot be collapsed into class and codetermining forms of economic/racial oppression that cannot be disaggregated. Contemporary researchers have identified how the state uses schools to perpetuate the racial order, one in which white people receive full civic benefits as they are socialized to become the leaders of the racial hierarchy; encouraged to form bonds with one another, not with students of color; elevated in the curriculum as white stories, logics, and narratives are centered; and rewarded materially through tests, assignments, and grading schemes designed in their worldviews (Carter et al., 2017; Donnor, 2011; Dumas, 2011; Gillborn, 2005; Green and Gooden, 2016; Haycock, 2004; Heilig and Darling-Hammond, 2008; Knoester and Au, 2017; Ladson-Billings, 1994, 2003; Leonardo, 2004, 2009; Mills, 2003; Orfield and Frankenberg, 2013; Rothstein, 2017; Vaught, 2011, 2017).

Studies into state-sponsored reproduction—how the workings of the state achieve intergenerational social divides—pose several challenges for researchers. As Michael Apple (2004) explains, researchers can overdetermine the relationship one state site plays in reproduction, such as elevating schools as *the* site and minimizing the role of other institutions like families. Paul Willis (1977) critiqued reproduction approaches for portraying students as agentless and unaware of their fate. Instead, Willis's research on working-class lads in British public schools found that lower-income students knew the schools were against them and intentionally rebelled in ways that sealed their fate in working-class jobs. If they were to remain working-class, they wanted to do so on their own terms. Further, reproduction has struggled to capture the interplay of multiple power structures and often reduces to elevating one—race, class, *or* gender—in the analysis providing an incomplete view of how domination truly manifests intersectionally (Crenshaw, 1988, 1991, 1992).

These criticisms have not deterred scholars from tracing the state's role in reproduction. Instead, new approaches retain the essence of the theory—a mapping of how the state coordinates across multiple institutions to preserve existing forms of power—but in ways that attune to the limitations of reductive, class-centric, and deterministic accounts. One of the major shifts in these updated accounts of power and reproduction is to examine how privilege is accumulated and conferred. Studies have uncovered how reproduction is not a passive or automatic process but instead requires active labor on the part of elites to activate and secure their benefits. Middle-class and elite families galvanize their privilege by marshaling their current capital and status and investing in new forms of it to advance within the education system (Calarco, 2014, 2018; Demerath, 2009; Kaufman, 2005; Khan, 2012; Lareau, 2011, 2015; Rivera, 2016; Weis et al., 2014). Schools accept and reward the additional investments by individuals, families, and communities in their offspring's educational outcomes. Schools provide these children with greater curriculum opportunities such as gifted and advanced programs, with more teacher time, higher grades, and more knowledge about the college admission process (Anyon, 1980; Calarco, 2014, 2018; Kaufman, 2005; Lareau, 2011; Weis et al., 2014). Students in these environments take for granted their individual, social, and community advantages and view their educational success as earned and deserved (Demerath, 2009; Khan, 2012; Weis et al., 2014). Simultaneously, schools penalize students who do not make these additional investments through less teacher time, lower grades, and increased disciplinary consequences (Carter et al., 2017; Kunesh and Noltemeyer, 2019; Morris, 2005; Vaught, 2011; Wun, 2016). The dynamic interplay between students, families, and communities with dividends to spend on school and schools confirming these dividends exponentially extends educational benefits to already advantaged groups.

The economic investments middle-class and elite families make in their children's educational futures have specific racial consequences. Across all features of American life, including housing, schools, political affiliations, employment, and sports, "whites are making life choices in a way that generally maintains and reproduces their domination and privilege" (Mills, 2003, p. 170). When white people purchase houses in majority-white suburbs with high-ranking public schools, they buy a future filled with white people living, studying, working, and playing in majority-white environments. White people are told they are entitled to safety and comfort in these spaces and are not required to question how and why the state continues to protect these entitlements. Working-class white people who are denied access to these economically exclusive enclaves and networks still consent to their existence. Working-class white laborers still receive greater material benefits than working-class Black laborers such as higher hourly wages, greater benefits, and union membership (Harris, 1993; Mills, 2003; Roediger, 2017; Rothstein, 2017). These benefits have flowed to white people due to their racial, not economic, standing. While these material assets are meager compared to those higher up the economic ladder, working-class white people have received and therefore may continue to invest in the benefits of adhering to a racial order.

College Admission: The Reproductive Prize

Reproduction approaches to education focus on the "pivotal" moments in youth and young adults' lives within schools that secure their social fate (Lareau, 2015, p. 4). School policies related to reading group assignments, testing, tracking, discipline, and course offerings create junctures to differently route students (Apple, 2004; Carter et al., 2017; Heilig and Darling-Hammond, 2008; McLaren, 2014; Oakes, 2005; Vaught, 2011, 2017). Concurrently, continuous and "small" moments such as college-educated parents providing nightly homework support to their children and coaching them to seek this support when in the classroom create cumulative education advantages (Calarco, 2014, 2018; Lareau, 2011, 2015). Thus, "academic achievement"—high grades and test scores that poise someone for college matriculation—is not intrinsic but instead reflects the "uneven rewards" doled out by "dominant institutions" to entrench existing class and race hierarchies (Lareau, 2015, p. 1).

College admissions is *the* pivotal education moment. Higher education promises an advanced curriculum, not present in K–12 education, with greater economic returns. College graduates are less likely to be unemployed, are paid higher wages, and are less likely to lose their jobs during economic downturns compared to those with a high school degree (Hoynes et al., 2012; Pew Research Center, 2014). A college degree on average produces over $830,000 more income over a lifetime than a high school degree (Daly and Bengali, 2014). College graduates also report higher rates of job satisfaction and are more likely to receive health and retirement benefits through their employer than are high school graduates (Pew Research Center, 2014). The admission process constricts access to college benefits.

As chapter 1 explores, for most of U.S. history, colleges limited access to only elite white men. Over the past sixty years these barriers have eroded. Today, the United States has more people in college than ever before as higher education institutions are educating twenty million students (NCES, 2018). These enrollment numbers represent a 100 percent increase from 1970 and a 30 percent increase in undergraduate enrollment since 2000 (NCES, 2018).

Not all groups have equally benefited from expanding higher education admissions. Asian-identified individuals have the highest rates of educational attainment: 53.9 percent of Asian-, 32.8 percent of white-, 22.5 percent of Black, and 15.5 percent of Hispanic-identified individuals have a college degree (Ryan and Bauman, 2016). In 2010, women of all racial categories became more likely than men to have a college degree (Ryan and Bauman, 2016). Since 1970, low-income college-going rates have risen from 10 to 20 percent. But higher income families have made even greater gains in college access. College-going rates for children in families from the top 25 percent of earners have risen from 40 to 80 percent (Piketty, 2014, p. 339). Furthermore, as women and as Asian-, Black-, and Hispanic-identified individuals enter higher education, they do not receive the same benefits as elite white men. As just one measure, expanded higher education access has yet to yield equal pay for women and racial minorities compared to their white male counterparts with similar education credentials (Hegewisch et al., 2019).

As historically disenfranchised groups fight for adequate access to and outcomes from higher education, these institutions redirect social change. Large-scale studies into the background characteristics of incoming college students show entrenched patterns related to race and income that shape college access. Factors such as where someone is born, what education level their caregivers achieved, and what state rank their high school achieved are strong measures of college access (Bowen and Bok, 1998; Bowen et al., 2009; Davies and Guppy, 1997; Dixon-Román, 2017; Haveman and Smeeding, 2006; Horn and Nunez, 2000; Ishitani, 2003; Jackson and Kurlaender, 2014; Teranishi and Parker, 2010; Terenzini et al., 1996). These studies show the lasting insights of Du Bois (1935) and Bowles and Gintis (1976) and the powerful connections between one's race, class, neighborhood, and parental education level and college admission. Do not conclude from the overrepresentation of white and Asian students who attend high-ranking schools and come from middle-income neighborhoods and have college-educated parents that they are more deserving of a college education. Rather, trends represent the many ways that college admission is designed to favor and select students with particular characteristics.

Shifting the Goal Post. One of the ways the state maintains inequality in college admissions while simultaneously expanding access beyond the privileged elite is through creating a system steeped in organizational complexity. Davies and Guppy (1997) characterize higher education as "a complicated mosaic, a richly differentiated tapestry, revealing a hierarchically arrayed system of institutions and programs" (p. 1417). The United States has approximately 4,300 degree-granting postsecondary institutions (Moody, 2019).

Within this mosaic are open-access two-year community and technical colleges; nonselective regional universities; selective public, private, and religious institutions; and highly selective elite public and private institutions. College selectivity—whether one must apply, and the expenses, rigor, complexity, and competitiveness associated with the application—has become a cultural and economic good, allowing individuals to differentially trade their degrees for greater or lesser social rewards (Davies and Guppy, 1997). The college admission process, therefore, is a gatekeeping enterprise, or a system designed to "control access to valued social positions" (Stuber et al., 2011, p. 431). Only those who can pass through the gate gain access to the valuable goods different institutions offer (Stuber et al., 2011).

Highly selective elite universities, the pinnacle of the higher education system, offer attendees higher graduation rates, greater placement of students in top graduate programs, and better labor advantages (McDonough, 1997; Weis and Fine, 2012). Those who hold the upper echelon of private- and public-sector occupations are predominately graduates of elite universities (Binder et al., 2016). Elite institutions are much less likely than open-access colleges to function as upward mobility institutions. Smaller, regional, technical two- or four-year colleges more often serve first-generation college students (Bowen et al., 2009; Haveman and Smeeding, 2006). A recent study into 342 elite public universities found that a third of students at these institutions come from families in the top income bracket, whereas 8 percent come from the families in the lowest income bracket (Halikias and Reeves, 2017). Put differently, 92 percent of students at elite public schools come from middle- and upper-income families and receive the school's corresponding rewards.

The higher education application process evaluates one's academic performance in two major areas: high school grades and scores on college entrance exams. These measures evaluate one's past academic competencies as a measure for college readiness. As Lani Guinier (2015) explains, measures of academic merit emerged in the early twentieth century to wrestle away the stronghold elites had on college access and, in turn, U.S. society. Yet their efforts to create and implement standardized tests to measure college readiness and academic merit "succumbed to a Trojan Horse" (Guinier, 2015, p. 17). The nationwide adoption and standardization of the SAT was forged through eugenics science that favored the knowledge and disposition of American WASPs. A century later, the SAT's own research proves it is a better measure of one's access to wealth than of one's college readiness (Dixon-Román, 2017; Guinier, 2015; Patterson et al., 2009; Patterson and Mattern, 2011, 2012, 2013).

Linking K–12 grades to college access is also a Trojan horse. Hiding within the façade of the merit associated with high school grades are a myriad of state policies related to curricula, testing, discipline, tracking, teacher training, and resource allocation that target and disenfranchise low-income students and students of color while simultaneously elevating and benefiting middle- and upper-income and white students (Anyon, 1980; Apple, 2004; Au, 2008; Calarco, 2014, 2018; Dixon-Román, 2017; Donnor, 2011; Dumas, 2011; Gillborn, 2005; Ladson-Billings, 1994, 2003; Lareau, 2011, 2015; Oakes, 2005; Orfield and Frankenberg, 2013; Roscigno, 1998; Vaught, 2011, 2017). Since higher education admission utilizes racially and economically unequal K–12 systems, college matriculation reflects these same patterns (Espenshade and Radford, 2009; Guinier, 2015; McDonough, 1997; Weis et al., 2014).

Anti–affirmative action state laws and Supreme Court decisions have also hamstrung universities' abilities to take proactive admission efforts to redress the racial inequality built within the K–12 system. Current case law says universities can consider race in their admission policies only if its use is narrowly tailored and if it presents a compelling state interest (Donnor, 2011). A program is "narrowly tailored" if no alternative race-neutral approaches exist (Spece and Yokum, 2015). A program rises to a "compelling state interest" if evidence exists of past or continuing racial discrimination "by an administrative, judicial, or legislative proceeding that necessitates the remedy" (Hendrickson, 2001, p. 121). These legal decisions have led to a color-blind approach to civil rights law that assumes institutionalized racism was eradicated and therefore any active attention to race is considered discriminatory and unworkable (Donnor, 2011; Hendrickson, 2001). These judicial logics uphold centuries-long legal opinions that protect white people's rights to maintain and benefit from their overrepresentation in all areas of public life (Harris, 1993). A wealth of research demonstrates that proactive measures that force white people to relinquish their centuries of accumulated racial benefits are needed to undo the systemic workings of white supremacy in our public institutions (e.g., Donnor, 2011; Dumas, 2011; Harris, 1993; Vaught, 2011, 2017). Race-neutral approaches maintain the status quo of white dominance in education.

College Admission Warfare. One of the peculiarities emerging from anti–affirmative action movements is that white people contend they are currently disadvantaged in college admissions and believe they need *more*, not less, protection from the state (Donnor, 2011; Dumas, 2011; Harris, 1993). Broader global state (in)actions over the past forty years have eroded the labor prospects, heightened the cost of living and education, and deepened the overall economic anxieties for white lower- and middle-income earners (Jury et al., 2017; Weis et al., 2014; Weis and Fine, 2012). The rewards associated with elite universities center college admission in the fight for the scarce resources created through these global shifts. In the 1970s, 28 percent of U.S. jobs required a college degree (Jury et al., 2017). In 2010, the share of U.S. jobs requiring a college degree grew to 59 percent, and in 2018, grew again to 70 percent (Blumenstyk, 2020). Just before the onset of the COVID-19 global pandemic, 91 percent of new jobs added to the labor market required a college degree (Goldstein, 2018). As of publication, with the pandemic still raging, the link between economic security and college education seems stronger than ever. The U.S. Bureau of Labor and Statistics (2020a) found that 67.5 percent of college graduates compared to 24.5 percent of high school graduates and 10.5 percent of non-high school graduates could work from home. The ability to work from home shielded college graduates from exposure to a deadly virus and job loss. Only 4.2 percent of college graduates compared to 7.7 percent of high school graduates were unemployed in November 2020 (U.S. Bureau of Labor and Statistics, 2020b). The pandemic also provided uneven economic restoration chances. Economists tracked a K-shaped recovery in which jobs and industries favoring those with a college education, like engineering, technology, and health care, grew while jobs and industries available to those without college degrees, like hospitality, childcare, and travel remained stagnant (Jones, 2021).

Rather than channeling economic anxieties to build a movement to destabilize global racial economic exploitation, white working- and middle-class communities redouble their efforts to retain preferential access to education (Khan, 2012; Weis et al., 2014; Weis and Fine, 2012). This results in a pattern of *race* and *class warfare* (Du Bois, 1935; Harris, 1993; Mills, 1997, 2003; Weis et al., 2014) in which privileged communities marshal and weaponize their accumulated economic and social resources to protect and defend their standing. This warfare is waged by defending routes to elite universities (Guinier, 2015; Khan, 2012; Rivera, 2016; Shamash, 2018; Weis et al., 2014; Weis and Fine, 2012).

Class and race warfare can manifest in obvious larger ways such as white people supporting an anti–affirmative action state law or graduates from elite colleges using their influence to raise tuition (in spite of ever-expanding endowments at selective universities) and admission standards and overvalue the potential promise for a family's capacity to donate (Piketty, 2014). More often, this warfare occurs in the smaller moments of cultural transmission (Lareau, 2015). Navigating the elaborate state-sponsored system of education requires "cultural knowledge" to negotiate the formal (e.g., publicized deadlines) and informal (e.g., norms about what is expected in the application materials) rules of the institution (Lareau, 2015). The competition and scarcity built within the system of college admission reward those with the knowledge, time, planning, and discipline to navigate and execute the admission process (Lareau, 2011, 2015; McDonough, 1997; Weis et al., 2014). As one example, students can improve their SAT scores through the "shadow curriculum," or doing activities outside of school, like private tutoring, prep classes, and workbooks (Buchman et al., 2010). Students from higher-income families use these testing services at higher rates, providing one reason for the connection between class and SAT scores (Buchman et al., 2010).

Collectively, studies into the economic and cultural transmission of privilege examine how members of dominant groups use their economic capital to shape higher education access. The reproduction of privilege is neither guaranteed nor universal. Upward mobility, as in the case of Caylin Moore, does occur. Weis et al. (2014) and Khan (2012) found elite high schools and colleges admit a small number of low-income students of color. These students become evidence that education is meritocratic and finds the best students regardless of their race or class position. In this way, elite groups exploit the success of Black people like Moore to maintain the status quo.

Tracing the complexities and contradictions of reproduction requires a "triple vision" to concurrently scrutinize three elements. First, we must focus on the larger moments of state action that create seemingly intractable conditions of inequality. Second, we must examine the smaller moments of how individuals enact the will of the state and work to secure and maintain elevated social positions. And third, we must scrutinize the exceptions.

Special Admission: Athletic Merit and College Access

The studies reviewed above describe the varied social, cultural, and economic processes and practices that position students to earn the *right* academic credentials to gain college access. Athletic admission disrupts these previously established modes of admission by favoring athletic over academic credentials. Chapter 1 looks at the history of intercollegiate athletics that began in Ivy League universities in the mid-1800s. The students who oversaw these matches debated whether athletes should emerge from the student body or be brought to campus to improve a sports team (Smith, 1988; Thelin, 2011). Today, the NCAA permits universities to bring students to campus for the specific purpose of competing for their teams (NCAA, 2017). Division I NCAA institutions use athletic recruiting and admissions different from their standard student enrollment process. In scrutinizing these policies, researchers have found that athlete admission policies often have lower academic standards and greater guarantees of admission (Eitzen, 2016; Shulman and Bowen, 2001; Smith, 2011; Sperber, 2000).

This book shows that special admission practices give coaches tremendous and almost unilateral discretion in how they define and evaluate athletic merit. The process also permits coaches to court and recruit athletes over several years, developing more intense, personal, and intimate relationships with athletes. The processes of athletic recruitment and admission are not widely available. No uniform *college athlete* application exists. Instead, each university, and each team, may have a different recruitment method. Athletic admissions also lack national assessments open to *all* hopeful athletes, akin to an SAT. Instead, athletic assessments remain individualized to the coach, program, sport, and university. A hopeful athlete must learn how each school conducts its unique process to start recruitment.

The nuance and irregularities built within athletic admission could disrupt the entrenched cycles of reproduction attached to the larger college admission process in at least two ways. First, by removing academic performance as the primary assessment, athletic admission could offer new, more equitable evaluations. In removing academic performance as *the* measure of college access, do new patterns of college attainment emerge? Is the opportunity structure for developing athletic merit more equitable than the opportunity structure for developing academic merit? Have coaches created a more just and fair admission system? Second, special admission removes layers of bureaucracy and oversight. Does devaluing academic measures like SATs create greater equity? Does eliminating several rounds or deliberations of an application generate more diversity? In sum, do athletic admissions function in a new way? Or do athletic admissions parallel, mirror, and/or corroborate the patterns and practices of privilege and exclusion that exist in the larger admission system?

To answer these questions, I conducted my own study into athletic recruitment and admissions. Despite the long history of exceptional admission and the public fascination with college sports, few researchers study this topic. Shulman and Bowen's (2001) *Game of Life* is the foremost account on college athletic admissions. Shulman and Bowen analyzed student data across thirty universities and found colleges provide admission advantages to athletes. Yet their inquiry assumed that the athletes who received the admission advantage were meritorious and deserved their college spot. They did not question the social or institutional processes that develop and assess athletic merit. Researchers who have studied athletic merit tend to offer physiological explanations for athletes' exceptional physical talent (Burgess and Naughton, 2010; Durand-Bush and Salmela, 2002; Gould et al., 2002; Ostojic et al., 2006). Others have examined athletes' effort levels in sport (Côté et al., 2005; Duda and White, 1992; Gilbert et al., 2001). These approaches position merit as a tangible, objective feature that resides at the individual level. The fields of education and sport studies have yet to consider the reproductive alignment between the cultural settings that enable certain groups to develop athletic talent, how universities assess athletic talent, and whether athletic talent facilitates mobility. To begin to answer these questions, let's first look at *who* college athletes are.

Rigging the Game: The Prevalence of White Middle-Class Athletes

A year before Moore was a national news story, I spoke to Monique, a white woman who grew up in a mostly white and wealthy suburb, about how she earned college admission and later a scholarship through her athletic talent. Monique is one of the 400,000 college athletes who play sports "but not on

TV" (Cooky et al., 2013, p. 203). Her story is unfamiliar to most sport consumers as she plays a sport without national broadcasts.

Monique's public high school is ranked in the top 700 nationally by *U.S. News and World Report* (see Appendix A for a breakdown of Monique's and all study participants' community characteristics). Over three-quarters of her fellow students took Advanced Placement tests, 70 percent took college-entrance exams, and 96 percent graduated. Only 7 percent of Monique's classmates qualified for free- or reduced-price lunch, and all but 30 percent were white. By attending this high school, Monique's odds for attending college were nearly 100 percent. She knew as much and instead sought even greater exclusivity, hoping to enroll in an Ivy League or elite public university. These schools boast 10 percent or less acceptance rates. She believed that these restrictive institutions would help her retain her parents' upper-middle-class lifestyle. She pursued sport as a route for educational and social access.

Monique joined a private rowing club after a family friend encouraged her to do so. After paying the club dues, Monique attended the first practice. She immediately disliked the sport and expressed as much to the coach. Monique recalled what the coach said to persuade her to come back to practice: "You know I went to Yale [for rowing]. You could be really good. This could help you get into college." Monique said that her coach's reference to Yale taught her that rowing could help her with college admission, and so she decided to continue in the sport. Monique used rowing to secure college admission and scholarship offers to Ivy League and elite public schools. In reflecting upon what role sport played in her college admission process, Monique concluded, "The more I think about rowing the more I think: I'm not that great at rowing, I just had the privilege to row. It's so difficult for people to get the chance to row . . . I'm sure there are more athletic people than I am, but they just didn't have the chance." Monique is a good rower. She contributed to national championship teams at the high school and college levels. Her feeling that she is "not that great" may emanate from her second observation that the pool of possible rowers is narrow and exclusive. The major purpose of this book is to describe how it is that individuals like Monique have the "privilege" to row—a privilege that increases their admission prospects.

Monique's "privilege" to row for a private club team is connected to broader structural changes to the U.S. economy. The rise of neoliberalism, beginning in the 1980s and accelerating into the present, further diminishes the already-minimal odds for one to ascend through mobility institutions (Brown, 2005, 2019; Fabricant and Fine, 2015; Giroux, 2014; Harvey, 2005; Weis and Fine, 2012, 2013). Neoliberalism "inject[s] marketized principles of competition into all aspects of society and culture" (Gane, 2014, p. 1093). Neoliberal logic transformed community-sponsored schools and recreational sports. In the past thirty years, privatized youth leagues supplanted low-cost community and school-sponsored athletic opportunities (Coakley, 2011a, 2011b, 2015; Eckstein, 2017; Eitzen, 2016; Messner, 2009). Coakley (2011a) characterizes neoliberal athletics as elite, organized, competitive, commercial sports (EOCCS). These sports cost more and uphold different values. EOCCS legitimate neoliberalism by elevating competition as *the* measure of merit, by conflating competitive success with "moral worth," and by legitimating current power brokers as the rightful economic "winners" who "deserve power and privilege" (Coakley, 2011a, p. 73). This model of sports assumes a pyramidal and hierarchical approach to access and ascendance. Over 22 million youth play sports (Aspen Institute, 2018). By high school that number drops to 8 million (NFHS, 2019). By college, only 490,000 play in the NCAA (NCAA, 2019). As I explore in subsequent chapters, elites influence each winnowing phase by shaping the criteria and assessment processes for individuals to upwardly ascend.

The demographic characteristics of college athletes result from these winnowing mechanisms. Athletes in the big-time, Power Five conference, revenue-generating sports, men's football and basketball, whose labor contributes to a $14 billion annual industry (Jacobs, 2019), compose 3.5 percent of all college athletes (NCAA, 2019). And 60 percent of athletes in revenue-generating sports are Black (NCAA, 2019). These are also the most visible athletes and sports. In the 2018–2019 season over 47 million people attended college football games, 366 of which were televised, reaching a total audience of 163 million during the regular season (National Football Foundation, 2019).

However, expanding the gaze to include the other 96.5 percent of college athletes shifts the demographics. While Black men are 60 percent of athletes in revenue-generating sports, they are only 14 percent of total athletes (NCAA, 2019). Within Division I athletics, 60.4 percent of scholarship recipients are white, and 67 percent of women scholarship recipients are white (NCAA, 2019). The 1990 Student Right-to-Know Act requires the NCAA to annually publish demographic and graduation rate reports. Congress passed this act in the wake of several high-profile cases where universities graduated Black men football players who had minimal educational proficiencies (Smith, 2011). To ensure greater public transparency and accountability for colleges to provide adequate educational opportunities to scholarship athletes, the law requires the NCAA to track the progress of athletes who receive a dollar or more in athletic aid. This state action multiplied the bureaucratic agencies and interventions that track, monitor, and surveil predominately Black men in revenue-generating sports (Baker and Hawkins, 2016; Branch, 2011; Eitzen, 2016; Grenardo, 2016; Hawkins, 2013; Sack and Staurowsky, 1998; Smith, 2011). But the framing and implementation of the law also permitted the majority of athletes—those who do not receive scholarships—to avoid public scrutiny and transparency. Only 160,000 of the 490,000 college athletes receive athletic aid (NCAA, 2018).

Therefore, two-thirds of college athletes are missing from the racial demo-graphics. Once again, state tactics of *removal,* in this case permitting the majority of athletes to not be tracked or monitored, have reproductive effects. A true accounting of college athletes' demographics remains undisclosed to the public.

Additionally, the NCAA is not required to publish athletes' socioeconomic standing. The closest national data on socioeconomic status come from the NCAA's voluntary reporting of college athletes who are first-generation college students—an indicator of class (Pascarella et al., 2004; Stephens et al., 2014). In 2015, the NCAA reported 14 percent of college athletes were first-generation college students (NCAA, 2016). Country club sports (those that require pay-for membership at the youth levels) had some of the lowest rates of first-generation students: lacrosse (2 percent), field hockey (3 percent), rowing (4 percent), gymnastics (7 percent), swimming (7.5 percent), golf (10.5 percent), and tennis (10.5 percent) (Farrey and Schreiber, 2017). These sports are also almost exclusively white (Butler and Lopiano, 2003; DeLuca, 2013; Leonard, 2017).

The incomplete demographic data still show white and middle-class athletes are overrepresented in college sports—suggesting intercollegiate athletics are not the NCAA's promised "pathway of opportunity." But the demographics of the institution cannot reveal *how* white and middle-class athletes became the majority and *how* they continue to retain their position in college sports. *Special Admission* looks within a broader segment of intercollegiate athletics—the nonexploited, non-revenue-generating sports—to understand *how* racially and economically privileged youth are overrepresented in college athletics. I contend that elites continue to secure their advantages in society through pro-tecting exclusive avenues of college access through sport.

College Athletic Admissions: Legitimating Unequal Social Outcomes

To understand *how* white suburban youth dominate college athletics, I outline the dynamic relationships between the state, elite groups, private entities, and educational and athletic institutions. *Special Admission* traces how state sup-port for college sports permits athletic recruitment to function as a *legitimat-ing institution* (Bourdieu and Passeron, 1977). French philosopher Pierre Bourdieu positioned cultural activities such as sports and education as central sites for the expression and maintenance of state power. Bourdieu (2011) defines capital as an accumulating resource that is objective (contained in objects like currency) and subjective (contained within humans). Governments can trace, quantify, and redistribute the objective form of capital—money. The largest college admission scandals in U.S. history indicated as much. Attempts by wealthy families to buy a spot on a college rowing team can be scrutinized. Instead, the "games of society" that create intergenerational inequality more often use *euphemized* forms of capital—like a high grade in an AP class—that are not immediately economically exchangeable (Bourdieu, 2011, p. 81).

Access to euphemized forms of capital flows from a lifetime of socialization or what Bourdieu called "habitus." One's habitus—a unique social and cultural orientation to the world—forms through a *durable training* occurring over time, place, and setting. Our habitus is inextricably linked to our position among varying power structures, our lifetime of interactions with socializers such as caregivers, peers, teachers, and coaches, and our continued exposure to various cultural representations such as particular technology, music, and religious rituals. Our habitus provides us with a "sense of what is comfortable or natural" as we encounter the social world (Lareau, 2015, p. 3). Importantly, habitus is not a static concept handed down to individuals from the state. Rather, habitus is a *process* that requires continuous work and does not always have predictable or replicable outcomes.

Institutions, like schools and sports, shape our habitus. Reproduction, according to Bourdieu, uses institutions to enable individuals to accumulate and later convert various capitals including economic, social, and cultural. Social capital offers individuals visibility in the world through symbolic relationships among group members. These networks often do not produce direct economic capital; rather they represent the potential for future action, interaction, and opportunities. One opportunity may be the development of cultural capital. Cultural capital represents one's attitudes, behaviors, preferences, and values. These attributes link to one's class standing and occur in embodied forms (which are accumulated within the body and cannot be delegated to someone else) and objectified forms (which exist within objects such as media, music, or literature). Cultural differences translate into class inequality through the institutionalized form of cultural capital (Bourdieu and Passeron, 1977).

While all social institutions (e.g., families, churches, sports) provide opportunities to accrue objective and symbolic capital, Bourdieu believed certain institutions rise in importance in the reproduction process. *Legitimating institutions* create the pivotal moments in one's life course to convert embodied capital into economic capital. Schools, more than any institution, transform euphemized capital into legible and consistent markers of "cultural competence" (Bourdieu and Passeron, 1977, p. 50). A college degree, or even admission to a prestigious university, offer "conventional, constant, legally guaranteed value" in the form of academic qualifications (Bourdieu and Passeron, 1977, p. 50). State bureaucracies ensure the *legally guaranteed value* of college degrees by creating and regulating educational and economic marketplaces in which not all credentials are equally valued. Admission to an Ivy League university has a higher value and exchange rate than admission to a regional state college. When an Ivy League university admits someone because of their euphemized capital, that person can enter elite economic, political, social, and cultural institutions when others cannot. This expression of state power validates existing hierarchies by conferring markers of merit onto those who occupy the upper rungs of society.

Bourdieu's approach to cultural transmission and reproduction has faced steep criticism for overdetermining the relationship between class and habitus, minimizing other power structures such as race, misrepresenting oppressed groups' habitus as mere reflections of the dominant group, and minimizing individual agency (e.g., Apple, 2004; Giroux, 1981; Leonardo, 2009; McLaren, 2014; Oakes, 2005). In this book, I take the methodological view that empirical inquiry can update and modify theories. I use a Bourdieusian view of reproduction to reveal how elites preserve their advantage through conferring cultural significance to *certain* forms of athletic merit. Athletic merit, therefore, is not neutral. The athletic merit universities desire represents one's access to interrelated forms of economic, social, cultural, and physical capital.

While Bourdieu positioned access to economic and symbolic capital as stemming from one's position with the class structure, I take an intersectional view. Intersectional approaches to power explain that oppression and privilege "cannot be reduced to one fundamental type" but instead "work together in producing injustice" (Collins, 2005, p. 18). As one example, in chapter 2, I position middle-class suburbs as white supremacist projects. The rituals of middle-class suburban lifestyles, like enrolling children in extracurricular activities, create racial logics of belonging, such as *certain sports are white*, that always come at the expense and exclusion of people of color.

Mapping the Path to Coastal-U

I did not set out to write a book about social mobility. I designed a study to complicate the notion that college athletes' educational compromises result from, and therefore are limited to, revenue generation (e.g., Branch, 2011; Cooper, 2012; Eitzen, 2016; Hawkins, 2013; Sack and Staurowsky, 1998; Singer and May, 2010; Smith, 2011; Sperber, 2000). As a former Division I nonrevenue college athlete and employee in academic support services, my background provided a unique vantage point in extremities; I achieved athletic and academic success, yet I witnessed many athletes who struggled to do so. The athletes overrepresented in our academic support services were lower-income Black men in revenue sports. But nonrevenue sports teams—filled with middle-class white athletes—also succumbed to the academic and athletic demands of college sports. These athletes struggled to find a major compatible with their practice schedule, complete the rigorous college course requirements, and find time for career preparation in anything beyond sports. If it's difficult for nonrevenue athletes to become "student-athletes," can anyone approach this ideal?

I embarked on a study using Dorothy Smith's (2005) institutional ethnography—a methodology that centers people's lived experiences within institutions, such as families, schools, or sports—to scrutinize the social world to examine the educational experiences of nonrevenue college athletes. As an education scholar, I knew that schooling experiences are cumulative and inform how someone engages with and navigates the next stage of their education. Thus, I incorporated life history interviews to allow participants to narrate, from their own perspective, the seminal athletic and academic experiences that informed their current college challenges. Life history interviews allow interviewees to drive the interview and construct their own meaning of events and allow researchers to center people's stories to understand cultural and social contexts (Gouthro, 2014; Ravitch and Carl, 2016; Smith, 2012). Interviews offer a window into how humans live within, construct, reinforce, and/or resist forces that constrain social outcomes (Creswell, 2013; Ravitch and Carl, 2016). Following the work of Gouthro (2014), Lensmire (2014), and Messner (1992), who demonstrated how in-depth life history interviews can reveal how social institutions shape the past, present, and future possible lives of individuals, I centered this approach as my primary methodological tool. Even when an individual does not speak directly to structural forces, researchers can place their stories in contexts that can enliven how institutions produce and reproduce the conditions and constraints that inform our realities (Crenshaw, 1992; Weis and Fine, 2012).

The pre-college athlete narratives I collected to contextualize in-college processes provided such rich accounts of privileged college access that the story required a book-length telling. To construct a people's vantage point, I contextualized the athletes' narratives by building a unique quantitative dataset (described in chapter 2) that examined the background characteristics of 1,487 collegiate rowers and track athletes. I also analyzed institutional documents such as university and NCAA handbooks, admission policies, and court cases. Collectively, these materials show the complex ways individual and familial sport preferences, interactions in school and sport settings, hierarchical models of athletic advancement and competition, and geographic and community resources converge in predictable patterns to preference white middle-class students in athletic recruitment.

The Destination: Coastal-U

Coastal-U (a pseudonym for the research site) is a highly selective Research 1, Tier 1 public university with forty thousand students. During the year of data collection, the university boasted a 17 percent undergraduate acceptance rate, placing it within *U.S. News and World Report*'s top fifty selective universities. Coastal-U is also a top athletic program as a member of the NCAA's Division I, Power Five, Football Bowl Subdivision. These characteristics make Coastal-U an optimal destination for athletes pursuing sports as a route to college. Rowing and track represent nonrevenue sports as they compose 25 percent of Coastal-U's athletes and they offered rich comparative potential. Rowing draws from elite white communities because participation requires tremendous resources, whereas track and field requires fewer resources and draws more participants from marginalized communities (Coakley, 2015; Eitzen, 2016). While I interviewed athletes enrolled at one university, these athletes came to Coastal-U from five nations and eleven U.S. states.

Coastal-U is a historically white institution. However, its present-day racial demographics are no longer majority-white. Racial minorities are now the majority of students, and 25 percent are from families in the bottom 25 percent of income earners. Yet the college athletes at Coastal-U do not mirror these demographics; 42.5 percent of Coastal-U's students compared to 6 percent of athletes are Asian-identified. Similarly, 10.6 percent of Coastal-U's student body identifies as Latino, but Latinos are less than 1 percent of athletes. In contrast, 28 percent of Coastal-U students are white-identified, whereas 47 percent of athletes are white. Students identifying as Black are also overrepresented as Coastal-U athletes. Only 3.4 percent of students but 23.3 percent of athletes are Black-identified. Due to the overrepresentation of white and Black athletes, my discussion of race centers white- and Black-identifying individuals. The demographic differences at the institutional level suggest a different admission and selection process for athletes. Studying this different admission process may reveal the entrepreneurial ways elite groups retain their power through college admissions.

I conducted the study from 2015 to 2016. I recruited participants by presenting the research opportunity at team meetings and disseminating research flyers (see Appendix A for a list of participants and their demographics and Appendix B for additional information on participant recruitment). I also asked volunteers to participate in snowball recruitment and refer their teammates as possible participants (Biernacki and Waldorf, 1981). These efforts yielded forty-seven participants.

The life history interviews were one to three hours in length. I began by asking that participants select their own pseudonyms to be used in all representations of the study. Some enjoyed the task and tried to think of an obscure name. Others found the task too difficult and requested I select one for them. Overall, this exercise provided an informal entry into how they narrativized their journeys to college. The interviews explored their pre-college athletic and academic journeys, including how they accessed sports, why they selected sports over other activities, what athletic/academic support systems they received, and how sports enhanced or limited their educational engagement.[2]

Participants described, in their own terms, their race, class, and gender positions. I was interested in the institutional processes that create the overrepresentation of individuals with certain identities and backgrounds. For instance, all participants in the study were cisgender or maintained the gender category assigned at birth (Schilt, 2010). Twenty-eight identified as women and nineteen as men. Regulations created the overrepresentation of cisgender people in the study. College sports enforces a segregated two-gender system of participation, governing the bodies of participants through sex testing and verification (NCAA, 2011; Pieper, 2016).

Similarly, institutional processes led to a majority of white and middle-class athletes in my study. Eleven classified themselves as "Black," "African American," or "mixed race," and thirty-six identified as "white," "European," or "Caucasian." The rowing teams in my study were nearly 100 percent white.[3] The smallest grouping of participants identified as low income. I created class categories through several lines of questions. During the interview protocol I asked participants to describe their neighborhood and school, their caregivers' education level, their extracurricular activities, and whether their family needed them to supplement the household income. I also used U.S. Census Bureau (2016) data related to their community characteristics to further contextualize their self-identification. Chapter 2 explores why the resources within a given community feature prominently in providing greater opportunities for athletic talent. In this sense, one's individual or family-level class position was less relevant than whether one lived in proximity to and could access the resources within middle- and upper-middle-class communities.

Special Admission: Format and Argument of Book

Throughout the book I document how college sport exemplifies the complex workings of the state. The athlete narratives, quantitative data, and reports depict one dynamic route co-constructed by white middle-class communities to access higher education and maintain their social standing. I focus my analysis at the community level instead of individual or familial levels because sport participation requires an "institutional web" of "schools, churches, community organizations, [and] after-school programs" (Sabo and Veliz, 2008, p. 2). As youth ascend in sports, the intricacies of the web increase to include private clubs, private coaching, athletic camps, and junior national team competitions (Coakley, 2011b; Eckstein, 2017; Messner, 2009). The forthcoming chapters describe how white middle-class communities are more likely to possess the infrastructure that creates *recruitable athletes*—those who develop the knowledge, dispositions, and relationships necessary to market themselves to college athletic recruiters. The route to college is co-constructed as suburban communities and college admissions change and adapt in response to one another's actions. For instance, as suburban communities increasingly support privatized sports, privatized sports become more valuable in athletic recruitment. By shifting analysis away from the individual level and toward the community level, I chart the historic and contemporary relationships between colleges, athletics, and white middle-class communities that ensure children from these areas have preferential access.

The first part of *Special Admission* reveals the structural supports that correspond white suburbs to college athletics. Chapter 1 describes how America became the only country to wed elite athletics and academics. I document how the state officiated this union and conferred greater college and athletic access to elite white men. I then trace how rules and regulations in college sports evolved in response to broader social, cultural, and economic changes in the United States and in response to political action from women and communities of color.

In chapter 2, I apply the historic analysis to the contemporary context. I discuss how the state aligned white suburban areas with greater opportunities to develop the athletic talent universities desire. To do so, I consider the shared background characteristics of college athletes, including geography, high median family income, infrastructure, public school rankings, and cultural traditions. In chapter 3, I complicate the notion of a singular pathway to college and discuss informal and formal patterns of race and gender segregation that limit women's and racial minorities' chances to become college athletes.

In the middle of the book, I look within the structure to explore the social interactions, knowledge productions, and successful strategies that white suburban communities engage in to maintain their advantages. Chapters 4 and 5 describe the social networks and capital that reaffirm stratification. Athletes discuss the social networks that assist them to develop athletic talent and later secure college admission. Caregivers, teammates, and coaches are all necessary for a young athlete to gain the particular skills, dispositions, and behaviors needed for college athletic recruitment. Athletes also describe the additional labor, tactics, and strategies they used to gain a recruitment and admission advantage. Strategies include selecting less competitive sports, paying to attend college-sponsored athletic camps, and taking a gap year to further improve their athletic ability.

In the last empirical section, chapter 6, I illustrate the moment of conversion. I overlay athlete narratives on athletic recruitment and admissions policies to show how the rules favor certain community characteristics, social networks, and strategies. Here, embodied capital is converted into economic capital (college access). This conversion is fluid as athletic merit is moldable, subjective, and visible only when universities confirm someone possesses it. As various groups compete for access, the university confirms the versions of merit white suburban athletes present, thereby legitimating their embodied capitals.

The final chapter summarizes the book's main themes, discusses the consequences of the *sports path to college*, and describes aspirational and tangible reforms to create more equitable school sports. As I reveal the implications for the sports path to college, I foreshadow findings from my second study that tracked participants' journey *through* college. I discuss the consequences of dedicating tremendous community, family, and individual resources to pursue an athletic route to college. Once in college, participants feel the institutions of sport and school turn against each other, no longer aligning in their favor. In this way, even track athletes and rowers fail to reach the NCAA's "student-athlete" model that requires individuals to simultaneously pursue elite athletics and academics. Several participants experienced short bursts of success in sport and school simultaneously through great physical, personal, and educational costs. Further, those who did achieve these fleeting moments were white and middle- or upper-class. The book concludes with aspirational reforms to create more transparent, equitable, and educationally compatible models of athletic participation and recruitment.

1

Gentlemen's Agreement

College Sports Become a State Institution

Around eight o'clock on a Sunday morning I drove across Lake Natoma Dam, just north of Sacramento, California. To my left spanned two thousand meters of race course for the women's rowing national championships. Large beach-ball-sized red buoys paralleled the dam to mark the finish line. Smaller softball-sized buoys ran perpendicular to the dam and separated the six racing lanes. Rowing requires large, calm, clean bodies of water. The rowing shells are not designed like canoes or outrigger crafts, which can ride over waves and through currents. Instead, these boats cut through the surface of the water, making them vulnerable to the slightest ripple or debris. These aquatic conditions rarely occur in the natural environment, which makes dammed rivers an optimal setting for rowing.

Once across the dam I drove to an overflow event parking lot located in a nearby office park. It was Memorial Day weekend, and the temperature was already close to ninety degrees. I walked about ten minutes to the main parking lot. The only security of note were three high schoolers wearing club rowing T-shirts who lounged on white fold-up chairs and accepted cash or check payments for event admissions. I paid them thirty dollars cash for a ticket. This monetary exchange caused me to pause. The admittance fee reminded me I was a paying spectator, not a rower, not a volunteer coach, not an event coordinator, and not an athletic department employee—all roles I held in my previous visits to this championship that granted me free admission. Once I passed through the gate, I was enveloped back into the familiar touchstones that characterize the sport.

I walked through the main parking lot, filled with boat trailers, which are multileveled apparatuses towed behind trucks and transport the two-hundred-pound delicate rowing shells from race to race. My eye was drawn to the sounds of plastic doors opening and closing. On my left athletes scurried in and out of their makeshift locker rooms, a row of temporary portable toilets. Between the parking lot and the race course a line of white pop-up tents crowded the finish area and divided the fans for each team. Imitation school logos, printed on paper, shirts, or flags, adorned the tents and marked the fans' territory. Parents staffed the tents and served each other an array of box-store snacks and beverages. The athletes could not congregate in this area until they received permission from their coaches—once their races concluded for the day. The first race would begin in an hour. Until then, the crowd—possibly too strong of a word, as I generously estimated one hundred people seeking shade under the sixteen tents—milled around quietly talking.

Three hours later, when the final race concluded, the crowd remained muted. No one erupted in cheers, hoots, or hollers. The winner of the final race needed to be determined by a photo finish. Officials also had to calculate the scoring of all the boats representing each school to total a final result for the team national championship. It took another thirty minutes for the results to be named. By then, only about a third of the crowd remained, as athletes and their families from lesser ranked teams exited early, knowing they would not receive a medal. The team that won that year ascended the podium to accept their award. They sang their school's fight song, hugged one another, and raised their trophies. Each woman on the podium appeared to be white. Most that I could see also had blond hair.

The NCAA, with help from athletic conferences and member schools, runs and operates the women's rowing national championship. The NCAA pays all the travel expenses for qualifying teams to compete in the event. The funds to support this championship come from the NCAA's largest revenue-generating event, the Men's Basketball Tournament. Hundreds of thousands of fans travel to the Final Four, or the last weekend of March Madness and its corresponding festivals and concerts. As this is one of the highest profile U.S. events, security requires coordination from private contracts, police departments, homeland security, and the FBI (Jones, 2019). In 2019, 23.5 million people watched the televised broadcast of the final game in which the University of Virginia beat Texas Tech to win the tournament (Patten, 2019). The television contract with CBS/Turner Broadcasting alone earns the NCAA over a billion dollars a year (Sherman, 2016). The University of Virginia hosted two stadium-filled public events, one of which charged admission, to celebrate the team's victory. The men's basketball tournament and women's rowing championship seem disconnected, but in reality they constitute two oppositional poles of college sports. At one end is a hypermarginalized sport that is barely visible to the public. At the other is a hypervisible and widely celebrated sport. Despite these outward differences, the athletes are subject to the same rules and governing structures, which contain them in polarized spheres. Neither represents the normed center of college sport.

State power flows and expands through bureaucracies like the NCAA. The state uses bureaucracies that crisscross and interlace diffuse landscapes of society to build collective agreement. Bureaucracies seem like neutral and bland organizations that decrease overt forms of state power (like military occupation). In reality, they increase the state's primary goal: social control (Brown, 1992). The trick of regulatory power is it uses mundane modes like cubicles and employee performance reports to produce violent ends akin to military might. As Brown (1992) explains, bureaucracies achieve "domination through regimes of predictability, calculability, and control" that "create disciplined, obedient, rule-abiding [state] subjects" (pp. 27–28). Bureaucracies need not achieve *all* the imperatives of the state; they need to only help the state enter public and private life. Thus, bureaucracies are "both an *end* and an *instrument* and thereby operate *as power* as well as *in the service of other powers*" (Brown, 1992, p. 28, emphasis original).

In this chapter, I discuss the historic co-construction of American leisure (exemplified through college sports) and the white supremacist, capitalist, heteropatriarchal U.S. nation-state. I center one form of state power, bureaucratic (Brown, 1992, 1995), to offer four ways that the state's expansion coordinates with and shapes college sports to maintain elite white men as the normed center of the institution: historical ties to the state, direct governing by the state, protections and benefits from the state, and state laws that shape the nature and makeup of the institution. First, I discuss how the NCAA arose from a mandate from U.S. president Theodore Roosevelt. The NCAA's historical origins shaped the bureaucratic impetus and logic that inform the current rules, regulations, and structures. Second, the origin of college sports—as reflected in the institution's name—placed athletics under the direct governorship of universities, many of which are *public* or state-run organizations. Third, the state granted college sport particular protections and benefits that enabled its rise, such as its nonprofit, tax-exempt status. In exchange for this benefit, the NCAA agrees to certain forms of state control and oversight. Finally, I describe how state laws such as Title IX shape the nature and makeup of the institution. These laws extended state control and power into private colleges and universities, formalizing the state's oversight of the composition and operation of intercollegiate athletics. College sport bureaucracies cement the sports path to college. The historical conditions of college sports shape today's regulations to favor white middle- and upper-class communities.

Presidents, Barons, and Tycoons: The Founding Fathers of College Sports

Unless you are a college sport historian, an avid fan of obscure trivia, or a current or former member of Harvard or Yale men's rowing programs, I imagine this next section will come as a surprise. The first college sporting event was a rowing race between Harvard and Yale on Lake Winnipesaukee in New Hampshire. The lake's name comes from the Winnipesaukee Tribe, members of the Pennacook and Algonquian peoples (Heald, 2001). As early as 1765 British colonizers built roads and occupied settlements along the lake area despite Native people living in the region (Heald, 2001). In the 1840s, two Massachusetts mill owners, Lowell and Lawrence, "bought" the rights to the water to run their factories. Today, five hydroelectric dams in the area still power nearby cities and industry (Weirs Beach, 2019).

In the mid-nineteenth century, railroad developers created new routes from the heavily populated Boston region to Lake Winnipesaukee, spawning tourism and vacation stays in the area. James Whiton Sr., a Boston merchant—a term of the era that signified either direct dealings with the slave trade or indirect dealings with economies of slavery (Wilder, 2013)—was a board member on the Boston, Concord and Montreal railroad company and oversaw one of the new routes. The company invested in the infrastructure in hopes the area would blossom into a resort community (Smith, 2011). In May 1852, Whiton Jr. rode his father's route for the first time. He had completed his third year at Yale and was traveling home to his family's New England "woodland" estate for the summer (Mendenhall, 1993). Whiton Jr. was seated next to the conductor, James Elkin. As they passed Lake Winnipesaukee, Whiton mentioned that the water was perfect for his college sport: crew (Mendenhall, 1993). Elkin responded with a proposition. If Whiton could organize a regatta between two premier universities, Harvard and Yale, his railroad company would cover all the costs of the event. Whiton accepted the challenge. In two short months, backers of the railroad and the new resort town used the upcoming regatta to advertise their capitalist projects and lure spectators to the region (Smith, 2011). Their efforts succeeded; the lake was packed with spectators eager to see the race (*New York Herald*, 1852). Rowing brought prestige, interest, and flare to the area. Within ten years the railroad network expanded, connecting Winnipesaukee to other nearby resorts and New England towns. Housing proliferated in the region without negotiation with or recognition of the Native people who lived there (Heald, 2001).

Harvard won the preeminent race between the selected top boats from each program. The rowers accepted a prize of silver-tipped walnut oars (Mendenhall, 1993). The democratic candidate for the presidency and soon-to-be-elected U.S. president General Franklin Pierce was one of the many notable celebrities in attendance (*New York Herald*, 1852). President Pierce was not the last U.S. president to attend the regatta. In 1911, President Teddy Roosevelt cheered on his alma mater, Harvard (*Harvard Crimson*, 2014). Two decades later, in 1934, Franklin Delano Roosevelt cheered on his son who rowed six-seat for Harvard (Otterbein, 2014).

Presidents attending the first intercollegiate contests reflect the early and continued state support for college sports. Their presence also indicates the restrictiveness of early American leisure practices. Newspapers published the names of prominent elites who attended these matches, only increasing the prestige and exclusivity of college sports (Oriard, 2001). The ability for athletes and spectators to partake in this first intercollegiate athletic event came through the legally sanctioned taking of land, labor, and resources from populations the state excluded from full civic rights—indigenous people, recent immigrants, Black people, working-class people, and most women (Crenshaw, 1988; Harris, 1993; Leonardo, 2004, 2009; Mills, 1997, 2003; Vaught, 2017). The spectators and athletes at these first contests—like Whiton Jr. and presidential candidate Pierce—secured their wealth, status, and prestige through *formal* state-secured exploitation practices. Early spectators and athletes could recreate because they were not subjected to the state-propagated economic, physical, and psychological harms endemic to the lower ends of the capitalist laboring and enslavement regimes (Mills, 2003; Roediger, 2017). In this sense, one's ability to be a fan or rower also came through the state *removal* of this ability from someone else.

The first college sports contests occurred at private schools, but this fact makes state support for college sports and, in turn, higher education no less relevant. The interrelationship between the state and higher education becomes obscured through terms like "public" and "private" institutions, where the former term connotes state support and the latter negates state involvement. State power expands by partnering with other institutions that align with and can validate the state's aims. More so than any other institution, higher education normalized and extended the aims of the white supremacist, heteropatriarchal, capitalist government (Crenshaw, 1988, 1991; Du Bois, 1935; Harris, 1993; Leonardo, 2004, 2009; Mills, 1997, 2003).

Colonizers, Enslavers, and Patriarchs: The Founders of Higher Education

Yale and Harvard predate the nation's founding. Higher education helped colonize the Americas as the campus founders sought money and resources from the British Crown to build a missionary presence (Wright, 1997). Harvard and Yale also provided the labor, knowledge, and infrastructure to expand the slave trade (Wilder, 2013). Harvard's early students, faculty, presidents, trustees, and patrons were slaveholders and traders. Yale used profits from a slave plantation in Rhode Island to create its graduate program. Philip Livingston, a second-generation Yale alum whose family earned their fortune in the slave trade, provided the funds for the first endowed chair at Yale (Wilder, 2013). After Massachusetts banned slavery, Harvard continued for decades to train their graduates to run and operate southern plantations (Wilder, 2013).

The Harvard and Yale professoriate also produced the research that justified the expansion of the U.S. white supremacist, heteropatriarchal, capitalist government. Harvard-trained Charles B. Davenport founded the twentieth-century eugenics movement. Davenport's *Heredity in Relation to Eugenics* (1911) was the leading book of the time and advocated for selected breeding between those with the greatest attributes and preventive breeding for those who could contaminate the race. Davenport warned of a "new plague that rendered four per cent [*sic*] of our population" "not merely incompetent but a burden costing 100 million dollars yearly to support" (p.4). He purported that only eugenics could solve the "crime, disease and degeneracy" associated with this plague (Davenport, 1911, p.4). G. Stanley Hall, the first person to earn a doctorate in psychology from Harvard, became the first president of the American Psychologist Association. Hall, a proponent of social Darwinism, espoused that children, nonwhites, and women occupied the lower rung of the evolutionary ladder, compared to white men (Ingrassia, 2012). Eugenicist and social Darwinist theories came from racial-difference scholarship, dating back to the eighteenth-century enlightenment thinkers who proposed that five categories of humans existed (Skiba, 2012). This same classification grounded race in immutable phenotypical and behavioral characteristics, of which the white race was the pinnacle and all four others "degenerated progressively" (Skiba, 2012, p. 5). Academics from top universities extended the early twentieth-century version of racial hierarchy science into national policy shaping all aspects of public life (Harris, 1993; Massey and Denton, 1998; Mills, 2003; Rothstein, 2017; Shabazz, 2015; Skiba, 2012).

Social Darwinism also limited women's education. Academics saw white mothering as a precious commodity that ensured national success. In 1873 Harvard medicine professor Edward Clarke published *Sex in Education; or, A Fair Chance for the Girls*, in which he argued that providing women the same educational opportunities as men is a "crime before God and humanity, that physiology protests against, and that experience weeps over" (quoted in Zschoche, 1989, p. 546). Clarke said that humans have a set amount of energy, which in women should serve their reproductive organs. Mental and physical activity, he claimed, depleted their supply and made them infertile. He aimed his fears toward elite white women attending the first women's colleges whose energy depletion could jeopardize future generations of elite white men. His book conjured fears of a "racial apocalypse" (Zschoche, 1989, p. 546). White women's colleges accommodated these anxieties by ensuring that their students had different curricula and activities suited to their roles as mothers and caregivers (Sadker and Sadker, 1994; Stanley, 1996).

The Proof! Athletic Prowess Legitimates White Men's Dominance

Within the academy, knowledge production and sport mutually informed the advent of one another. Sport provided the empirical "evidence" to support emerging eugenic and social Darwinist knowledge. For instance, G. Stanley Hall saw sport as a safe way for young boys to learn and enact the processes of evolutionary struggle. Through sport boys could learn how to "withstand modern society's mental pressures, remain sexually viable, and reproduce white civilization" (Ingrassia, 2012, p. 77). Likewise, William Graham Sumner, a social Darwinist from Yale, believed that the British successfully conquered the world because they embraced aggressive and violent forms of sport such as rugby (Ingrassia, 2012). Eugenic and social Darwinist knowledge drove university leaders to incorporate and expand athletic opportunities. As one example, in 1903 the president of Princeton and future U.S. president Woodrow Wilson courted the notorious robber baron Andrew Carnegie to fund the construction of a law school. Carnegie gave Wilson a counteroffer: He would give $150,000 to dam a nearby river and create a lake for the young, elite white men to row on and build their character (Halberstam, 1985). To this day, the Princeton crews and the U.S. National Rowing programs train on Lake Carnegie.

It is no accident that Carnegie suggested and Wilson supported a terrain altering infrastructure project to bring rowing to Princeton. Both men advocated, funded, or enacted eugenics-based policies in their respective roles as state and industry leaders (Rust, 2013; Whaples, 2005). Carnegie's philanthropic contributions to Princeton came through state *inaction*. Carnegie amassed his steel fortune through exclusive contracts with public and private railroad companies, through union busting (exemplified in the numerous worker deaths during the 1892 Homestead strike), and through horizontal and vertical monopolistic efforts (Ris, 2017; Whaples, 2005). While Carnegie is cited as a generous titan of the Gilded Age, he turned to philanthropy to stave off the growing socialist movement in the white working class (Morey, 2014). Carnegie used his wealth and influence to develop business-friendly practices and curricula in higher education that legitimated the American oligarchy (Ris, 2017). Rowing, once again, became the perfect vehicle to display and legitimize elite white masculinity as the virtuous characteristics of rulers of America.

Robber barons like Carnegie funded and produced the "science" informing restrictive college admission practices. The first college athletes were elite white men not because they were physically superior to other groups but because universities restricted access to all others. Eighteen years *after* the Harvard-Yale rowing race, Harvard admitted its first undergraduate Black student, Richard

Theodore Greener (*Journal of Blacks in Higher Education*, 2014). Twenty-two years *after* the Harvard-Yale race, Yale admitted its first undergraduate Black student, Edward Bouchet (*Yale Alumni Magazine*, 2014). Twenty-seven years *after* the Harvard-Yale race, Harvard opened a separate-and-unequal annex to educate women. The first students were white middle-class women and mostly teachers. Almost a century passed until Harvard permitted women to enroll in its mainstream curriculum. Yale did not admit women into their undergraduate program until 1969 (Cummings, 2019).

Academics, administrators, and politicians used intercollegiate sport to reconcile the contradiction of the exclusionary practices within a newly formed democratic society. Through displays of physical strength, endurance, and overt violence, college sport demonstrated the virtues of masculine Anglo-Saxon supremacy (Gems, 2000; Oriard, 2001). The physical performances by elite white men normalized and justified the exclusion of working-class white men, all women, and the vast majority of people of color from the first iteration of college economies, knowledge production, curricula, and sports. Competition among colleges drove some to look beyond this narrow recruitment pool and recruit working-class white men as athletes. This crack in access gave rise to the sports purity movement and formalized state control of intercollegiate athletics. State control of sport came through efforts to contain the encroaching evils—depicted in racists and sexist terms—that threatened to topple masculine Anglo-Saxon supremacy.

Amateurism: Athletics for Gentlemen

*Inter*collegiate refers to a contest *across* colleges. Sports existed *within* colleges at least a hundred years prior to the first Harvard-Yale regatta. Sports began in college as a cultural rebellion from what students perceived as the dull, overbearing, and dehumanizing curricula of eighteenth-century colleges (Pope, 1997; Smith, 1988; Thelin, 2011). Students stole time from their faculty-prescribed schedules and partook in spontaneous games, often pitting one class against the other, under the threat of punishment and rebuke from faculty if caught (Smith, 1988). These digressions, while irksome to faculty, were characterized within a raucous spirit of a "boys-will-be-boys" ideology. These boys inherited the right to college—a right resilient to antics. Two hundred years later, a highly evolved bureaucratic state apparatus of college sport governance offered conditional invitations into the institution to those without birthright claims. This conditional membership could be revoked for the slightest deviation from the college sport rules.

As a cultural practice, sports bore no inherent form or regulation but were instead invented, modified, and infused with human interests. The games, internal to the college, started to organize around particular moral orders such as fair and uniform rules to even the field of play. The students who negotiated the terms of fair play were a small, select, elite group, reflective of the recently established white, masculinist, settler-colonial regime of the United States (Guinier, 2015; Smith, 1988, 2011; Thelin, 2011). Up until the late nineteenth century nearly all the students from seven elite male boarding schools in New England matriculated to Harvard, Princeton, and Yale (Guinier, 2015). These preparatory schools mirrored the goals of the colleges and aimed to cultivate "character, manliness, and athleticism" (Guinier, 2015, p. 14). The American boarding schools and universities used the British model to design athletic structures and regulations.

British school reformers cultivated sports in boarding schools to prepare young boys for their future roles as leaders of the settler-colonial empire (Messner, 1992; Miracle and Rees, 1994). Sport held far greater potential than the academic curriculum to cultivate the core values of colonial rules of "dominance over others and deference to the authority of leaders" (Messner, 1992, p. 10). Organized competitive team sports largely remained the purview of the elite until the mid-nineteenth century. The rise of industrialization and the corresponding rise of the middle class and the democratization of leisure threatened the ruling classes' exclusive access to and control over athletics (Llewellyn and Gleaves, 2014). By the 1860s popular forms of sport such as boxing enabled various forms of recreating for the working class including playing, gambling, and spectating the sport (Llewellyn and Gleaves, 2014; Miracle and Rees, 1994; Pope, 1996). Without a centralized governing bureaucracy like the British school system, these more democratized sports expanded public participation (Pope, 1996). The ruling classes invented the principle of amateurism—an ideological concept with diffuse and ambiguous meanings depending upon time, place, and culture—to differentiate, denigrate, and divide their sport form from the rising popular and commercialized athletics of the white working class (Eitzen, 2016; Llewellyn and Gleaves, 2014; Pope, 1996, 1997; Thelin, 2011).

College students at Oxford and Cambridge first used the term *amateurism* and defined it "synonymously with 'gentleman'" (Pope, 1996, p. 295). The elite college students "alleged that their 'social inferiors' could not comprehend the ethos of amateurism and fair play" and therefore did not deserve to compete against the Oxford and Cambridge gentleman (Pope, 1996, p. 295). British adult athletic leagues soon adopted the Oxford-Cambridge version of amateurism (Pope, 1996). The public campaigns around amateurism in Britain and later in the United States inscribed amateurism with social meanings along the lines of morality, cleanliness, and purity (Carter, 2006; Pope, 1996). In *Imperial Leather*, Anne McClintock (1995) recounts how the British Empire invented gentlemanliness in the nineteenth century to reconcile emerging political conflicts from women, white laborers, and colonized peoples who attempted to gain greater rights. Elites pointed to filth, disease, and moral corruption of "degenerate classes" who were constructed as "departures from the normal human type" (McClintock, 1995, p. 47). Only the English middle-class gentleman—in part through birth and in part through training—possessed the moral and intellectual aptitude to be "the white father at the head of the global Family of Man" (p. 234), a "family that admits no mother" (p. 4).

Gentlemanliness, thus, exists in the ideological and material terrains. McClintock (1995) traces how the state, in partnership with private companies like soap manufactures, developed and propagated images of the gentleman throughout their colonial empire. By transferring the gentleman into commodified forms through advertising and products, the values, dispositions, and characteristics attached to his rule were widely disseminated. The ideological spread of gentlemanliness necessitated and expanded the British state's infrastructure and wealth. The gentleman broadened the British global conquest, all the while creating new terrains for private companies to mine resources for their products and new markets to off-load said products. The wealth and success that flowed to actual British gentlemen materially and ideologically buttressed their rule. Therefore, the gentleman represents how ideology cements the interrelated foundation of state, private, and elite social, economic, and political power (McClintock, 1995).

Similarly, the rise of amateurism in ideological and material forms reflects the interrelationship between state, private, and elite power. Sport leaders in England and America used elites' fears of state domestic degeneracy to justify the ideology of amateurism. This ideology had material consequences. Elite white men banned from sport anyone who did not meet the strict and ever-changing definitions of amateurism. These bans sought to keep sport *pure*, or free from the corrupting influences of undesirable groups like the white working class, colonial subjects, and the formerly enslaved. Edward Said (1978) posed the ironic conundrum attached to a norm: the gentleman exists only in his relationship to the degenerate. In constructing boundaries around sports participation, the gentleman amateur invited rebellion. Their concerted efforts to keep people out gave excluded groups a platform for political action.

Capitalism and Containment

One major difference between the American and British models of amateur athletics is the former monetized their intercollegiate competitions. American college sports were the first major athletic spectator events to be widely popular and accessible (Kaliss, 2013). Universities charged admission to matches and used the profits to fortify their operating budgets (Smith, 2011). The commercial possibility and public popularity of college sports also became a sign of degeneration and contamination. The professional elements of sport had a taint of working-class ambitions. University leaders feared colleges would lose their "respectability as a middle- or upper-class institution" if commercialized sports persisted (Pope, 1996, p. 298). In the 1870s, as sports became a popular spectacle, progressive reformers started a sports purity movement centered around amateurism. Sports purists spent their time critiquing how commercialism corrupted the athlete, not the institution. This movement created an inescapable closed circuit of taintedness. Those sports purists deemed as inherently impure (women and people of color) or behaviorally impure by their association with commercialism (working-class and professional athletes) could never cleanse their beings and gain entry into the institution. Sports purists had to contain impure athletes so they would not contaminate pure athletes.

Sports purists targeted proselytizing—today known as recruitment. In the 1870s, universities began to hire professional coaches who scouted beyond their campuses for the top athletes (Oriard, 2001; Smith, 2011). Athletic recruitment created a cadre of "working-class ringers" or students brought to a university to improve the football program (Flowers, 2009, p. 353). By the 1890s, football rosters featured students of Irish and German descent, which the press deemed as proof colleges strayed beyond the New England prep school feeder pools (Flowers, 2009). Colleges created separate admission and curricula for these "ringers" to attend school (Smith, 2011; Thelin, 2011). The press named these students "tramp athletes" or those who "offered their services to the highest bidder" (Flowers, 2009, p. 354). Even university presidents used such rhetoric. George W. Gregory was a prominent high school football player at the turn of the twentieth century. Stanford and Michigan tried to lure him to their campuses. After Gregory selected Michigan, Stanford's president and an academic leader in eugenics (Skiba, 2012), David Starr Jordan, called Gregory a "tramp athlete" who accepted bribes to go to Michigan (*Topeka State Journal*, 1908, p. 12). Gregory refuted the charges.

By virtue of their economic position, working-class athletes had to *work* to attend school. Until the 1950s, universities could not offer athletic scholarships. The "ringers" sought jobs in several areas including coaching or playing on teams in the summer (Furrow, 2013). Baseball, in particular, offered opportunities for college athletes to play for pay at summer resorts that hosted games to entertain guests. College players knew this practice violated amateurism, so they used fake names to disguise their identities (Furrow, 2013). Muckrakers uncovered this ruse and reported on the tactics as evidence that working-class men were inherently deceitful and corrupted sport (Brown, 1907). Today, public suspicion is often invoked around the character of Black football and basketball players. Recall the sanctions levied against Ohio State for players selling their jerseys and memorabilia to supplement their athletic scholarships. Public sympathy seemed on the athletes' side so long as they spent the earnings on necessary items such as food and shelter. But when details broke that some players spent the money on cars and tattoos, the press turned on the athletes and nicknamed the players the "Tattooed Five" (Dirlam, 2011) or referred to the scandal as "Tattoo-gate" (Grove, 2011).

In February 1898 several East Coast universities—which later formed the Ivy League—met in Providence, Rhode Island, to curb professionalism in sport. The resulting Providence Rules defined amateurism by stating who should be *excluded* from college sports.

> No student shall be allowed to represent the University in any public athletic contest, either individually or as a member of any team, who, either before or since entering the University, shall have engaged for money in any athletic competition, whether for a stake, or a money prize, or a share of the entrance fees or admission money; or who shall have taught or engaged in any athletic exercise or sport as a means of livelihood; or who shall at any time have received for taking part in any athletic sport or contest any pecuniary gain or emolument whatever, direct or indirect, with the single exception that he may have received from his college organization, or from any permanent amateur association of which he has at the time a member, the amount by which the expenses necessarily incurred by him in representing his organization in athletic contests exceeded his ordinary expenses. (Needham, 1905, p. 1)

Eight years later, the NCAA formed and nationalized this definition of amateurism. The formation of the NCAA expanded bureaucratic power in college sports. Amateurism permitted universities to earn revenues in sport unfettered. Universities created markets around the already commercialized sport of football. Simultaneously, amateurism preserved the elitist nature of higher education by requiring universities to regulate and restrict how schools compensated athletes. The bureaucracy contained the commercialized and corrupted features in segments of the university, allowing sport leaders to claim most sports were pure. Amateurism clarified three facets of college sport governance and access that still structure today's organizational features. Amateurism signified the norm, or who belongs in sport; the degenerate, or who does not belong in sport; and the boundaries, or how to contain the degenerate to protect the norm.

Nationalizing Amateurism: Rough Riders as Gentlemen

The NCAA emerged as a centralized governing apparatus for college sports along similar imperatives as other state bureaucracies. The threat of violence is one tool the state uses to retain control of the public. The state offers protection from violence by creating additional layers of governance to exercise authority (Brown, 1995). Colleges ceded some of their autonomy to the national, state-sponsored bureaucracy of college sport, the NCAA, because the organization promised to protect and contain the violence in football. The NCAA's governing principles, stated in their first constitution, closely resembled the amateur language in the Providence Rules. Amateurism guided the resulting regulations, which were seen as a rational and calculable alternative to student stewardship of a rowdy game. Through amateurism and the expansion of bureaucratic power in college sports, the state helped universities contain potential threats to their national elitist standing.

At the turn of the twentieth century an increasing number of deaths in football drew public attention and concern to reforming the sport's rules. In 1905, 25 players died and 137 suffered major injuries (Branch, 2011; *The Call*, 1905). At that time football did not permit a forward pass. Players lined up against one another as the offense tried to force the ball through a wall of defenders. With no reason to fear a ball flying overhead, the defense could "link arms together or stay in close formations to obtain extra force or leverage against opponents" (Carter, 2006, p. 216). In a call to action, the *Chicago Tribune* listed the types of injuries that resulted from this style of play: "Body blows, producing internal injuries, were responsible for four deaths, concussions of the brain claimed six victims, injuries to the spine resulted fatally in three cases, blood poisoning carried off two gridiron warriors, and other injuries caused four deaths" (*The Call*, 1905, p. 1). Harvard and Columbia suffered student deaths, leading the presidents of these universities to consider banning the sport (Columbia later did so). Yale and Penn, both with profitable football programs, said football should remain with few changes (Carter, 2006; Pope, 1996). With no clear, uniform action on the part of universities, the *Chicago Tribune* sent a telegram to President Teddy Roosevelt urging him to act. The telegram was widely reported in the press.

The *Chicago Tribune* strategically appealed to Roosevelt because he was America's "sports president" (Swanson, 2011). More so than other presidents, Roosevelt wedded sport, masculinity, and colonialism (Bederman, 1995; Swanson, 2011). Throughout his life Roosevelt promoted a unique white, masculine American identity that was forged through the violent takeover of Native peoples and lands. As historian Gail Bederman (1995) describes, "Roosevelt constructed the frontier as a site of origins of the [white] American race, whose manhood and national worth were proven by their ability to stamp out competing, savage races" (p. 178). Prior to his presidency, Roosevelt became known for forming a voluntary army to follow him into war with Spain. The group, called the Rough Riders, included former athletes from Yale and Harvard (Bederman, 1995). Roosevelt, a proud Harvard boxing team alum, attributed his military strength to his athletic experience (Pope, 1997). In the late nineteenth century, white settler-colonizers had already taken most of the continental United States, in effect closing the frontier and, with it, opportunities to display and cultivate whiteness and masculinity (Bederman, 1995; Pope, 1997). In campaigning for president, Roosevelt promised a reinvigorated western white manhood under his presidency through the interrelated terrains of imperialism and sport (Bederman, 1995; Pope, 1997).

Roosevelt also created distinctions among these categories. Amateurism ensured that *certain* white men accessed sport and in turn Americanness. Writing in 1890, Roosevelt explained that amateur sport, not professional, could save the republic: "the amateur, and not the professional, is the desirable citizen, the man who should be encouraged" (p. 190). Roosevelt believed that amateur sport could "develop such qualities as courage, resolution, and endurance" (p. 188) and could cultivate "the good man who is ready to strike a blow for the right, and to put down evil with a strong arm" (Roosevelt, 1890, p. 187). By invoking amateurism, Roosevelt divided his already exclusive club of national belonging, eliminating white men who needed money to play sports. While Roosevelt personified white, rugged, individual masculinity, he did not originate these beliefs. Roosevelt merged his biography with preexisting social Darwinist and eugenic movements to address the dominant group's anxieties about their potential decline. Sport facilitated and concretized this merger, thereby expanding state power into new terrains of higher education governance.

In December 1905 Roosevelt responded to the *Chicago Tribune*'s call for action regarding violence in football and scheduled a meeting with the leaders of Ivy League football—Bill Reid (Harvard), Walter Camp (Yale), and Arthur Hillenbrand (Princeton)—to discuss how to reform the game. After the meeting, Reid told reporters that their goal was to "purify football but don't weaken it" (*Chicago Tribune*, 1905, para. 1). This meeting ignited a movement that transformed not only football but college sports generally. Roosevelt's decision to intervene in college students' games set in motion a chain of continued state intervention and regulation of college sports that continues to this day.

Purifying College Sports: The NCAA

Later in the month, the original three universities met with the U.S. Naval Academy, the University of Chicago, the University of Pennsylvania, and Cornell University, under the name Football Rules Committee, to draft national regulations to reform football (Carter, 2006). Simultaneously, the chancellor of New York University, H. M. McCraken convened his own meeting to reform the game. McCraken was spurred to action after football player William Moore died during a game against NYU (Carter, 2006). McCraken, along with the leaders of sixty-eight other institutions, met in New York to form the Intercollegiate Athletics Association of the United States (IAAUS). The New York group decided to look beyond football and reform all college sports. They drafted a constitution and elected a president: Captain Palmer E. Pierce, a representative from West Point, the U.S. Military Academy. And they invited the Football Rules Committee to join their organization (Carter, 2006). The two groups merged and convened their first national meeting to ratify the constitution in March 1906. Only twenty-eight of the original sixty-eight attended (Carter, 2006). The founders and the press framed the central objective of the newly formed organization to *purify* college sport.

After the organization's first meeting, Pierce told reporters that national collegiate athletic rules would reform football into a "gentleman's sport" (*New York Daily Tribune*, 1906, p. 8). IAAUS formed to set "a standard of purity in amateur college sport which will not only be recognized, but faithfully lived up to by all the organizations affiliated in their movement" (*Washington Times,* 1909, p. 10). The initial regulations to "purify" sports targeted the athlete, not the university—which today remains the NCAA's modus operandi. The original bylaws of the organization set out the "principles of amateur sport." Following the Ivy League model, the IAAUS did not define amateurism; rather, they defined what amateurism is *not*. This oppositional definition created a norm of those included in college sports (those who could prove their amateur status) and degenerates (those who could not). All IAAUS member institutions agreed to police their athletic programs by prohibiting athletic recruitment, inducements (any form of compensation for athletic talent), unsportsmanlike conduct, and the participation of athletes who were not full-time students (Carter, 2006; Smith, 2011). The original rules also required that athletes fill out an "eligibility card" to certify their amateurism—a process that continues to this day. The original eligibility card asked, "Have you ever at any time competed for a money prize, or against a professional for any kind of prize? Have you ever received money or any other compensation of concession for your athletic services, directly or indirectly, either as a player or in any other capacity?" (quoted in Carter, 2006, p. 224). The card concludes with the following language: "On my honor as a gentleman I state that the above answers contain the whole truth, without any mental reservation" (quoted in Carter, 2006, p. 224). To pass the amateurism purity test, one had to be an amateur and a gentleman.

But the original and lasting NCAA regulations never limited universities' athletic profits. In 1906 the salary and expense account of William T. Reid, Harvard's football coach, approached that of President Eliot (Smith, 1988). Similarly, Yale had an athletics reserve fund of $100,000 ($2.9 million in 2019 dollars), and revenues from athletics composed one-eighth of the school's total revenue (Smith, 1988). These profit-centered objectives conflicted with amateurism defined as *sport for pleasure, not for profit.* How did the founders reconcile the original contradiction within college sports, or that everyone but the athletes could profit?

The founders settled these tensions by instituting amateurism in certain sectors of the institution. A year after the NCAA formed and announced their amateur regulations, many press accounts celebrated the reforms as victorious. As journalist Elmwood Brown (1907) explained, "Today college athletes are practically free from the taint of professionalism. A few years ago there were many abuses, but the recent purity agitation has done much to wipe these things out.... The average college athlete is a gentleman, and will refuse offers if he suspects that they are being made to him because of unusual athletic ability.... Tennis, golf, and swimming are sports all comparatively free from professionalism" (p. 4). Brown's article shows how reformers reconciled amateurism with commercialism: quarantine.

Reformers claimed a moral victory for amateurism by quarantining the transgressions—including the background and behavior of athletes—to football. In 1906 Harvard president Charles Eliot derided the corrupt elements of football and noted the differences between those who played on the gridiron and those who played on the tennis court. "Rowing and tennis are the only sports in which honorable play altogether is practiced.... You can no more cheat in those two sports than in a game of cards; you would be crowded out of society if you tried.... Not only is there an absence of cheating [in rowing], but it is the most healthful and interesting as well as one of the two most honorable sports. Tennis can be played with profit by any one. All it requires is individual skill and brains" (*Evening Star*, 1906, p. 9).

Eliot's exaltation of rowing ignores how the original "sins" of commercialism came from Harvard and Yale crew programs. These teams invented tactics such as slotting graduate students or even nonstudents into their lineups, seeking out commercial sponsors, training beyond the specified limits, and hiring professional coaches (Smith, 1988, 2011; Thelin, 2011). But these facts cannot disrupt the general feeling and attitude that prevailed then (and I suspect now), that sports with restrictive barriers to entry, such as rowing, golf, and tennis, retain a different class character. When the NCAA was founded, college athletes largely came from preparatory schools with the funds and facilities to train their students in a wide variety of sports (Flowers, 2009; Pope, 1996). Most primary and secondary schools had yet to adopt even physical education programs, let alone fund sports programs (Larned, 1909). The primary way that a working- or middle-class person could access sport was through professional associations, in effect negating their NCAA eligibility. By preventing sports access to the majority of the public, Harvard and the other NCAA membership institutions could truthfully say they adhered to amateurism. These *pure* and *clean* sports gave colleges and the NCAA the institutional legitimacy that amateurism did exist and that their organizations should continue to run, monitor, and govern college sports to ensure the persistence of these moral values (Flowers, 2009).

The NCAA began as an organization to allay national fears about the pollution of higher education from the contamination of violence, working-class ringers, and tramp athletes. Terms in the original amateur policies—*pure, gentleman, honor, sportsmanship*—resonate with eugenic and social Darwinist ideologies. The notion of a *gentleman* invoked a particular worldview—he who could run, operate, and represent the nation's main institutions, politics, and economies. Those who embodied *un*gentlemanly behavior—*the ringer, the tramp, the professional*—tried to access college sport. In doing so, colleges justified the expansion of bureaucratic power to remove these threats through surveilling college athletes. No longer could college men design and run their own games. Instead, the state regulated and monitored college games to preserve higher education's reputation as the producer of civilization. This national bureaucracy formalized faculty and university control over the student-run athletic organizations (Flowers, 2009; Pope, 1996). This resulting partnership placed athletics under the stewardship of colleges, securing the governing and organizing relationships between elite athletics and elite academics. The gentleman ideology enlivened the abstract regulations needed to enforce the terrain of sport. Notions of who could and could not be a *gentleman* restricted college sport access well into the late twentieth century.

Exclusion: Gentlemen's Agreements

The exclusion and later partial inclusion of women and Black people in college sports challenged and solidified the NCAA's quarantining strategy. From 1900 to 1946, no school in the United States, outside of historically Black colleges and universities (HBCUs), had more than seven Black men in their athletic program at one time (Lumpkin, 2013). The University of Pennsylvania track team and University of California, Los Angeles (UCLA) football team were the only instances where a predominately white university had up to three Black men on the same roster (Lumpkin, 2013). Prior to 1972, *if* a school had women's sports, they played on a gender-segregated team, with modified rules and with little or no dedicated funding (Stanley, 1996; Suggs, 2005). After 1972, white women and some Black women and men became NCAA athletes. These token inclusions contained women in gender-segregated spaces and Black men in revenue-generating sports.

Working-class white men were accepted and contained into college sports at a time when all women and virtually all Black men were denied access. As political philosopher Charles W. Mills (2003) reminds us, poor white men may be at the bottom of the social ladder, but they are still *on* the ladder. Existing on the ladder, even at the bottom, provided poor white men with a "public and psychological wage," or the intrinsic benefits of group membership denied to women and Black people (Du Bois, 1935, p. 700). The United States was founded on beliefs in inherent race and gender differences that still structure today's social world (McClintock, 1995; Mills, 1997, 2003; Skiba, 2012). The manifestations of state power—ideologies, identities, knowledge systems, and bureaucracies—that exclude and contain Black people and women are primarily located in the physical body (Mills, 2003). In this way, "political domination *becomes* incarnated" as it "roots itself *in* the biological" and "invest[s] the physical with social significance" (Mills, 2003, p. 168). Sport uniquely displays the physical body. Controlling sport participation, such as containing women into different, unequal, and gender-segregated athletic venues, reproduces *root* apparatuses of power.

The NCAA arose when the federal government used its policy and military strength to ensure that women and people of color remained off the white man's ladder. But the nation, in part because of college sports, faced a seismic realignment. Prior to the 1950s, institutions like college sport could ensure that the state would partner and support their efforts of overt exclusion and containment. But the military effort required to mobilize the nation for World War II provided new motivations and openings for widespread racial and gender justice movements that threatened the state's policies of overt exclusion and separation of women and Black Americans. The mid-twentieth-century civil rights movements used athletics to demand their inclusion in a democracy formed and predicated upon their exclusion (Cahn, 1994; Kaliss, 2013; Martin, 2010; Skiba, 2012; Stanley, 1996). A multitude of forces, crises, and movements unfolded throughout the twentieth century that I cannot adequately and justly explain here. These crises set in motion a set of tensions that universities had to reconcile. How would universities preserve elitism all while increasing access to those constructed in opposition to said ideals? Would the state-mandated changes in student enrollment impact sport? And if so, how would universities fund these efforts? Here, I briefly describe how universities embraced the impending hegemonic crisis and reformulated the gentleman amateur to accommodate the partial inclusion of women and Black athletes.

The White Norm and Black Exclusion

Sports in the nineteenth and early twentieth centuries publicly displayed white physical supremacy. Eugenicists pointed to white men's football victories as clear evidence for the race's inherent superiority (Bederman, 1995; Gems, 2000; Paxson, 1917). Many white people believed that Black people were not fully human and therefore not worthy of competition (Bederman, 1995; Du Bois, 1935; Skiba, 2012). Most northern universities denied enrollment to Black students well into the 1920s (Martin, 2010). The token Black students permitted into northern universities had to display tremendous academic and athletic potential (Kaliss, 2013; Martin, 2010; Skiba, 2012). When northern universities began to admit token Black students, they could still retain their majority-white status by relying upon students to police and enact the values of white supremacy. The state often emboldens and supports individuals who commit such acts on its behalf (James, 1996). This is certainly true within college sports.

White athletes policed the terrains of sport committing violence against Black athletes. On October 24, 1903, Dartmouth played Matthew Bullock, a

Black player, in a football contest against Princeton. Princeton had an all-white team and university, banning Black students until 1940 (Martin, 2010). During the first minute of the game, Princeton player Howard Henry and several of his teammates attacked Bullock and broke his collarbone. Later, in press accounts, the Dartmouth team accused Princeton of organizing the attack against Bullock. As evidence, they cited that Princeton refused to house Bullock on their campus the previous night. Dartmouth players also reported that prior to the attack they heard a Princeton player say, "Remember what you are to do with the n[*****]" (*Washington Times*, 1903, p. 8). Dartmouth players accused Henry of then saying, "We'll teach you not to bring n[*****] down to play against us" (*Washington Times*, 1903, p. 8). Henry denied these charges and said "he was not a bit sorry how roughly he handled the other members of the Dartmouth team" (*The Sun*, 1903, p. 8). That same year, Henry was selected for the all-American football team.

Today, white athletes and coaches still use racial violence to maintain white control of sport. One form of racial violence is coaches who overdiscipline Black compared to white players. Studies have found coaches hold Black players to higher physical standards, more often surveil Black players' outside-of-practice actions and behaviors, and more often call the police on their Black athletes (Ferber, 2007; Leonard, 2017). These strategies help maintain minority-white rule over majority-Black athletes.

Along with condoning physical violence, universities used bureaucratic functions to limit and control Black people's presence and behavior in college sport. During the first part of the twentieth century universities brokered deals known as "gentlemen's agreements" to ensure limited or no interracial contact; men's teams with Black athletes would agree to bench their players if the opposing team was all white. By the 1920s these agreements had become the "informal governing policy" or a "widely shared private understanding among [white] gentlemen" (Martin, 2010, p. 18). Yet again, the *gentleman* was invoked to mark the acceptable terrains of sport participation. While the term was first used as a tool to prevent working-class athletes from entering, it emerged in the 1920s to limit Black participation. Here marked the beginning of the hegemonic crises in college sports. In the twentieth century, part of northern gentlemanly behavior included partial racial tolerance (Martin, 2010). These universities contrasted themselves to the southern schools by having ever so slightly more progressive admission practices. The gentlemen's agreements indicated just how fragile racial progress was at northern universities. Northern schools did not sever the bond of whiteness that transcended regional and political difference.

By adhering to gentlemen's agreements, northern universities condoned the southern state-sponsored racial apartheid system enacted through Jim Crow laws. In 1940, NYU cut their lone Black basketball player, Jim Coward, from the team prior to a matchup against North Carolina. The NYU chancellor justified his decision through the following logic: "The time has not arrived when we can ask Southern schools to play against Negro players on southern campuses" (Martin, 2010, p. 46). As basketball increased in popularity following World War II, universities adopted a quota system known as "two at home and three on the road" (Martin, 2010, p. 152). This policy contained Black players to ensure white players always were the majority on their home court. Southern teams also formalized these agreements through "no Negro clauses" in game contracts that required northern teams to bench their Black athletes (Martin, 2010, p. 31). These gentlemen's agreements illustrate how the bureaucratic features of college sports, such as opportunities for coaches and universities to set the terms of play, create contracts, and decide the terms of access, are infused with ideological notions of who is the normed, desired athlete and who is the degenerate, suspect athlete who must be contained and controlled.

The NCAA did not ban HBCUs or Black athletes from participating in their national tournaments, but they permitted universities to do so. It was not until 1966 that Texas El Paso broke the racial quotas in basketball and played an all-Black lineup against Kentucky's all-white team (Lumpkin, 2013). Texas won the national championship. That same year, an all-white NCAA rules committee banned dunking in the league in response to the playing style of Lew Alcindor (also known as Kareem Abdul-Jabbar), a Black starter for UCLA. Dunking was associated with a "street ball approach to the game" (Lumpkin, 2013). Alcindor was also part of a growing Black athlete activist movement (Smith, 2009). He spoke openly about the racism he faced on and off the court as a UCLA student (Smith, 2009). Two years later, Alcindor earned and refused a spot on the United States basketball team to compete in the 1968 Olympics. When asked on NBC's *Today* show why he boycotted the Olympics, he replied, "Yeah I live here, but it's not really my country" (quoted in Smith, 2009, p.224). The dunking ban remained in place until 1976.

Linking Black athletes to the "streets" simultaneously denigrates Black forms of athletic access and elevates white forms of athletic access. To learn a sport in informal and free settings outside of the technocratic, rational, and bureaucratic reaches of the state poses a threat to social control. Forcing athletes to conform to the more desired approaches to the game that align with the "gentlemanly" style of play is one tactic to contain the potential threats of Black inclusion to white control of sport. These rules live on in the NCAA's unsportsmanlike conduct rules, which target excessive celebration—displays that became popular during the rise of the majority-Black University of Miami football team and live on in NFL games—prohibiting players from bowing, taking off portions of the uniform, and jumping into the stands (Kirshner, 2018; NCAA, 2017). Yet each new rule invites resistance. The dunking ban never stopped Alcindor. He developed and popularized a new style of play, the "skyhook," enabling him to simultaneously defend and shoot the ball (Smith, 2009). He went on to anchor three NCAA and six NBA championship teams.

The Manly Norm and Womanly Exclusion

The overt and covert tactics by universities to prevent Black access to college sport meant HBCUs were the primary venue to develop Black athletic talent. In the 1920s, Tuskegee started hosting women's sports and produced some of the greatest athletes of the era. The Tuskegee Flash track team broke national and international records and produced a host of Olympians. Alice Coachman, one member of the team, won twenty-six national titles (Lumpkin, 2013). The athletes' unique experience as gender and racially marginalized provided conflicting opportunities for Black women. HBCUs provided more athletic opportunities for Black women than women's colleges did for white women (Lansbury, 2001). The social anxieties that sport could harm white women's reproductive organs were not applied to Black women. As Angela Davis (1981) explains, one of the "supreme ironies of slavery" was "the black woman had to be released from the chains of the myth of femininity" as the master sought to extract the "greatest possible surplus labor of the slaves" including women and children (p. 7). Plantation rule subjected Black women to the same brutalizing labor conditions as Black men. These conditions normalized the physicality of Black women in ways that permitted partial athletic access (Lansbury, 2001).

In the late nineteenth century, white women challenged white femininity as inherently fragile and invalid by pursuing sports. Many of the first women's colleges created physical education departments and hosted sports programs (Sadker and Sadker, 1994). Women who were admitted into private and land-grant universities also formed their own physical education departments and sports teams (Stanley, 1996). In April 1896, the basketball teams at the University of California (Cal) and Stanford University competed against each other in the first women's intercollegiate contest. In front of a reported crowd of seven hundred, the women competed in full-length bloomers and sweaters, or what amounted to heavy, restrictive, and suffocating clothing. Before the game began, the athletes clipped their fingernails, a ritual that delighted a reporter as "good policy, as a precaution to ensure that the game shouldn't turn out a scratching match" (*The Sun*, 1896, p. 5). Reporters ignored the play-by-play and instead covered the beauty of Stanford's athletes, who were "small, slender, and sinewy" compared to Cal's "bigger, stronger, and heavier" team members (*The Sun*, 1896, p. 5). Reporters concluded Stanford's physique contributed to their 2–1 victory. The infantilizing press coverage of white women's sporting interest was (and remains) one such way to contain women in sports separate from men (Messner, 2002; Musto et al., 2017; Travers, 2013).

Infantilization is one of many tropes attached to white women athletes. In the 1920s, women's colleges and leagues adopted the paternal concern that athletic activity masculinized women and made them unfit for motherhood (Stanley, 1996). Doctors provided "evidence" that certain sports—track in particular—strained women's bodies (Lansbury, 2001). The press also characterized the rise of several white working-class women in track such as Babe Didrikson, Helen Stephens, and Stella Walsh as mannish (Stanley, 1996). These characteristics led white women to flee from track and toward more socially acceptable feminine sports contained within private country clubs like tennis, golf, and swimming (Lansbury, 2001).

Even after the abolition of slavery, the state-sponsored economic deprivation of the Black community ensured that Black women could still never achieve the ideals of white femininity and become full-time homemakers (Davis, 1981; Harris, 1993; Lansbury, 2001). Racial and economic repression created unique conditions for Black women that informed their athletic access. Living under racial apartheid, Black communities formed their own gender norms that aligned with athletic participation (Lansbury, 2001). Yet under racial apartheid one is never free from the political systems enacted by the oppressing group. When Black athletes achieved national recognition for their success, their performance was translated in white supremacist, patriarchal logics. In 1948 Alice Coachman became an international superstar after seventy thousand people watched her set a world record in the high jump. Yet press coverage in white and Black newspapers undercut her performance. The white press largely described her "mannish" features (Lansbury, 2001). One reporter spoke to her professors at Tuskegee and stated that she was "an outstanding forward on the basketball team" but "'just a fair student' in home economics" (Lansbury, 2001, p. 238). This account diminishes her success by invoking the in vogue eugenics thinking of Black inherent mental inferiority, positioning Coachman as a subpar student. But the account also frames her as violating the standards of femininity through a poor performance in home economics (Lansbury, 2001). The Black press, perhaps in trying to counter the racist stereotypes, played up Coachman's and the Flash's femininity (Lansbury, 2001). These forms of press coverage—which continue to this day—amplify women athletes' *womanness* while sacrificing their athleticism (Musto et al., 2017). Doing so bifurcates femininity and athleticism, recentering masculinity as the prime feature of the normed athlete.

Governing leagues orchestrated the marginalization of *all* women athletes by creating separate, different, and unequal sporting opportunities at HBCUs and beyond. In 1964 several women's groups lobbied the NCAA to sponsor women's national championships. The organization rejected their request. Afterward, the NCAA passed legislation clarifying that all championship events "shall limit participation to eligible *male* athletes" (quoted in Carter, 2006, p. 258, emphasis added). Without national college championships, women's elite amateur athletic opportunities came through the Olympics. The first Olympics excluded women. In 1900, women were invited to compete in only four country club sports (equestrian, golf, sailing, and tennis), whereas men had nineteen sports, ranging from football to tug of war (Keuk Ser, 2016). Track and field became the battleground to enforce notions of women's inherent inferiority. For much of the twentieth century, women competed in a fraction of the track and field events offered to men, often in shorter distances. In 1928 the Olympic committee removed the 800-meter race for women under the premise that women could not run the distance (Cahn, 1994). Women could not race 800 meters again until 1960. Not until 1972 could women compete in the 1,500-meter event (the closest distance to the mile), and not until 1984 could they compete in the marathon. Also in 1984, the Olympics introduced a middle-distance event for women, the 3,000-meter race, yet it was 2,000 meters shorter than the men's middle distance event (International Olympic Committee, 2019). Twelve years later, in 1996, women could compete in the 5,000-meter event. The Olympics provide a global stage for nations to symbolically compete for global supremacy. When nations collectively agree to place their women athletes in separate, different, and unequal events, they support a global alignment of male supremacy.

In 1976, four years after Congress passed Title IX, the NCAA sued the Office of Civil Rights to contest whether the law applied to their league (Suggs, 2005). The court refused to hear their case. In response, the NCAA began to sponsor women's championships, a choice that killed the recently established national women's collegiate athletic league (Suggs, 2005). The NCAA enacted a segregated, regulated, and medically monitored two-sex system that presents the categories of "man" and "woman" as fixed rather than as socially constructed, fluid, and vulnerable (Messner, 2002; Milner and Braddock, 2016).

Gender segregation is premised under the "fair play thesis," or the notion that *all* men are physically superior to *all* women (Sullivan, 2011). Thus, "fair" competition cannot occur if men compete against women. Athletic organizations have measured and quantified athletes to count as "women" through genitalia inspections, chromosome markers, phenotype inspections, and hormone tests (Sullivan, 2011; Travers, 2013). These practices neither are original nor were invented for women athletes. The same systems that categorize, measure, and hierarchically rank human beings—originating from eugenics—are deployed and granted legitimacy through the sex testing of athletes. Sex testing remains infused with social and cultural understandings of performance and superiority. These tests center testosterone as *the* performance-enhancing feature that men inherently possess (Dworkin and Wachs, 2009; Pieper, 2016).

Women testing with medically defined *abnormal* rates lose their status as women athletes (Pieper, 2016; Travers, 2013). These policies do more to support male superiority than the advancement and equality of women (Sullivan, 2011).

The two-gender sport system also protects and naturalizes the right for men to access spaces free from the corrupting influence of women (Anderson, 2008; Messner, 2002, 2009). Following Roosevelt's frontier thesis, if sport is one of the last spaces to develop aggressive masculinity, the presence of women might neuter these efforts. This view was codified in a judicial opinion the year prior to Congress passing Title IX. Girls at a Connecticut high school desired to form a cross country team. With no support from the school to do so, they hoped to join the boys' team. The school denied them access. The girls sued, with the judge siding with the school for the following reason: "The present generation of our younger male population has not become so decadent that boys will experience a thrill in defeating girls in running contests, whether the girls be members of their own team or an adversary team. . . . Athletic competition builds character in our boys. We do not need that kind of character in our girls, the women of tomorrow" (quoted in Dunkle, 1974, p. 9). The judge's language invokes Roosevelt's speeches. Sport is once again a unique site for boys to develop their masculinity—a masculinity that cannot be cultivated in the presence of women. Thus, men need the state's protection to keep women out of their sacred masculine spaces.

A year later, Title IX gave state legitimacy to the fear that men's sports were under threat from women. During the hearings for Title IX, Senator H. Dominick from Colorado asked whether the bill would desegregate athletics. Senator Birch Bayh, the bill's sponsor, assured Dominick this would not happen. "I do not read this [bill] as requiring integration of dormitories between the sexes. Nor do I feel it mandates the desegregation of the football fields. What we are trying to do here is provide equal access for women and men students to the educational process and the extracurricular activities in a school, where there is not a unique facet such as football involved. We are not requiring that intercollegiate football be desegregated, not that the men's locker room be desegregated" (quoted in Suggs, 2005, p. 41). Title IX preserved the centrality of men's sports and offered no modifications to men's institutional dominance. Instead, the law contained women in low-profile, underfunded, and male-controlled gender-segregated sports.

Inclusion: Brokered by the White Gentleman State

The overt tactics universities used to exclude women and racial minorities became an increasingly unstable way to maintain power as the twentieth century wore on. Decades of political consciousness raising and organizing on the part of disenfranchised groups started to change public sentiment toward the eradication of overt segregation. Marginalized groups strategically harnessed the public spectacle of athletics to draw attention to persistent race and gender discrimination (Kaliss, 2013; Lumpkin, 2013; Martin, 2010; Suggs, 2005). Various political movements attempting to change the elitist origins of college sports coalesced in securing state intervention. These movements led to two direct state interventions to expand athletic access: *Brown v. Board of Education* and Title IX (Martin, 2010; Suggs, 2005; Thelin, 2011).

Prior to *Brown* universities could prohibit and/or limit the number of students of color who could enroll. In 1954 the Supreme Court overturned the long-standing *Plessy v. Ferguson* (1896) precedent that permitted segregation. *Brown* considered whether separate educational institutions could be equal. The justices unanimously decided that no, separate does not lead to equal education experiences. Under *Brown*, university admission policies that banned the admittance of Black students were no longer legal. However, *Brown* did not require universities to ensure equal racial representation within their institutions or across the subsets of student life, like athletics. So long as a university's admission policy did not *prohibit* the entrance of Black students, large swaths of the campus—including athletic teams—could remain all white (Martin, 2010). In this way, *Brown* did not (and has never since) address processes that inherently advantage white students, such as how coaches recruit and select athletes.

Brown also permitted white people to retain their leadership and control of college sports. Eradicating separate-and-unequal athletic spaces led to a massive decline in leadership opportunities for Black people in sport. After *Brown*, HBCUs' athletic programs dwindled and more than two thousand Black coaches lost their jobs (Edwards, 1979). Even as more Black athletes entered NCAA programs, white people kept control over sport. In 2017, 44.2 percent of football and 53 percent of basketball Division I athletes were Black (Lapchick, 2018), whereas only 9 percent of students at Division I institutions were Black (NCAA, 2018). Yet white people remain the decision makers, as 86.5 percent of Division I coaches, 86.1 percent of athletic directors, and 89.2 percent of university presidents are white (Lapchick, 2018).

Gender integration did not flow from *Brown*. Black women could now enter universities, but they faced institutionalized hurdles of gender discrimination. Prior to 1972, universities could limit or ban women from entering their college, certain majors, and certain activities (Sadker and Sadker, 1994; Suggs, 2005). Title IX, an amendment to the 1964 Civil Rights Act, clarified that educational institutions receiving federal funds could not discriminate on the basis of gender. Whereas racial desegregation incorporated Black men into portions of white athletics, no such effort was made to integrate women. White liberal feminist approaches to gender equity shape the nature and interpretation of Title IX. They embraced separate-but-equal approaches that created gendered separate-but-equal K–12 schools, colleges, dormitories, locker rooms, and athletic programs (Grant et al., 2006; Hextrum, 2014, 2017b; Lorber, 1994; Milner and Braddock, 2016). They argued that inherent biological differences between men and women exist, and therefore women could never receive equal treatment in the presence of men (Milner and Braddock, 2016; Suggs, 2005). As a result, Title IX deviated from prior civil-rights-era logics that *separate is inherently unequal* and instead embraced the separate-but-equal approach. This approach had profound consequences for college sport access.

Since 1972, three federal laws, nine federal interpretations, and twelve U.S. Supreme Court rulings have shaped the meaning and enforcement of Title IX. Two interpretations, in 1975 and 1979, clarified that Title IX applied to school-sponsored sports and offered guidelines for compliance. The 1979 interpretation banned schools from providing sports just to men and required them to provide separate sports programs for women. How athletic departments could and should comply with Title IX was not fully clarified until the 1996 Supreme Court ruling *Cohen v. Brown*.

Title IX has yet to create a panacea in athletic participation for *all* women. In colleges, although women remain the minority of athletes, their teams receive fewer resources, they are underrepresented in coaching and leadership positions, and many schools remain noncompliant (Hattery, 2012; Lapchick, 2018). In 2018, high schools offered 1.2 million more roster spots to men than to women (NFHS, 2019). At the collegiate level, 56 percent of athletes are men, despite women composing 54 percent of college students (NCAA, 2018). Additionally, Title IX requires *parity*. If a school is underfunded and offers no resources for men, then they need not offer resources for women (Cheslock, 2008; Hattery, 2012). White middle-class women receive greater educational benefits than other women (Fields, 2008; Hattery, 2012; Pickett et al., 2012). Therefore, white middle-class women disproportionately benefit from Title IX. The current college sport participation number reflects this legal statute: 71.7 percent of all college women athletes are white, 9.3 percent are Black, 5.2 percent are Latina, 2.5 percent are Asian or Pacific Islander, 0.4 percent are Native Americans, and 10.9 percent identify as racially "other" (Lapchick, 2018).

College sports provided a public spectacle to disseminate narratives of civic membership. U.S. and college presidents alike used college sports to cultivate mutually informing meanings about who belonged on campus and the nation. For a century, the NCAA and universities legislated to preserve sport for the (white) gentleman amateur. Elite white men's athletic accomplishments signified they earned their spot atop U.S. hierarchies (Gems, 2000). But cultural ideals remain open to reinterpretation and contestation. While amateurism elevated elite white men, it also created the opportunity to expand access beyond this elevated group. By placing sports within a direct arm of the state—schools—marginalized groups could mobilize for inclusion.

Brown and Title IX grant the state authority to monitor and dictate terms of access to college sports. Both state actions defined what constituted membership in a discriminated group (race and gender) and offered protection from discrimination in educational settings. But the state brokered these protections (Crenshaw, 1988) and, therefore, did not disrupt the underlying features of exclusion I described in the preceding sections. To maintain legitimacy as a governing body, the state offered concessions to activists in the form of antidiscrimination legislation. These concessions further enshrined the state's legitimacy as a ruling order and "foreclose[d] greater possibilities" (Crenshaw, 1988, p. 1368). The resulting antidiscrimination laws such as the 1964 Civil Rights Act centered opportunities (i.e., disallowing schools to actively prohibit access to certain groups), not outcomes (i.e., ensuring greater representation of marginalized groups within higher education) in seeking equality (Crenshaw, 1988). College sports as a whole did not change. These populations, long constructed as social and cultural degenerates who could contaminate white men's spaces, were contained in specific institutional spaces. Black men entered the already-corrupted revenue sports where the NCAA and universities still exploit their unpaid labor. Women, white and Black, entered culturally devalued women-only sport spaces. White men govern and control both terrains. Chapter 3 describes how these containment practices structure today's sports path to college.

Amateurism Revised: The Gentleman Becomes the "Student-Athlete"

During the mid-twentieth century, amateurism faced new challenges as technological and commercial innovations such as radio increased the revenue stream for the NCAA and universities (Oriard, 2001; Smith, 2011; Sperber, 2000; Thelin, 2011). With greater revenue potential, universities began to violate the NCAA's amateur rules to find athletic talent. In 1948, seven institutions (Boston College, University of Maryland, Virginia Military Institute, University of Virginia, the Citadel, Boston College, and Villanova) violated regulations by recruiting nationally and offering students scholarships. The resulting Sanity Code attempted to strengthen amateurism and ban these seven colleges. The Sanity Code failed, and instead in 1952 the NCAA permitted limited recruitment and scholarships or "grants-in-aid," for room, board, tuition, and fees (Thelin, 2011). Permitting scholarships represented the biggest compromise to amateurism to date. Sports purists saw the new regulations as professionalizing college sports by permitting pay for play (Byers and Hammer, 1995; Smith, 2011; Sperber, 2000). These changes to amateurism did not eliminate the *gentleman amateur*. Instead, the state stepped in asked the NCAA and universities—not students—to redefine college sports access and its corresponding benefits (Carter, 2006). The U.S. legal system helped the NCAA establish the collegiate model of amateur athletics and positioned college sport as a state-sanctioned profit-taking educational institution. Nearly seventy years later, the *student athlete* legal maze still governs college sport.

By granting scholarships to athletes, the NCAA created a new threat to its governing structure: athletes began to sue for employee rights. In 1950 the University of Denver (DU) gave Ernest Nemeth a football scholarship. The scholarship covered his room, board, and tuition. Shortly after, Nemeth was injured at practice. He sued the school for workers' compensation, claiming that the university paid him for his football skills and he therefore was an employee. In *University of Denver v. Nemeth* (1953), the Colorado Supreme Court agreed and granted Nemeth benefits. Seven years later, California State Polytechnical College football player Edward Gary Van Horn died when the team's plane crashed. Van Horn left behind a widow and children. His widow sued for rights to death benefits, claiming that Van Horn, a scholarship athlete, was a university employee. In *Van Horn v. Industrial Accident Commission*, the courts agreed and ruled his scholarship was an employment contract.

Walter Byers, the recently appointed NCAA president, initiated a marketing campaign to combat these two legal defeats. Byers sought to convince member institutions and the public that even with scholarships, college athletes remained *students* and therefore were not eligible for workers' rights (Byers and Hammer, 1995). The lawsuits united universities behind Byers in an unprecedented collusion that had yet to be achieved through the NCAA (Byers and Hammer, 1995, p. 69). Universities allied with the NCAA as they feared additional lawsuits would grant severance packages for players cut from a team and workers' compensation for injured players. Byers explained how he implemented the plan: "We crafted the term *student-athlete,* and soon it was embedded in all NCAA rules and interpretations as a mandated substitute for such words as players and athletes. We told college publicists to speak of 'college teams,' not football or basketball clubs" (Byers and Hammer, 1995, p. 69). In doing so, Byers cemented the difference in public and legal opinion between college and professional sports.

By 1983, two resounding defeats of college athletes claiming employee status vindicated Byers's strategy. In *Rensing v. Indiana State University Board of Trustees* and *Coleman v. Western Michigan University*, the court recognized that scholarships are contracts but also said these contracts do not rise to the definition of employment. A year later, in *NCAA v. Board of Regents of the University of Oklahoma*, the Supreme Court provided the first and lasting precedent for universities to retain the right to earn revenue on college athletes' labor. While the case largely examined whether the NCAA could broker and control television contracts for football games for individual universities (and found the NCAA could not), the court did permit the NCAA to unilaterally govern the behavior and rights of college athletes. The court offered this benefit to the

NCAA because the organization "plays a critical role in the maintenance of a revered tradition of amateurism in college sports. There can be no question but that it needs ample latitude to play that role, or that the preservation of the student athlete in higher education adds richness and diversity to intercollegiate athletics. . . . The role of the NCAA must be to preserve a tradition that might otherwise die" (*NCAA v. Board of Regents*, 1984, p. 468). Here the court endorsed the NCAA's eligibility rules that maintain the "purity" of sport and endorsed amateurism—something the NCAA alone can defend—as central to higher education. Underlying this *tradition* of amateurism is the white colonizing gentleman.

In *NCAA v. Board of Regents*, the court began an era of judicial deference toward college sports (Carter, 2000). The ruling endorsed the NCAA's self-definition as inherently educational, and therefore the organization was entitled to different rights and protections. As Carter (2000) explains, the court established judicial deference for education institutions, and higher education in particular, in cases related to college admission and affirmative action. The court ruled that judges should not decide admission criteria, as colleges are better suited to do so. By aligning themselves with higher education, college sports received the same judicial deference to set their eligibility criteria, including all rules related to amateurism (Carter, 2000). This precedent informed a dozen subsequent cases challenging the NCAA's legal right to restrict athletes' behavior. Until 2015, athletes lost these cases. In later rulings, the court clarified the NCAA can pass and enforce regulations that deny college athletes constitutional rights including the right to free speech, due process, employment, and compensation (Boliek, 2015; Branch, 2011; Carter, 2006). The court cited the NCAA's own logic—amateurism is a "revered tradition" conserved through restricting athletes' behavior—to justify their rulings (Carter, 2000). The court did not consider that Byers and universities fabricated the student athlete.

The state-backed *student athlete model* gave unique protections to universities not offered to professional sports. By sanctioning amateurism, the state said even revenue-generating sports are educational and therefore free from paying taxes (Byers and Hammer, 1995; Carter, 2006; Colombo, 2010). Much of these benefits are secured under current tax law. Private colleges are tax exempt under the IRS's section 501(c)(3) rule, which relieves charitable organizations (e.g., religious and educational entities) of tax obligations (Colombo, 2010). Academic institutions govern athletic departments, granting athletics the same tax protections as schools. In 1976 Congress amended section 501(c)(3), stating that organizations that support "national or international amateur sports competition" are considered charitable in their works (Colombo, 2010, p. 118). This amendment solidified the NCAA's status as a nonprofit entity. Through state-backed amateurism, universities created a state-backed two-tiered system of college access. In one tier, the socially undesirable elements of commercialism proliferated with contaminated working-class and/or Black athletes. In the second tier, universities could claim amateurism existed by pointing to the pure, uncontaminated sports white and middle-class athletes play.

Conclusion: College Sports Legitimate Inequality

College athletes have continued to fight each legal advantage the state granted to the NCAA. Their efforts have posed a new crisis for the NCAA. Two cases deviated ever so slightly from past judicial deference to the NCAA's amateur model. In 2015's *O'Bannon v. NCAA* and in 2019's *Jenkins v. NCAA*, Ninth Circuit Court judge Claudia Wilkins examined whether and how the NCAA could restrict scholarships for athletes. Wilkins ruled first in *O'Bannon* that colleges could offer scholarships that cover the true cost of living and later in *Jenkins* that the NCAA cannot collude with universities to limit scholarships. *Jenkins* is currently under appeal. However, Wilkins did grant the NCAA continued authority as a regulatory body over college athletes and reaffirmed amateurism. Her rulings stated that the NCAA can require college athletes to remain full-time *students* and limit their compensation to educational expenses.

In 2019, California—home to the Ninth Circuit Court—passed a state law that limited universities' power to restrict compensation for athletes. The law raised questions of whether the NCAA would eject California schools from its ranks for violating amateurism. Instead, the NCAA modified its amateur regulations. In October 2019 the NCAA voted to permit athletes to "benefit from the use of their name, image, and likeness in a manner consistent with the collegiate model," signifying a potential crack in long-standing amateur standards (Osburn, 2019, para. 1). As of this writing, the NCAA has not yet adopted specific rule changes but has reiterated that all forthcoming changes will ensure athletes cannot become "employees of the university" (Osburn, 2019, para. 3). Without employee status, athletes have no right to guaranteed payment or legal protections like workers' compensation. Thus, the state once again offered concessions to activists to preserve the exploitive model of collegiate athletics.

The current crisis in college sport also reflects an expansion of state power. The recent legal opinions and laws reflect the *formal* dimensions of the state. By stepping in to regulate college sport—in this case the compensation for athletes—the state re-legitimated amateurism and its own oversight and authority to monitor athletes. The state's authority over athletes is secured through the *relational* form of state power. The fight over name, image, and likeness has momentarily concluded with the state transferring regulatory authority to the NCAA, universities, and private companies. It is up to these agencies to determine whether and how an athlete's potential contract aligns with the "collegiate model." In the case of California, universities must view and approve a contract before an athlete signs with a private company. This nuance preserves universities' decision-making power and ability to broker private athletic partnerships. It is in the state's interest to support the NCAA, higher education, and private companies as these organizations preserve long-standing hierarchies. These predominately white organizations retain the power and control over Black men who remain contained in revenue-generating sports.

Further, these court decisions, laws, and NCAA policies reflect the third mode of state power: *removal.* The long-standing racial containment practices of the state and college sports are upheld as these state actions do not address college access. Yet to be challenged is the NCAA's sway over college admissions. The NCAA dictates the eligibility, recruitment, and admission criteria for college athletics. The NCAA permits universities to design different criteria, rules, and practices specifically for athletes (NCAA, 2017). The NCAA monitors athletic admission by ensuring that potential athletes adhere to amateurism, fair recruitment, and academic minimums. The NCAA's current definition of amateurism mirrors historic terminology. Athletes who receive payment "of funds, awards or benefits not permitted by the governing legislation of the Association for participation in athletics" cannot compete within college sports (NCAA, 2017, bylaw 12.02.9, p. 62). Before a potential athlete can be recruited, the NCAA must certify their amateur status by examining an athlete's compensation (amateurism) and if they meet minimal academic standards (NCAA, 2017). Prior to college, athletes cannot receive money and/or compensation beyond necessary expenses (NCAA, 2017). Fair recruitment also remains central to amateurism. *Fair recruitment* is defined as "minimizing the role of external influences on prospective student-athletes and their families and preventing excessive contact or pressure in the recruitment process" (NCAA, 2017, p. xi). The subsequent chapters of this book describe how these regulations disproportionately benefit those from white middle- and upper-class areas. A prospective athlete must also reach minimum academic marks to start recruitment. The NCAA Qualifier established a sliding scale system in which the lower one's SAT or ACT score, the higher one's high school GPA must be to "qualify" as a potential NCAA athlete. So long as an athlete passes initial certification, universities retain discretion over evaluative criteria in admitting athletes (NCAA, 2017; Smith, 2011).

Legal backing for the NCAA's recruitment and admission processes is embedded within investigations and precedents for general college admission. Current legal standards forbid universities from creating admission criteria aimed to rectify past racial discrimination (Donnor, 2011; Dumas, 2011; Green and Gooden, 2016; Guinier, 2015; Long, 2015). In the 1978 decision, *Regents of the University of California v. Bakke,* the court affirmed that white people have a right to compete for *all* admission slots, and therefore universities cannot allocate certain slots for minority groups (Harris, 1993). Simultaneously, the court affirmed that universities can allocate certain slots for student characteristics including categories for legacy admits or athletes (Harris, 1993). In 1990, the Department of Education clarified that universities can earmark slots for athletes or legacy admits—even when these categories favor white people—so long as the categories align with "legitimate institutional goals" (Jaschik, 2018, para. 34). In 2018, Harvard's admission processes were once again subject to public scrutiny through the trial of Students for Fair Admissions (SFFA). SFFA claimed that Harvard used race-conscious admission practices that discriminated against Asian applicants. SFFA produced internal documents that revealed other forms of preferential admission: legacy students, recruited athletes, and children of Harvard faculty members. Students in these categories are "overwhelmingly white" and "make up roughly 29 percent of students at the College" (Franklin and Zwickel, 2018, para. 27). By protecting universities' rights to create special admission processes that favor white applicants, the federal government secured the three-hundred-plus-year accumulation of benefits for white people as a "legitimate and natural baseline" (Harris, 1993, p. 1714).

State support for college admissions allows universities to function as *legitimating institutions* (Bourdieu and Passeron, 1977). College admission practices validate the symbolic and embodied characteristics of those admitted to university. By doing so, universities give accepted applicants cultural and economic value that they can exchange in greater society. Throughout this chapter I have argued that college sports value characteristics that align with the *gentleman amateur* (repackaged today as the *student athlete*). I described how the origin of college sports, rooted in the ideal of the gentleman amateur—a wealthy white man who has the privilege to participate in sport for pleasure—informs the practices, policies, and hierarchies in today's institution. From the original support and mandate of President Roosevelt through recent federal court cases, the state legitimates the amateur ideal and marks college sports as inherently educational in nature and therefore entitled to certain rights and benefits.

Today, college athletes no longer uniformly reflect the positionalities of elite white men. College sports weathered several hegemonic crises, including changes to amateurism to maximize profits and liberalize recruitment by offering admission to white working-class *ringers*, and federal action, which prohibited universities from banning women and racial minorities from admission. Women and racial minorities accessed college sports by partially adhering to the *gentleman amateur*. For white women this meant playing in segregated, underfunded, and underrecognized sports. For Black men, this meant playing in the highest profile but most exploitative commercial sports. For women of color, this meant remaining on the athletic sidelines as they have no guaranteed legal protections. Containment did not end but instead refashioned amateurism.

The forthcoming chapters reveal how the *gentleman amateur* persists in contemporary sports as a *habitus*. The ideological and material characteristics of the gentleman amateur remain the desired and required entry criteria into most college sports. In subsequent chapters, I describe how *formal* state laws and infrastructure projects imbued white middle-class communities with greater opportunities to develop the gentleman amateur habitus. The state's *relational* dimension partners with white suburban communities and higher education institutions to maintain race, class, and gender hierarchies through athletic admissions. Through the state, higher education receives the legitimation power to reward the gentleman habitus with special admission. In turn, this encourages members of white suburban communities to pursue sports to accelerate their advantages. The public's consent to the state's power, higher education institutions, and current social hierarchies is solidified through tactics of *removal*. Special athletic admission is an inherently exclusionary system that removes most hopeful athletes from the benefits of elite higher education. Narratives that present athletes as *deserving* admission disguise the underlying elitist architecture.

While the forefathers of college sports gazed upon the colonized Lake Winnipesaukee region and imagined their amateur rowing contests, the contemporary leaders gaze out into the suburban landscape looking to fill their current athletic rosters. Underlying these two seemingly interrelated points in time are state exclusionary practices. Those who can ideologically and materially traverse the suburban landscape secure the benefits within.

2

The State Alignment

White Suburbia and
Athletic Talent

In the months leading up to the 2016 Rio Olympics, several media stories positioned Jenny Simpson as a hopeful to become the first American woman to medal in the 1,500-meter race. Simpson began her running career at a public high school in a Florida suburb, from which the University of Colorado, Boulder recruited her. She had an immediate impact on the team, winning four NCAA titles during her college career. While Simpson was training for the Olympics, journalists asked her how she became a world-class athlete. "I think I'm probably one of the old-school people who would say to be a great runner, all you need is a pair of shoes that doesn't fall apart," said Simpson (Woelk, 2016, para. 3).

The American colloquialism—repeated here by Simpson—that track success *requires only a pair of shoes* supports the notion that sports are upward mobility vehicles. As discussed in the previous chapter, American college sports weathered several hegemonic crises by appearing as upward mobility vehicles while still preserving elitism. Simpson embodies the compromises that arose through the twentieth-century amateurism crises. As a woman from a middle-class instead of an upper-class background, she does not possess the original features of the *gentleman amateur*. However, her ability to become a top-level athlete still flowed through elitist and restrictive channels similar to the previous generations of gentleman amateurs. Despite her statement to the contrary,

Simpson required far more than a pair of shoes to become first a college and later an Olympic athlete.

Athletic talent displayed by athletes like Simpson emerges at the communal, not the individual, level. Framing athletic talent as a communal property reveals the diverse workings of the state to preserve social hierarchies. In this chapter, I discuss how the state secures the broad correspondence between race, class, and intercollegiate athletic participation. I begin by reviewing the *formal* state actions that create white suburban neighborhoods and permit these areas to secure and concentrate a disproportionate amount of state resources. This is not to say that other neighborhoods lack state infrastructure or support. Rather, I discuss how the resources that the state permits white suburban areas to concentrate better prepare suburban youth to develop the talent college athletic programs value.

Next, I discuss the manifestations of state *removal* (the absence of state regulations) and state *relational* (the state partnerships with private entities) tactics that have flourished under neoliberalism. These state workings increase disparity across suburban, urban, and rural communities. For instance, I explore how the state has privatized formerly "public" lands for the benefit of those with higher incomes.

I conclude the chapter by examining how public schools align white suburban areas with college sport access. I illustrate how public schools rely upon all three workings of the state—*formal*, *relational*, and *removal*—to host athletic programs that prepare high school athletes for college-level sport. I show how suburban schools are more likely than urban and rural schools to sponsor the sports offered by colleges. By hosting more sports as well as the particular sports sponsored by universities, public suburban schools grant their students greater opportunities to test out and refine their abilities until they find their athletic fit.

By outlining *how* the state secures greater opportunities for college athletic access for white suburban communities, I offer two broad arguments. First, I position athletic success as a process that begins with one's access to a wide range of sports. Second, I argue that the state restricts access for youth to develop the athletic talent universities desire. The state does so by narrowing the pool of potential athletes. While college sports are seemingly available to *all* youth, the state imbues certain communities with far greater opportunities than others. As a result, youth growing up in a white suburban community doubly benefit from state support: they have more athletic opportunities and less competition for the scarce college roster spots.

Lagoons and Leagues: The Spatial Terrains of Youth Sport

I began my interviews by asking participants, "Can you recall your earliest memory of sport?" Despite their regional and international differences, college athletes recounted striking similarities in how they accessed, and later incorporated, sport into their lives. Their first memories evoked fun or spontaneous forms of physical activity. Many recalled "playing tag" with their siblings or friends as their earliest memory of sport. These physical movements are "play," not formalized "sport." Sports are supported by social institutions with hierarchical relationships and governing bodies (Guttmann, 1978). Participants' first encounters with "formal" sports began when they entered the school system. All but three participants played a formal sport by kindergarten. Participants recalled that their caregivers enrolled them in sports that required membership fees, regularly scheduled practices and competitions, and coaches instructing them on the proper way to play—and they began these sports when they were as young as four years old. Access to formal sports at this age required certain physical and geographic infrastructure. Organized sport requires a *playing field*, albeit not an equal one.

Their sporting memories were anchored in their communities. Participants, across sport and racial identity, described their hometown as "affluent" or "suburban." Their communities included local parks, recreational centers, public fields, and blacktops. CM, a white woman and Coastal-U distance runner, began our conversation saying, "Running literally runs in my family." CM's mother and her older sisters were college runners. One of her sisters likely competed against Jenny Simpson. Even with these hereditary ties, CM's entry into sport did not begin with her genetics or in the sport of her relatives. Instead, like with many participants, CM's community infrastructure influenced her earliest memory of sport. While CM was too young to recall the details, she knew from family stories that her first athletic exposure came at "age one and a half," when her mom "threw me into the pool" during her sisters' swim lessons. In her telling, CM's journey to college as a track runner meant she "started off as a swimmer." A few years later, her mother enrolled her in community swim lessons, then soccer, softball, and horseback riding. She did not join a track team until her freshman year of high school.

The community features that littered study participants' early memories of sport—parks, playgrounds, and pools—are not naturally occurring and instead arise from specific state action. CM's community infrastructure enabled her to try numerous sports before selecting running. She believed swimming was her first sport because her neighborhood had abundant pools. "My community [has] twenty-seven pools and two lagoons and two man-made lakes. It's literally as suburbia as you can get. In between the two lakes there was a [recreational] center." In addition to the lakes, lagoons, and twenty-seven pools, CM's hometown has equestrian facilities. Local zoning regulations created a town of ranch-style homes where residents can keep large animals on their expansive lots. One of the neighborhoods hosts a notable equestrian center with a large indoor arena, professional riding lessons, and stables available to residents. The city also built equestrian trails for residents to ride horses outdoors.

The details of CM's community coalesce into a *spatial awareness* linked to social hierarchies (Kirby, 1996). Details such as walking to school without fear of violence, living in a community with a grocery store, and living in a neighborhood with parks and playgrounds all contribute to someone's chances to achieve a relatively free, dignified, and just life (Kirby, 1996; Shabazz, 2015). As Kathleen Kirby (1996) explains, the state informs our spatial awareness because as state subjects "we vary widely depending on the actual *place* we came from and the subsequent *places* we occupy" (p. 11, emphasis original). The characteristics of the space "largely dictat[e] our degree of mobility and our possible future locations" (Kirby, 1996, p. 12). Sports are spatialized terrains that use community infrastructure. Don Sabo and Phil Veliz's (2008) national study of youth sports found that a child's proximity to parks, playgrounds, gyms, and other athletic facilities led to greater athletic participation. They found that suburban communities, like CM's, have more sport opportunities than urban and rural areas, and thus white suburban youth become overrepresented in sports.

As a member of an upper-middle-class white suburban community, CM's default spatial awareness brought greater mobility prospects. CM's community had safe, open, and diverse athletic infrastructure that granted her multiple sporting options. CM was not forced to settle on running because of no other opportunities. Rather, she could *choose* running after testing her interest and proclivities in a range of other sports. The corresponding spatial awareness that CM's community affords its residents comes through the state neglecting and depriving other communities of such athletic abundance. Of course, members of lower-income, urban, and rural communities play sports, as physical activity is a foundational part of all human communities across time, space, nation, and culture (Miracle and Rees, 1994). Rather, my focus here is *how* the state elevates *certain* sports forms—those that rely upon community infrastructure—in ways that benefit white suburban communities.

The State of White Suburbia

CM's suburb, like all American suburbs, is a *formal* state product. Suburbs exist through centuries of state property laws that permitted the U.S. government the right to "seizure and appropriation" of Black labor and Native land (Harris, 1993, p. 1716). Law professor Cheryl Harris's (1993) theory of *whiteness as property* describes how contemporary racialized hierarchies of settlement, schooling, and economic stratification are rooted in historic definitions of property. Harris (1993) explains that the U.S. government's foundational prerogative was to expand the nation's territory and protect individual and private property rights.

The government intertwined legal definitions of what constituted a citizen (and therefore what entitled a person to property rights) and property (a resource with accumulating value that citizens can own and use) with an emerging racial hierarchy. Whiteness filtered legal claims to labor and land, conflating property ownership with "the cultural practices of whites" (Harris, 1993, p. 1721). State laws legalized and justified the seizure of Black labor and Native land. Those white by law received rights to develop land, to profit off of land, and to own and profit off the unpaid and extracted labor of enslaved peoples. These are just some examples of the evidence that W.E.B. Du Bois (1935) used to conclude that the precondition of the U.S. economy is whiteness. The state created the legal and institutional environment that permitted white people to use the U.S. land, resources, and racially minoritized populations to enrich themselves.

The three-hundred-year history of U.S. state-sponsored white supremacist political economies does not guarantee the continuation of racial/economic hierarchies (e.g., Harris, 1993; Leonardo, 2004). The benefits granted to contemporary white people are not passively accumulated over centuries. Instead, these benefits are actively maintained through contemporary formal state action that supports white people's continued domination of people of color. In the hundred years following the end of slavery, the state passed laws in all areas of public life, including housing, schooling, and employment, that permitted white people to retain the wealth earned through colonialism and slavery and transfer that wealth intergenerationally (Donnor, 2011; Dumas, 2011; Gillborn, 2005; Green and Gooden, 2016; Harris, 1993; Haycock, 2004; Heilig and Darling-Hammond, 2008; Hirsch, 1983; Katznelson, 2005; Knoester and Au, 2017; Kurashige, 2008; Ladson-Billings, 1994, 2003; Lassiter, 2012; Leonardo, 2004, 2009; Massey and Denton, 1998; Mills, 2003; Orfield and Frankenberg, 2013; Perry et al., 2018; Rothstein, 2017; Vaught, 2011, 2017).

Suburbs are a state-designed product for white middle-class communities to retain their colonial goods. In the mid-twentieth century, the state funded suburban housing projects to accommodate white flight (Kurashige, 2008). Cities subsidized these projects by offering developers discounted land and permitted communities to have tacit racial covenants to maintain all-white neighborhoods (Kurashige, 2008). Federal home loans and redlining policies permitted white people to increase their property values in suburban areas by virtue of excluding people of color (Kurashige, 2008; Lassiter, 2012; Rothstein, 2017). In the fifty years after *Brown v. Board of Education*—the Supreme Court ruling intended to desegregate American public schools—the state permitted suburban areas to create and oversee their own (mostly white) school systems with no obligation to integrate across neighboring communities (Donnor, 2011; Dumas, 2011; Green and Gooden, 2016; Harris, 1993; Knoester and Au, 2017; Nelson, 2008; Rothstein, 2017). These state actions permit today's white suburban communities to have disproportionate access to physical land, natural resources, and manmade infrastructure such as buildings, schools, and athletic fields. These state-secured benefits make suburban communities prime incubators for athletic talent.

Community Income: Concentrating Athletic Opportunities in Suburbia

The disproportionate resources and opportunities in white suburban communities are products of racial economies. Racial economies interrelate race and class (not separate), are communal (secured at the individual and group levels), and are relational (secured through struggles among unequally positioned groups). Through interrelated, communal, and relational race/class struggles, an individual's chances to access and navigate U.S. winnowing mechanisms are constricted or expanded. Thus, it is important to view social opportunities as not confined to the individual or familial level and instead at the communal and group level.

Participants recounted long athletic histories that involved playing in local parks, gyms, and pools; joining low-cost recreational leagues; competing for school teams; paying for privatized teams and coaches; and switching sports season by season. All of these athletic memories require communal engagement, whether with a park funded by local tax dollars or with a team coached by local parents whose jobs permit them the flexible schedules to volunteer. To contextualize participants' reflections, I examined whether their accounts of growing up in resource-rich areas were broadly represented. I was surprised to find that college athletes were even more likely than college students overall to come from wealthy communities.

While the educational literature is flush with studies that examine how community income shapes college access, few studies consider how it shapes college athletic access (see Hextrum, 2018, 2019a, 2020a, for related literature reviews). To address this gap, I created a database, Athlete's Hometown Stats, of Coastal-U track and field and crew rosters from 2005 to 2015 to identify demographic trends for athletes. The database included 1,487 Coastal-U track and crew athletes with a nearly even representation across sport and gender.[1] Rosters offered each athlete's hometown, high school, sport, and gender. I paired their high school and hometown with U.S. Census Bureau and Department of Education data to create measures for income and high school rank. I then used Coastal-U institutional reports to compare how community income and high school rank differ among the groups: Coastal-U students, Coastal-U track athletes, and Coastal-U rowers. I used the database to generate descriptive statistics and point to trends in *who* accesses college via athletics. Findings revealed that athletes came from wealthier communities than the average Coastal-U student.

Table 2.1
Estimated family median income across student and athlete populations

Income[a]	Students (%)	Crew (%)	Track (%)	Crew/track combined (%)
Less than $45,000[b]	25.80	0.26	0.55	0.43
Less than $50,000	24.00	0.78	2.77	1.94
$50,000 to $79,999	14.00	23.50	36.60	31.17
$80,000 to $124,999	23.00	42.03	44.73	43.61
$125,000 or more	38.00	33.68	15.90	23.27

[a]U.S. Census Bureau (2016) in 2014 dollars.
[b]Measure for state low income, used for financial aid distributions.

Measures for family incomes and secondary education quality yielded stark differences between the backgrounds of Coastal-U students and Coastal-U athletes. As table 2.1 shows, 0.43 percent of athletes (rowers and track athletes combined) compared to 25.8 percent of students qualified as low-income. Since median income varies across the country, I compared the income of athletes' communities to the median income of their respective states. Again, athletes pervaded middle- or upper-middle-income communities, as 71.2 percent lived in areas above the state's median income.

While athletes as a whole seemed more socially advantaged compared to students, differences across sports remained. Rowers attended higher ranked, often private, and majority-white high schools. Rowers also came from neighborhoods with greater median incomes than track and field athletes. But even track athletes, who are supposed to participate in a low-cost and accessible sport, were clustered in upper incomes. Less than 3 percent of track athletes came from communities where family incomes averaged less than $50,000 per year. Instead, track athletes were more often from communities with incomes ranging from $80,000 to $124,999 per year.

Table 2.1 suggests that Coastal-U Olympic sport athletes are more likely to live in higher-income areas than their nonathlete peers. The correspondence between community income and access to college via athletics raises additional questions. Why do certain communities have more sports than others? What state processes permit communities to shelter resources? And how do these processes restrict access to athletic talent? To answer these questions, I looked at the spatial properties of college athletes' communities that are secured by the state.

The Playing Fields of the State

Youth sports have become a staple of twenty-first-century suburban living (Messner, 2009). Suburbs now advertise the rankings of their public schools and their extensive sporting infrastructure. The government website for CM's hometown advertises amenities such as youth sports leagues; equestrian, bike, and pedestrian trails; and a "sports complex" that includes a skate park, baseball, soccer, and softball fields, and even a roller hockey rink. The seemingly benign infrastructure that characterizes a twenty-first-century suburb—high-ranked public schools, cars tucked into driveways and garages, homogenous homes, and extensive sporting fields—constitutes an exclusive lifestyle. Suburbs promise residents (the majority of whom are middle-class white families) that they provide the tools necessary to raise successful children in an increasingly competitive economic context (DeLuca and Andrews, 2016; Lareau, 2011, 2015; Messner, 2009; Weis et al., 2014).

Suburbs are built through iterations of state power. State bureaucracies, all while appearing fair and neutral to the public (Brown, 1992), created and contained the suburbs, allowing middle-class white residents to hoard resources within their borders. State bureaucracies allow residents to transfer formerly public lands into privatized communities, altering and restricting the natural environment to fit their needs. State bureaucracies empower private citizens to become state representatives, who go on to enact the state's will and protect social hierarchies. The paradox achieved in suburban living is that the state's invasions and orchestrations disappear into the monochrome backdrop. By distributing its power through bureaucracies, citizens, and private corporations, the state is omnipresent and absent. Scrutiny of the underlying characteristics that constitute suburban life reveals how the state creates the optimal conditions for *certain* youth to develop the athletic talent that aligns with university admission.

Bureaucracies of Containment: Zones, Maps, and Taxes

State-sponsored public housing projects are often characterized as dangerous units filled with undeserving and unworthy Black and Brown residents who are unwilling to work for a living (Shabazz, 2015; Vaught, 2017). In contrast, suburbs are built and maintained by private companies and filled with residents who can purchase their own dwelling. Even though the state does not build, fund, or manage most U.S. suburbs, it still constructs them. The spatial features of suburban life are shaped by city governments, which are *formal* state entities. Private developers must seek approval for housing projects through city bureaucracies like zoning boards. The 1926 Supreme Court case *Village of Euclid v. Ambler Realty Co.* permitted cities to dictate land use in their region. Following this case, cities enacted zoning codes to allocate certain portions of their territory to specified use like industrial, residential, or commercial properties. These codes concentrated low-income and people of color in areas close to industrial and hazardous production and isolated wealthy white families on larger properties farther from the dangers (Hirsch, 1983; Kirby, 1996; Kurashige, 2008; Massey and Denton, 1998; Perry et al., 2018; Rothstein, 2017; Shabazz,

2015; Zonta, 2019). As sports purists in the early twentieth century used amateurism to contain undesired populations (working-class white and Black athletes) and elements (commercialism) in revenue-generating sports while leaving the majority of sports pure and untainted for the desirable populations (elite white men), the state used the same fears to reach into private housing. Zoning is the twenty-first-century equivalent of redlining and racial housing covenants.

CM's suburb with twenty-seven pools uses containment language to construct their infrastructure. The city enacts zoning ordinances to "protect, promote, and enhance the public health, safety, and general welfare." CM's suburb is outside of a major urban center in which low-income Black and Latino people are concentrated. The suburb spans 4,234 square acres, 49 percent of which is dedicated to "estate residential," or low-density, large-lot, single-family homes, and "low-density residential," or single-family homes on large to medium lots. Zoning even within the suburb has created more exclusive tiers of access. The low-density region is home to more public infrastructure than the high-density region and has ten public parks (open to anyone) and seven private parks (open to fee-paying residents). Her suburb also has winding, disconnected streets that often end in cul-de-sacs, preventing through traffic and creating quieter living spaces. The smallest portion of the town, 14 percent, is allotted to "high-density residential," with lower-cost apartment and condominium units. Zoning has neglected the high-density region. This part of the community lacks parks and borders a noisy freeway.

CM's earliest memories of sports occurred in the public spaces of her suburb. Recall how she believes she was younger than two the first time she went in a public pool. She also played soccer, softball, and one season of basketball—despite her height, she never picked up the game—in her community parks. The "public" parks in CM's community are operated and monitored by local government bureaucracies. To schedule an athletic event in the park, a representative from the team must acquire a permit through the city. The permit request form asks the name and address of the applicant, the days and times of use for the facility, the estimated number of participants, and the estimated percentage of participants who are residents of the community. City bureaucrats evaluate the permit request and can request "any other information that the City finds reasonable or necessary to safeguard City Facilities and the public," including proof of residency. While city policy does not *require* that the applicant reside in the community, the city grants preference to community members and retains the right to refuse a permit to anyone who applies. Additionally, the city retains the right to inspect the permitted activity and revoke the permit if they observe policy violations. Requiring permits to use public land is one expression of what Wendy Brown (1992) characterizes as the bureaucratic form of state power. On the surface, these policies seem to permit universal access. But the layers of paperwork, surveillance, and discretion allow state actors to tailor and funnel resources to those who live within city limits.

Property taxes funded CM's community infrastructure. Local and federal governments permit communities to collect taxes and store revenue within their bounds. These funds can be immune to redistribution across other cities and counties (Nelson, 2008). As Lise Nelson (2008) explains, white communities created and utilized the phrase *taxpayers' rights* to successfully argue in court that those who pay taxes in a given area can control how the money is used regarding land use and facility construction. When the state permits property taxes to be stored within a community, instead of redistributed across communities, it reprivatizes public monies. This is one way the state helps secure relational forms of economic stratification. The community income patterns associated with the class structure persist as the state permits certain communities to keep, protect, and accumulate resources within their borders while depriving other communities of much-needed public funds (Johnson, 2014; Kirby, 1996; Nelson, 2008; Shabazz, 2015).

Taxpayer rights is one way the state grants legal cover to white suburbs who take racist/classist action. For instance, CM's suburb borders a community with a higher portion of lower-income Black residents. If a majority-Black youth soccer team from the neighboring city requested a permit to use the fields in CM's suburb, the city could deny them access due to inadequate residency. If the Black youth soccer team sued, CM's city would likely win because their permit process evaluates people's residency, not race. The courts have permitted these legal arguments, ignoring complex correlations between race and residency, in favor of elevating taxpayers' rights (Donnor, 2011; Dumas, 2011; Green and Gooden, 2016; Harris, 1993; Knoester and Au, 2017; Nelson, 2008). By granting taxpayers greater status, the state empowers them to defend their borders. These state actions permit white suburban areas to privatize public land for exclusive athletic facilities.

Bureaucracies of Infrastructure: Altering the Natural Environment

The playing fields and racing courses of organized team sports sponsored by colleges occur on altered physical terrain. A basketball court is a flat and level outdoor paved surface or an indoor polished wooden floor. A football field is flat and level turf, stretching over one hundred yards long including the end zones. A baseball diamond is both a field and dirt terrain, often bordered by dugouts and fences. Track and field and rowing are no different. Track requires a track—a flat and level quarter-mile circular multilane course. A component of track, cross country, uses dirt courses, often in wooded, hilly terrains. The throwing and jumping events also require specific facilities. Long jump and triple jump require a sand pit. The hammer and javelin throw into a large field. Shot putters heave their metal ball into a large, flat, marked area of compacted dirt, sand, or grass. High jumpers and pole vaulters need smooth runways, raised bars to ascend, and mats to cushion their decent. Rowing needs long, calm, flat bodies of water. The specificity of each sporting event invites state action. A state agency cuts down trees and clears brush to create a cross country course and paves a grassy field to install a basketball court. A state agency levels uneven terrain and seeds the ground to make a soccer field. When the state directly or indirectly creates athletic terrains in suburban communities that align with college sports, the state tips the scale in favor of the community residents' college recruitment chances.

Rowing is conducive to the state's alteration of the natural environment. As discussed in the previous chapter, the type of rowing sponsored by universities requires calm, flat water. Dams, significant state-infrastructure projects, tame rivers, which rowers can later exploit for their sport. During their construction, dams are a visible state action. But the passage of time can mute the state's presence.

Morgan, a white woman who grew up in New York State, saw joining the local rowing community as a "natural choice." Rowing, she explained, was central to her town's history. "Everybody at one point or another in their life does [a] learn-to-row." A "learn-to-row" is just as it sounds—an instructional session hosted by rowing clubs to teach new participants how to perform the sport. She went on to explain why learn-to-rows are so common in her community: "Our town was built because of the Erie Canal. We were like a port I guess but not anymore. It's just a decorative little thing that moves through the State. But that's what we row. [The canal] goes through the whole town. So, everybody knows about it. It's a very family-oriented, homey-suburban town. And so, everybody knows everybody. And rowing is in the middle of it all."

What Morgan sees as a "natural" choice of athletic opportunities is instead state engineered. In the early 1800s New York State funded the Erie Canal to connect Buffalo to Albany through 363 miles of artificial waterways (Finch, 1998). This infrastructure project cost the state $7 million in funding ($1.1 billion in 2018 money) and transformed New York City into an industrial port hub (Finch, 1998). The gains and harms of the Erie Canal were unequally felt. The resources produced through the canal were not redistributed to the low-paid Irish immigrants who built the project, nor were the land rights of Native peoples respectfully honored or negotiated (Finch, 1998). As the state modified the natural environment, it also modified the economic conditions to favor an influx of white European settlers. Rowing, which thrives on state-modified waters, was transported from the English to the Americans through imperialist takeover. As discussed in the previous chapter, amateur rowing rose to prominence in colleges and communities across the East Coast because it exemplified the elitist, masculine, white supremacist ideals espoused by academic eugenicists, politicians, and robber barons. Thus, the state's coordination of terrain, knowledge, industry, and citizenship creates damned waters for rowing. Whether Morgan realized it, she accepted these state benefits when she tried a learn-to-row and began her journey to college.

Morgan's access to a dammed waterway created centuries prior came through her community. Both the *removal* of state regulations and the state's *relational* strategies to partner with private companies and citizens restrict access to the clean, calm waters that crisscross the United States. Three thousand miles away, in the Pacific Northwest, burgeoning rowers encounter a similar spatial reality to Morgan's. Bays, lakes, jetties, and estuaries pervade the region. One area resident recalled seeing rowing shells tied to the tops of Subarus driving through the city streets. Property values in this part of the country are some of the nation's highest. Land in proximity to oceans, reservoirs, and bays is pricier than the open agrarian plains of the central and midwestern United States. Under capitalism, the U.S. government has chosen to deregulate housing markets and permit exploding housing prices in areas like Seattle. This has led to the rampant displacement of the predominately Black and Brown residents who previously inhabited cities, replacing them with predominately white upper-middle-income residents.

Yet again, rowing is at the center of it all. Seattle remains home to the nation's preeminent rowing clubs. The Pocock Rowing Center, a club known for producing future college and Olympic rowers, is located on the shores of Lake Union in Seattle's Eastlake district. According to Zillow, the median home price in this neighborhood is $631 per square foot, more than $100 more than the rest of Seattle, which is already one of the priciest cities in the nation. The median price for a home in Eastlake is $839,000. Astronomical housing costs function as their own containment mechanisms, permitting those with financial means to enter and access Seattle's resources.

Rowing has more commonsense associations with elitism and exclusivity than does track. Track, after all, is the sport that *requires only a pair of shoes.* But just as the state need not always operate in overt ways to achieve reproductive results, so too is the case for sport. Even seemingly accessible sports like track require state-mediated community resources.

Duane, a Black man who grew up on the West Coast, explained how financial investments are required in his sport, cross country running. Duane occupied a unique position. He straddled a middle-class mixed-race community and a predominately low-income Black community. He lived and went to school in the former, whereas his extended family lived in the latter. In witnessing many of his cousins drop out of sport, he noticed they lacked the necessary resources. "If you don't put a lot of money into it, you're not going to get the most out of it. . . . A lot of the inconsistencies or difficulties for people in track [occur] because they're not using proper equipment or they don't have the proper nutrition, they don't have the proper tools. . . . I can see why people would think, 'Oh you don't need a lot of money. You just throw on your shoes, throw on your shorts and run.' It's not that simple. Not if you want to save your body the terror."

Here Duane recounts how a superficial glance at track makes the sport appear to require minimal infrastructure—a pair of shoes and shorts. Reducing track to items of clothing that most people may already own makes the sport appear as if it is free of barriers, particularly compared to a sport like rowing, which, at minimum, requires a rowing shell fitted with sliding seats, riggers, and oars. Duane went on to explain why "it's not that simple." To save his body from the "terror" associated with training, he took certain measures to remain healthy. One of these measures was to "drive up to [dirt running] trails" to limit the amount of miles he ran on "concrete." This meant he needed access to a car and money for gas. The costs added up over the summer when he "trained individually and drove up to the trails twice a day to do distance runs."

Duane's precarious position on the boundaries of race and class made him an astute narrator for the litany of costs involved in track. As he points out, success within track and cross country requires communal investments. Duane notes that technically someone could do his sport in a concrete urban center. But this decision would wreak "terror" on the body in the form of physical injuries. Instead, Duane and his team trained and competed on dirt running trails in the state and national park systems nearby. As an endurance athlete, Duane sought long distances to complete his runs. The expansive trail systems in the parks provided him such space to optimize his trainings.

Duane, Morgan, and CM recount how their first encounters with athletics required community-level investments. Sport is a territory vocation. It occurs on swaths of natural resources modified by and through state interests. CM's suburbs artificially constructed concrete-lined pools and mowed grass fields to ensure the children in the area had spaces to learn sports. These spaces were sanctioned through zoning codes and bureaucratic permit processes that protected access for residents. Morgan and Duane played sports in a "natural" environment created by the state channeling water and clearing brush. As the state enters and organizes sport, so too does it control who is welcome to participate.

The People's Bureaucracy: Community Athletic Leagues

The public fields that characterize today's suburbs could be multiuse. A large grassy expanse can become a place for children to play tag, for adults to throw Frisbees, and for groups to meet for outdoor barbecues. Organized sports commandeer these public spaces and limit field use. Cities have granted sports leagues the authority to reserve public spaces for their use, denying other members access when sport is in session. In CM's community, bureaucrats grant permit preference to nonprofit recreational leagues. If a resident wanted to reserve a field for a birthday party the same day that a community soccer team wanted to host practice, the policy states the bureaucrat should grant the permit to the soccer team, not the resident. The city's preferential treatment for these teams is one indicator of the communal value suburbs place on athletics.

Community-sponsored athletic leagues were most participants' first exposure to organized sport. These local organizations are subsidized by the community. They use the community's physical infrastructure at little or no cost. The community leagues permit youth residents to learn and try various sports, encouraging them to find their niche. Brandon, a white man and college track athlete, spoke at length about how his community recreational facilities shaped his athletic success. Like Morgan, Brandon lived near a community park system that came through state action. His community, a suburb of a major midwestern city, founded a public park organization in 1908. In the early twentieth century, a state-sponsored water project created a landfill area that had yet to be classified for city use. One of the city leaders utilized a state law that said community park districts could "take possession" of unoccupied land for their purposes. And so Brandon's community formed a local bureaucracy to expand their city territory and create parks for local residents. A local university enlarged Brandon's park district by donating unused campus land to the residents for their recreational use. Throughout the twentieth century, city residents voted in favor of several multimillion-dollar referendums to build athletic facilities and maintain the parks. Today, the district has more than three hundred acres of land that includes nature trails; picnic areas; basketball courts; baseball, soccer, football, and softball fields; an indoor and outdoor ice rink; a golf and tennis club; a dog park and a dog beach; a fitness center; a child play area; sailboat rentals; a library; an aquatic center; and a skate park. The park district also hosts youth leagues, including soccer, basketball, and flag football for children as young as five.

Brandon recalled how the members of his community organized their free time through the athletic activities hosted by the park league, which varied season to season. The league hosted soccer in the fall, basketball and hockey in the winter, and volleyball in the summer. He recalled his childhood athletic experiences as composed of "a lot of variety." He went on to explain that "even through high school I was trying to still engage with a lot of different sports . . . I played basketball a lot, volleyball on the beach, tennis, and soccer after cross country practices."

Brandon recognized the low-cost youth sports were subsidized by the community's collective time and income. The sports were not free. "I mean, you had to pay to do it," he said, "but as a resident of the town, it was maybe like a hundred fifty dollars to join a league for the year, and it was like ten games or whatever that pays for like referees." He went on to clarify how his town's collective income further supported the park league. "There's a lot of money obviously. Lots of free time. People [could] make their kids practice or get better, playing these summer travel teams. . . . It was something that [is] really obvious. Every Saturday morning if you had a kid aged four to ten then your kid does athletics." Brandon sensed how his community operated and defined itself through the shared athletic activities of its members. Brandon's immersion in a white suburban community—one that was resource-rich with state-secured athletic opportunities—led him to view sports participation as an "obvious" choice. Like Morgan (for whom rowing seemed "natural"), Brandon's decision to play sports was orchestrated as the state denied these same opportunities to a neighboring community.

Brandon's suburb is just a few miles away from one of the nation's lowest-resourced Black communities. Brandon's suburb has its own city government and is not affiliated with the major metropolis it borders. This allows his suburb to function like CM's and create its own zoning codes, land-use policies, school districts, and funding schemes. Brandon's suburb is 84 percent white and 1.1 percent Black, with a median family income of $152,778. The urban center of his neighboring city is 67 percent Black and 10 percent white, with a median family income of $33,095. This urban area hosts the greatest density of Black people in the United States, as Black people comprise 97 percent of residents in one neighborhood. This neighborhood also has the area's lowest median income, at $27,355 per family.

Brandon's community athletic leagues and parks did not share their resources with the neighboring city. Instead, his youth and high school sport teams, even track, were "entirely white." It was not until he reached the high school state track meet that he noticed other teams had members of other racial groups competing. "But that was not characteristic of my high school at all," he noted. Brandon's athletic experience remained predominately white because his community league, like many across the country, asked for proof of residency in the area to join the league. Brandon's league, therefore, reflected the racial composition of his nearly all-white suburb. These residency requirements, which are monitored through state bureaucracies, allow resources to be contained within already-affluent suburban communities.

State mechanisms like community leagues, zoning laws, and property taxes intervene at the formative stage of youth. State containment policies permitting white citizens to accumulate resources in their regions create suburbs. These policies increase opportunities for white middle-class communities to develop athletic talent. Denying young children access while simultaneously herding resources and protections to another group creates an accelerating disparity in opposite directions. As the next section describes, local public schools—the supposed social safety net that should reverse these disparities—further the already-advantaged suburban youth's athletic opportunities.

Community Schools: Sponsoring College Sport Opportunities

Public schools are the last chance for children without recreational sports to join athletics (Sabo and Veliz, 2008). The sports that are (and are not) sponsored by community schools widen (or winnow) the athletic opportunity structure. Children growing up in communities with plentiful low-cost recreational sports, private youth leagues, community facilities, and school-sponsored sports have multiple chances to find a sport that fits their aptitudes and interests. Equally important, if local schools sponsor the same sports that colleges do, students can learn sports that offer special admission.

Yet again, the state has linked community income to educational opportunities. *Formal* state laws link public school funding to property taxes (Bucy, 2013). This funding scheme favors majority-white communities. The properties in majority-white communities hold greater economic value (Bucy, 2013; Harris, 1993; Rothstein, 2017). White people are more likely to live in larger houses, on larger lots, and in recently built or renovated homes (Perry et al., 2018; Zonta, 2019). White communities also retain the symbolic elements that translate to greater property values, such as safety, prosperity, and security (Harris, 1993; Kurashige, 2008; Leonardo, 2009). By tying school funding to community property values, white neighborhoods can raise greater revenues for their schools.

The state also allows white suburban communities to keep resources within their boundaries and not redistribute them to areas with lower property values (Green and Gooden, 2016). In 1973's *San Antonio Independent School District v. Rodriguez*, the Supreme Court reviewed Robin Hood laws, or practices in which states reallocated the property taxes accrued in wealthier neighborhoods to fund the schools in poorer regions. The Supreme Court deemed these practices unconstitutional, as the U.S. Constitution does not position education as a fundamental right (Moran, 1999). States learned to overcome the *San Antonio* decision by revising their state constitutions to define education as a fundamental right (Moran, 1999). The Supreme Court later ruled that if a state requires education in their constitution, then it must provide an "adequate" education to all residents (Moran, 1999, p. 35). But the state does not have to ensure that all students in the state can access the *same* schooling experience. The court has no standard for what constitutes an "adequate" education. This *removal* of state accountability for equitable compulsory schooling heightens race and class disparities.

The state relies upon *relational* powers, in this case relationships with white communities, to entrench hierarchies. White people have continuously chosen to move to and invest in majority-white areas over minority-majority areas. The resulting formal, removal, and relational powers of the state have returned U.S. education's race-based segregation and corresponding inequality to pre-1954 levels. Today, the U.S. educational system is more racially segregated than before

Brown v. Board of Education (Green and Gooden, 2016; Knoester and Au, 2017). White people are more likely to attend higher funded, majority-white schools than are people of color (Haycock, 2014). Racial minorities are more likely to attend underfunded schools in high-poverty school districts (Haycock, 2004; Heilig and Darling-Hammond, 2008; Knoester and Au, 2017; Orfield and Frankenberg, 2013). High-poverty schools where the majority of students are racial minorities are more likely to have emergency credentialed teachers, weakened infrastructure, larger classrooms sizes, outdated curriculum materials, and non-college-preparatory courses (Haycock, 2004; Knoester and Au, 2017).

This unequal race/class educational structure creates vast disparities in the extracurricular offerings of schools. It is no great leap to assume that if schools do not have the resources to pay teachers, it is unlikely they will sponsor a rowing team. Therefore, the public school system offers yet another opportunity for suburban communities to marshal and protect resources for their members. Both the quantity and quality of athletic opportunities offered in a given school increase the likelihood that someone becomes a college athlete.

Alignment: School and Sport Prospects across Secondary and Tertiary Education

Students who attend schools mirroring the college curriculum—providing Advanced Placement, International Baccalaureate, or college-preparatory courses—are advantaged in college admission compared to students who attend schools without these resources (Khan, 2012; Oakes, 2005, Shamash, 2018; Weis et al., 2014; Zarate and Pachon, 2006). Similarly, students who attend schools mirroring the college athletic curriculum are advantaged in athletic recruitment. Humans could organize sports in infinite ways as a cultural practice. A public school could design their own sport. A school could sponsor a noncompetitive sport like hiking without organized governing leagues. A school could sponsor one of the hundreds of organized sports that exist across the globe. Or a school could sponsor a sport commonly played in universities. When a high school sponsors an NCAA sport, they sponsor the sports path to college. A student who attends a high school with NCAA sports is positioned to develop the athletic talent universities desire.

The sports in my participants' high schools aligned with the NCAA. Division I fields thirty-eight sports (eighteen men's and twenty women's). I used institutional data from the NCAA and the National Federation of State High School Associations (NFHS) survey to compare the frequency of Division I sports across U.S. public high schools (Appendix C). In aggregate, U.S. high schools offer a wide range of sports that are not sponsored by the NCAA. For instance, bass fishing, Ultimate Frisbee, surfing, snowboarding, badminton, and squash are just some sports not examined here because they are not currently NCAA-sponsored sports. Of those sports opportunities offered at the high school level that correspond to college sports, there are 137,759 spots on college women's teams and 3,041,131 female high school athletes, and 147,302 spots on college men's teams and 4,368,425 male high school athletes (NFHS, 2019). The comparison shows that not all sports sponsored by Division I colleges are evenly and equally represented across American high schools.

To assess the opportunities available for high school athletes in a given sport to matriculate to college as a Division I athlete in that same sport, I compared the number of teams and roster spots offered across high school and college (per sport). Both comparisons were necessary because a given sport may have many more spots on a team than another sport. Interestingly, across all sports, the odds of matriculating are far from infinitesimal. The lowest odds hover around 1 percent, which translates to one person from every high school football team becoming a Division I football player. Importantly, the odds are not evenly distributed across sport or region.

Certain sports are more prevalent in high school, suggesting they are more accessible than others. Basketball is the top high school boys' sport, with 18,510 programs offered in fifty states and the District of Columbia. Track is the top girls' sport, with 488,592 athletes. Football has the most boy participants with 1,035,942 athletes. Yet colleges host sports that are rarely offered in high school. Rowing is the scarcest high school boys' sport, with 73 teams across seven states. Gymnastics has the fewest participants, with 1,570 male athletes across twenty-seven states. Rifle has the fewest female athletes, with 1,285 participants across ten states. Sports are also unequally represented across the United States. Beach volleyball is offered in schools in two states, fencing in six, water polo in six, rowing in seven, and rifle in ten. Put another way, forty-eight states (and the District of Columbia) *do not* offer beach volleyball at the high school level. Further, eleven college sports exist in thirty states or fewer.

The mismatch between the presence of sports in U.S. high schools and colleges shapes the odds for college recruitment. Men's wrestling, soccer, and track have the *fewest* teams at the college level relative to the high school level (0.68 percent wrestling, 1.6 percent soccer, and 1.7 percent track). Women's bowling, softball, and basketball have the *fewest* teams at the college level relative to the high school level (1.2 percent bowling, 1.9 percent softball, and 1.9 percent basketball). The scarcity of teams at the college level compared to the high school level suggests competition may be greater in these areas for college recruitment. It also suggests that these sports are widely offered at U.S. high schools compared to other college sports. Men's wrestling is one such case. It is the eighth most common high school sport, with nearly eleven thousand high school teams, yet merely seventy-three college teams.

It is necessary to look beyond team numbers and toward the number of roster spots to gain more accurate insight into the scope of opportunity at the college level. On average, football has the most roster spots (114 participants per team), whereas rifle has the fewest (6 participants per team). A school that sponsors rifle and football will have more spots open for aspiring football athletes compared to aspiring rifle athletes. Further, opportunities are shaped by the number of kids interested in playing a sport. Football may have more roster spots available, but the overall number of aspiring football players compared to rifle athletes is exponential. Combining available roster spots with interest in the sport, we see the *fewest* opportunities for participation in college men's programs are wrestling, basketball, and track (1 percent wresting, 1 percent basketball, and 1.7 percent track). The sports with the *fewest* roster spots for women's programs are bowling, volleyball, and basketball (1.1 percent bowling, 1.2 percent volleyball, and 1.2 percent basketball). Again, the likely assumption from this finding is that these sports have plentiful opportunities at the high school level and that the smaller team size at the college level may create greater competition for athletic recruitment.

High schools also sponsor sports that are relatively noncompetitive in college recruitment. Men's rowing, fencing, and gymnastics have the *most* teams at the college level relative to the high school level (40 percent rowing, 17 percent fencing, and 15 percent gymnastics). Women's rowing, beach volleyball, and fencing have the *most* teams at the college level relative to the high school level (119 percent rowing, 43 percent beach volleyball, and 22 percent fencing). Put differently, these are the rarest high school sports. In women's rowing, the percentage exceeds 100 percent, which shows that colleges are *more* likely than high schools to sponsor rowing. The sports with the *most* participation opportunities based upon available roster spots for men's programs are rowing, fencing, and gymnastics (55 percent rowing, 20 percent fencing, and 19 percent gymnastics). The sports with the *most* roster spots for women's programs are rowing, beach volleyball, and fencing (264 percent rowing, 54 percent beach volleyball, and 20 percent fencing). These trends suggest dramatically different odds of recruitment in certain sports over others. In the extreme case, a high school rower nearly has a guarantee to attend college for their sport.

It is worth noting that crew is a new NCAA sport. A 1994 gender equity investigation of the organization revealed that college sports had yet to create equal athletic opportunities for men and women in university-sponsored sports (NCAA, n.d.). The investigation motivated the NCAA to create an *emerging sport* category to encourage member institutions to add women's sports. In the intervening years, five sports were added to women's programs: ice hockey, water polo, bowling, field hockey, and rowing (NCAA, n.d.). As of 2020, the NCAA is supporting three emerging sports that may receive official sponsorship in the coming years: equestrian, rugby, and triathlon (NCAA, n.d.). As the above section illustrated, adding a new sport at the college level will not create greater equity in opportunity to become a college athlete. The 2017–2018 NFHS sport participation survey indicates that equestrian, rugby, and triathlon show even more restrictive patterns of access than rowing. Triathlon is not tracked by the survey, but equestrian and rugby are and are offered in only a few states. Equestrian has advantages in college recruitment similar to rowing. Equestrian has some of the greatest percentage of college teams relative to high school teams (83 percent) and greatest percentage of college roster spots relative to high school roster spots (127 percent). Like rowing, equestrian has *more* college roster spots than high school roster spots. If colleges added rugby, triathlon, and equestrian, the rare students with access to these sports in high school would have an immediate advantage.

These comparisons are a starting point to capture the availability of high school sports relative to college sports. The comparisons demonstrate broad trends in which sports may be more or less competitive for college recruitment. Schools that sponsor sports like rowing, fencing, and beach volleyball assist their students in the athletic recruitment process. Students who play these sports have greater odds of recruitment than students who play sports like wrestling, which are common in high schools but uncommon in college. Only 0.06 percent of U.S. public high schools offer a rowing team. This translates to a six in ten thousand chance that a youth growing up in the United States attends a public school with a rowing team. If you are a woman who attends such high school, you are almost guaranteed a spot on a college rowing team. But these odds are not evenly distributed across the country. Instead, state policies have ensured that communities and schools across the nation are unequally resourced. White suburban communities have more opportunities for youth to develop athletic talent. Public schools in these communities provide yet another chance for youth to further their athletic development. Families with the financial means to purchase a home in these communities are paving their child's path to college via sport.

Conclusion

Jenny Simpson made it to the 2016 Olympics. After competing in the 1,500-meter race, she ascended to the third-place podium and accepted the bronze medal. For a moment, the direct tie between her athleticism and the American state was visible. As she represented the United States on an international stage, the state's multilevel investment in Simpson paid off. Simpson embodied America's version of success—hard work, determination, grit, fortitude—all features endemic to long-distance running. Simpson embodied upward mobility—as a woman from a middle-class community, she did face credible barriers to become an Olympian. She could not directly purchase her Olympic medal and likely faced gender discrimination as a woman in a men's sporting world. Simpson disseminated the narrative that *all she needed was a pair of shoes* to reach such heights. These are just some of the ways the Olympic Games represent one of the greatest contradictions of state power. In a moment of heightened state visibility—nations competing against each other for athletic and, in turn, global supremacy—the state's role in creating these athletes recedes. Athletes' success is distilled to their own, not the state's, work. These moments permit the state to credibly claim it offers fair opportunities to all Americans, all the while it disproportionately invests in white suburbanites.

The state's role in athletics begins with establishing and preserving unequal residential communities. The racial and economic disparities that constitute American housing are not naturally occurring, do not arise accidentally, and are not the products of an individual's work ethic. Instead, historic and contemporary state practices have built and maintained white, resource-rich suburban communities. Through varied and multifaceted workings of the state such as *formal* practices like zoning and tax laws, *relational* practices like relying upon private citizens to take on bureaucrat roles and monitor land-use permits, and *removal* tactics like the state's inaction to define and execute equitable educational funding, the state, in partnership with private citizens and agencies, has ensured white communities are elevated and enriched at the expense of racial and economic equity. In this chapter, I positioned athletic talent as a communal property that is connected to these broader state workings and partnerships. Scrutinizing the state reveals how opportunities to develop athletic talent are maldistributed to favor white middle-class citizens.

White middle-class communities have far greater physical infrastructure, recreational leagues, and school-sponsored sport teams than communities whose residents are majority low-income and/or racial minorities and rural areas. These community-level differences manifest in differential opportunities. Narratives from college athletes revealed that access to resource-rich communities is a precondition to developing athletic talent. Examining ten years of Coastal-U athletic rosters bolstered their insights and revealed a broad correspondence between white middle-class communities and athletic participation. College athletes at Coastal-U came from neighborhoods with higher median incomes and higher ranked schools than their student peers. The state brokered this correspondence by *containing* opportunities to develop athletic talent in white suburban areas. These containment practices protect the underlying features of college sports amateurism: exclusion. While contemporary college athletes are no longer required to prove their gentlemanly lineages, for many their path to college still originates in exclusive enclaves.

The community-level athletic inequities shaped by the state set the backdrop for the intergenerational transfer of privilege. Those born into white suburban areas are imbued with advantages. I have indicated how the state secures the conditions that permit white middle-class communities and schools to marshal disproportionate resources. Suburban residents can access these resources to develop athletic talent. But not *all* members of white suburban youth become college athletes. We must look within these communities to understand how sport opportunities are even further restricted. In the next chapter, I describe how the state supports racial and gender segregation to further distort and restrict opportunities to develop athletic talent. State support for segregation ensures that not all paths to college within suburbia are equal.

3

Build a Wall

The State Segregates Sports

The Physicist, a proud science major who selected his pseudonym to reflect his accomplishments, grew up in an affluent white suburb on the West Coast. The family median income of his area was $135,587, nearly triple the state's average. His community was also 83.8 percent white—in a state that was 37 percent white. His first exposure to organized sports came through community leagues where he played soccer, baseball, and basketball. His caregivers also enrolled him in tennis lessons through a private sports club, of which they were members. He soon joined a private tennis club team and competed against other clubs in the region. After several years of competing, he found he liked the conditioning aspect of tennis more than the game itself. He especially enjoyed the chance to race his classmates during PE class: "I always loved the PE mile. We had these wood slat boards up in the locker room for the records—the top-ten records in the mile. It was always my goal to be at the top of that list. And I worked my way up and worked my way up. And eventually ran 5:22 and the record was 5:20, so I was number two on the list. I almost got there."

The Physicist's middle school facilitated his first taste of running success. The competition encouraged youth to best one another, pushing their bodies to the limit to reach the top of the records chart. Through these seemingly innocuous moments within a public school—walking into a gender-segregated locker room to change, glancing up at the record board, finishing a timed mile run, rearranging the names on the record list—the state's investment in race, class, and gender structures reemerges. Aggression, competition, and hierarchy, all fundamental characteristics of whiteness, masculinity, and capitalism, are engraved in the names on the wooden slats in the middle school boy's locker room.

Climbing the mile record boards ignited the Physicist's running career. His middle school sponsored a cross country team, which he joined to improve his mile time. He became an undefeated middle school runner, and his confidence swelled. By high school he quit all other sports to specialize in cross country and track.

The Physicist landed in his college event after testing his abilities in half a dozen sports. As he traversed recreational, private club, and school-sponsored sports teams, he encountered "a lot of white kids" as his teammates—even on his track team, a sport historically and culturally reclaimed by Black athletes (Edwards, 1979; Eitzen, 2016; Lansbury, 2001). The Physicist also found his athletic fit within a gender-segregated sporting world. His recreation, private club, and school teams restricted participation to those who are categorized as male, not female. When he competed to become the best miler, he knew the athletes to beat were boys, not girls. When he joined the cross country and track and field teams, he competed in boys-only not coed events. The Physicist encountered mostly men as the officials and coaches across athletic spaces. He saw versions of himself reflected in the top athletes and sport leaders. His gender never limited the sports he could play or informed the kinds of training he did.

The Physicist could not recall a time when his race or gender limited his sport participation. The freedom to *not* face race or gender barriers when navigating America's institutions reflects the entrenched and "rarely apparent" "assumptions, privileges, and benefits that accompany the status of being white" under the U.S. racial order (Harris, 1993, p. 1713) and male under the U.S. gender order (Messner, 2009). The Physicist could freely choose among a myriad of athletic options and focus on finding the sport that best fit his interests and aptitude. The freedom to choose is one of the greatest benefits retained by dominant groups in the post–civil rights era. U.S. law disallows private or public agencies to deny access to someone because of their race, ethnicity, national origin, or gender. Yet the unfortunate lesson from the civil rights era is prohibiting discrimination does not equate to equal opportunity (Crenshaw, 1988; Harris, 1993; Mills, 2003; Vaught, 2017). When the state offered greater legal protections to historically disenfranchised groups, it also preserved the legal mechanisms that elevated capitalism, whiteness, and masculinity. As a result, the disparate opportunity structures—reflected in the *choices* Americans have to live a free and dignified life—remained.

The 1954 Supreme Court ruling *Brown v. Board of Education* exemplified how the state, under the guise of extending greater choices to Black Americans, protected the advantages white Americans hold under the U.S. racial order. The court overturned the separate-but-equal precedent established in *Plessy v.*

Ferguson (1896). *Plessy* examined whether formalized segregation enacted by state actors (defined as local, state, and federal governments) violated Black Americans' Fourteenth Amendment rights, or equal protection under the law. The *Plessy* ruling affirmed the constitutionality of segregation and granted states and private business the right to separate individuals by race.

Fifty-eight years later, the Supreme Court revisited whether segregation violated the Fourteenth Amendment, this time applying the question to public education. The unanimous *Brown* decision disagreed with *Plessy*'s findings and ruled "the evil of state-mandated segregation was the conveyance of a sense of unworthiness and inferiority" (Harris, 1993, p. 1750, quoting *Brown*). *Brown* rejected the logic that separate could ever be equal, as separation telegraphed to children of color that their presence harmed white children. In turn, white children received *superior* legal treatment from the state, or the protection *from* the supposedly harmful children of color, through all-white schools. Children of color received no such protections. *Brown* was revolutionary because it deviated from centuries of legal precedent that sympathized with and supported white people's claim to superior treatment under the law.

Brown's aspirations to desegregate America were undercut by the court's unwillingness to define or dismantle the legal advantages white people accrued until that point in time. The court conflated banning segregation to achieving equality. To see how and why this approach failed, let's return to the Physicist's mile test. The PE mile is four, 400-meter laps around a flat track. Imagine if the state sponsored a mile test in which only white children could enter the race. After concerted protest and public dissent from Black communities, Black children earn their right to enter the race. At this point, the white children have completed three of the four laps. While the state permits Black children to enter the race, they route them onto a different track, one covered in hills, potholes, and hurdles. The state also invites white spectators to line the Black-only track and attack Black children as they race. After additional protest and public dissent declaring that the race remains unfair, Black children once again gain the attention of the state. The state returns to survey the race and decides that separate mile races are unconstitutional. The state now permits Black children to compete on the same smooth, flat track as white children. While this decision leads to far superior conditions for Black children compared to when they started, the state takes no responsibility for its role in creating the unequal races. As a result, the court does little. The court does not stop and restart the race so that all children can compete fairly on the smooth, flat track. Instead, the court permits white children to retain their multi-lap advantage and keep running the race—at this point most white children have already crossed the finish line. The court does not punish the white spectators who physically harmed (and in some cases killed) the Black children who raced. The court does not dictate *how* Black children can leave their segregated, barrier-ridden track and enter the smooth, flat track. The court does not invalidate the superior times white children earn in this race. Instead, the white children's names and times are engraved on wooden boards and hung in the locker room. Their race results are celebrated as victories and achievements, earned through their hard work and effort. The court then permits white children to use these achievements to access other institutions like higher education and employment. Any protests by the Black children that the race is unfair are met with disdain and skepticism by the state and white children alike. Instead, Black children are told their failure to catch white children is due to their poor life choices, not a race invented and rigged by the state to always end with white victors. The mile metaphor showcases how *Brown* failed to remedy the centuries of harm enacted by the state in partnership with white communities. The inadequacy of *Brown* also created a new form of white advantage: white people retained their historical head start and disseminated the lie that Americans compete under the same conditions.

The state's apocryphal commitment to equity extends into the fight over women's access to education. Here, the state reversed its own stance on segregation—no longer viewing it as a "conveyance of a sense of unworthiness and inferiority" to the subordinate group. Rather, segregation became the state's remedy for gender equity, particularly for women athletes.

Women's educational access flowed through Title IX, the 1972 amendment to the 1964 Civil Rights Act. Title IX prevented federally funded education programs from discriminating on the basis of sex. Whereas *Brown* rejected the notion of inherent racial differences, Title IX codified inherent gender differences (Milner and Braddock, 2016). Legal interpretations of gender equity were filtered through a Western view of gender binarism that constructs men and women as biological opposites. Under this frame, men retain corporeal tendencies such as a proclivity toward sexual and physical violence from which women (viz., white women) must be protected (Brown, 1992, 1995; Hood-Williams, 1995; Milner and Braddock, 2016). Women become incapable of protecting themselves, other women, and other men from men's violence. This view of gender has justified men's monopolistic control of the private household and political arena for centuries (Brown, 1992).

When considering whether and how to offer educational access to women, the state incorporated this view of inherent, violent, masculine supremacy into their approach to gender equity. Like white people under the *Brown* decision, men were not punished or discouraged for their supremacist benefits. Rather, the state normalized this view of masculinity and forced women to accommodate it. The 1975 and 1979 federal interpretations of Title IX clarified that it applied to sports and that schools could host sex-segregated athletic programs. Over the next thirty years, court precedent reaffirmed schools' rights to uphold gender-segregated sports under the belief that women would be harmed if they competed alongside or against men (Milner and Braddock, 2016; Suggs, 2005). As I discuss later in the chapter, this sex-segregated system instituted men's athletic dominance by permitting men to retain greater athletic opportunities in higher funded sports with more media investment and retain the majority of leadership and power positions over women's sports. To return to the mile metaphor, women were also invited into the race once white men had completed three laps. They could not compete on the same smooth, flat track as white men but were relegated to a segregated, barrier-ridden terrain. Within these conditions, women never catch up to the men's mile pace. Women do not protest segregation, but instead embrace the opportunity to play. They see participating on a separate and unequal track as the only *choice* they have.

This chapter explores how the civil rights era never undid the structural advantages of white people, men, and, in particular, white men. I track one thread of civil rights rulings—segregation—to discuss the contradictions that arise for disenfranchised groups seeking protection through the state. How the state defines and administers race and gender segregation reflects one such contradiction that pervades the sports path to college. In the case of race, the state defines equity as the *absence of* state-instituted segregation. In the case of gender, the state defines equity as the *presence of* state-instituted segregation. These differential framings are united through the language of *choice*. Any resulting race and gender hierarchies are reduced to individual decisions, not to state action. The language of choice breathes new life into the *gentleman amateur*. Just as the *gentleman amateur chose* to play sports for pleasure, not for profit—a framing that disguised the allegiance between colleges to actively prevent most women, people of color, and working-class athletes from joining their teams— today's athletes cannot freely *choose* to play sports.

Instead, white suburban men like the Physicist retain the greatest number of choices. They are materially and culturally eligible for *all* sports. In contrast, women and people of color are relegated to choose from *certain* sports. The "choices" individuals make within their narrower selection pools substantiate essentialized notions of race and gender—that these categories of difference are inherent, natural, and fixed rather than produced through and within specific historical, cultural, economic, and social contexts (e.g., Butler, 2011; Collins, 2005; Crenshaw, 1988, 1991, 1992; Harris, 1993; hooks, 1984; James, 1996; Lorber, 1994; McClintock, 1995; Messner, 1992, 2002, 2009; Mills, 2003; Naples, 2003; Vaught, 2011, 2017; Weedon, 1997). Therefore, a central task of this chapter is to showcase how the sports path to college contains different routes for people of color and women. Their pathways are limited not by desire, biology, or preference but rather by state-constructed walls that direct and restrict their college-going options.

Racial Segregation on the Sports Path to College

One of the largest benefits that white people retain in our current racial order is to live and recreate in majority-white settings (Harris, 1993). Over several decades of reviewing remedies to de jure or state-sponsored racial segregation, the courts concluded that the state cannot fix de facto segregation, or the "choice" of white people to live in all-white areas (Donnor, 2011; Dumas, 2011; Vaught, 2017). Nearly 87 percent of study participants lived in predominantly white communities. Sixteen of the forty-seven athletes, half of whom were rowers, came from communities that were 80 percent or more white. Eight—most of whom were people of color—came from communities less than 50 percent white. Study participants described their white communities in positive language. They noted how their neighborhoods had "a good school district" (Sanya) and were "pretty calm, not a lot happening" (Boris), "very secluded" (Kayla), and "safe" (George). Concepts of safety, quality, opportunity, and comfort as proxies for whiteness reflect how white people come to expect and, in turn, defend their greater access to institutional benefits (Leonardo, 2009).

When whiteness becomes the default characteristic, white people learn to see themselves as raceless or devoid of a racial subjectivity. When I asked participants to define their racial identity, people of color spoke definitively and in nuanced terms. Sometimes, they contextualized their answer, explaining to me why they identified in one category over the other. In contrast, white athletes spoke tentatively about their racial identity. Many answered with a question mark and expressed confusion about the question or their answer.

REGGIE: I'm Caucasian? Anglo-Saxon? Which one? Caucasian. Don't know.
ICEMAN: Caucasian? Right?
SANYA: I hate this—like, I guess, white? Is that a race?
VICTORIA: White? [pause] Canadian?

White athletes struggled to name their racial identity and privilege because segregation enables white people to see themselves as raceless, not as active racial participants (Du Bois, 1935; Harris, 1993; Leonardo, 2004, 2009).

Amanda's story of sport involvement reveals how racially segregated communities and sports create underdeveloped notions of race and racism in white athletes. Amanda, a white woman from a community over 77 percent white, described her upbringing in race-neutral terms until pressed. Amanda's first athletic activity was community-sponsored soccer. She recalled joining the team because "everyone in my kindergarten class was going to play soccer." Her taller-than-average height made her uncoordinated, and her coach relegated her to the goalkeeper position. She loved playing goalie and developed strong connections with her teammates. But she knew she had only a small chance, if any, to play soccer beyond the recreational level. Amanda learned about rowing while watching a television show featuring someone attending Stanford on a rowing scholarship. She also wanted to attend a school like Stanford. She researched rowing clubs and convinced her parents to pay the dues.

When asked about the racial demographics of her sporting experiences, Amanda replied, "[Race had] never really been on my radar until we [had] one Black girl on the [club] team. . . . [In college] I remember [during one regatta] looking over at the start line and, and there was like a Black girl . . . racing against us. And I was like, 'Whoa.' It was surprising to me. And then I was mad at myself that that was surprising. That shouldn't be surprising, but it is in this sport. . . . And it was something of note." While Amanda chastises her own racial ignorance, she does not consider how white communities, and her subject position within one, also arise from racial processes. In all-white venues, white people do not think about their race, about how they accessed the setting, or about how the venue became, and remains, exclusively white. Only in fleeting encounters with the rare person of color in the sport does Amanda consider how white athletes' overrepresentation in spaces like rowing is achieved by excluding Black athletes.

How Sports Become White

In April 2019, during the "Weekend Update" segment of *Saturday Night Live*, host Michael Che made the following joke about the emerging college admission scandal: "Lori Loughlin appeared in court to face charges that she bribed college officials. It's amazing that people are so shocked by this story. Rich people have been finding loop-holes to get their kids in college forever. For example: lacrosse." Che did not mention Loughlin's race or the race of the hypothetical lacrosse players. But as he told the joke pictures of both flanked the screen. The actress and the lacrosse players were visibly white. Che has also made jokes that conflate race and class throughout his tenure on "Weekend Update." In Che's telling, to call someone a "rich person" is to call someone white. More importantly, Che did not need to waste airtime to name the race of the lacrosse players. This joke lands because the *SNL* audience already imagines a sport like lacrosse filled with white athletes. Like most contemporary racial associations, colonialism facilitated white people's affiliation with the sport. Lacrosse originated in North American tribal cultures who played the game for spiritual and recreational purposes. White colonial settlers learned of and later stole the sport for themselves as they violently traversed the Americas (Clayton, 2020).

Today's commonsense notion linking lacrosse and whiteness emerges through racial processes that infect every facet of American life. While race primarily roots itself in the physical body (Mills, 2003), it also transcends the body and becomes located in the physical world. Physical infrastructures such as schools, houses, streets, storefronts, and athletic facilities become encoded with racial logics (Shabazz, 2015). While these spaces are no longer marked with signs that demark "whites only," we learn to encode these spaces with racial synonyms that still tell us as much. As we navigate physical spaces, we encounter particular racialized beings, messages, and symbols that become grounded in the material places we occupy. In the previous chapter, CM described her suburb, which included twenty-seven swimming pools and a recreational center. Films, television shows, and novels about suburban living tell us that upscale neighborhoods like this are filled with white people. We do not need CM to tell us the racial demographics of her community; the physical infrastructure has already said as much.

The physical infrastructures used by sports—swimming pools, tennis courts, lacrosse fields—are racialized. These terrains exist in neighborhoods and country clubs marked by histories of racial segregation. According to Anthony Kwame Harrison (2013), these physical environments become encoded with racialized collective memories of pleasure or trauma that inform access. The white racial group has predominantly positive memories of swimming. Pools feature in white lifestyles as signs of affluence, leisure, and pleasure. In contrast, for members of the Black community pools may invoke memories of collective trauma. Public recreational spaces like pools were some of the last spaces to desegregate (Mowatt, 2009). White people fought desegregating public pools because swimming represented a "moderately sexualized recreational activity," which could ignite miscegenation (Mowatt, 2009, p. 518). Many towns in the South filled their pools with dirt so they would not have to permit Black people to swim alongside white people (Hackman, 2015). Once again, terrain alteration—in this case dismantling leisure opportunities—demonstrates how whiteness is defined through its distance from Blackness. Here, white people destroyed their own backyards to avoid playing with Black people. These tactics persist in today's fights over swimming pools. In 2009, a predominately white swim club denied access to Latino and Black children, citing concerns of safety and overcrowding (Mowatt, 2009). The club did not raise these concerns when white children sought access. This more benign language of "safety" produces the same effect as turning to the shovel: exclusion. The latter example is even more dangerous because white communities have found a way to protect their privileged access. They can have their white-only pool and swim in it too.

These exclusionary tactics are further justified by rooting race in the body. A 1969 study claimed that Black bodies were less buoyant and could not perform as well in cold water as compared to white bodies—a racist myth that still plagues swimming (Wiltse, 2014). These myths disguise the partnership between the state and the white community to actively exclude Black people from athletic opportunities. Instead, we learn that overrepresentation of white youth across all sports and the lack of representation of Black youth in most sports results from individual choices, not from the racist removal of opportunity.

Rowing: The Whitewashed Sport

Boys in the Boat (2013), the *New York Times* best-selling sports book, tells the history of the 1936 U.S. men's rowing team. Author Daniel James Brown narrates the success of the men's program as largely due to grit, determination, and fortitude in a grueling sport. The story centers on a class struggle, one in which the crews on the West Coast and East Coast battle it out for a chance to represent the United States in the Olympics. As discussed in chapter 1, colleges, particularly on the West Coast, had deviated from the strict amateur rules of the day and permitted limited access to white working-class men for the first time. The West Coast wins, signaling a victory for the American mobility narrative. But through this class-based battle, whiteness, masculinity, and elitism in rowing were solidified.

The American crews were fighting for a chance to attend the Hitler Games. Adolf Hitler used the 1936 Olympics to gain international legitimacy for the Third Reich. Despite this white supremacist backdrop, *Boys in the Boat* has only one reference to race. As the U.S. team is preparing for the Olympics, Brown invokes the parallel story of African American boxing great Joe Louis to contrast America's racial order to Germany's. Brown (2013) framed Louis as a world-class boxer whose athletic achievements helped "erode the racial attitudes of many—though far from all—white Americans" (p. 259). In 1938, Louis started his decade-long reign as world heavyweight champion—a title he held "long after [Nazi propaganda minister] Joseph Goebbels's charred body had been pulled out of the smoldering rubble of the Reich Chancellery" (p. 261).

Brown's (2013) account of Louis singularly defeating global white supremacy is a familiar whitewashing of American history. Details of America's racial order are glossed over in favor of painting the Nazis as the true white supremacists. America's eugenics movement, which inspired Hitler's concentration camps; America's Jim Crow South, in which Louis was born and raised; America's segregated and unequal armed forces, in which Black Americans gave their lives fighting against Hitler; America's white sport leaders and tax collectors that appropriated the millions Louis earned, leaving him nearly penniless at his death: these are just some of the racial plotlines erased in Brown's story. Ignoring America's founding role in global white supremacy frees the U.S. government, and its Olympic sporting apparatuses, from rectifying racial inequity.

Louis, like the Black rower who showed Amanda most rowers are white, becomes the one concrete racial object in Brown's story. As philosopher Richard Dyer (1993) explains, whiteness expunges the specific and concrete workings of racial dominance because it has no "particularizing quality" and instead, paradoxically, encompasses both everything and nothing (p. 142).

Brown mentions Louis's race, as only people of color can become racial actors in white stories. The other main actors in the story—the rowers, their families, their coaches, the referees, the reporters, and the Olympic Committee—receive no such racial modifiers. White people are permitted to be all the actors in the story—the villains, heroes, and bureaucrats. In this case, the raceless "boys" in the boat are also relieved of their racial benefits. The white-segregated communities and athletic worlds that transformed the "boys" into world-class rowers become inscrutable details in this narrative.

The workings of whiteness in *Boys in the Boat* disguise how the central sport in the story, rowing, is an almost exclusively white sport. As of 2019, only two Black women have rowed for the U.S. Olympic team (Bruggeman, 2019). Anita DeFrantz became the first when she competed in the eight-person boat event in the 1976 games (DeFrantz and Young, 2017).[1] Patricia Spratlen followed Anita the next cycle but could not compete due to the 1980 boycott. Black men did not enter the Olympic levels of the sport until the twenty-first century. Aquil Abdullah because the first Black U.S. men's rower when he competed in the single scull event in 2004 (Norris, 2004). Despite DeFrantz, Spratlen, and Abdullah's achievements, the three last Olympic eights for U.S. men and women were exclusively white. Most college programs across the country are completely white.

As members of the dominant racial group, white people consistently receive messages that they belong in, and are entitled to, all sectors of society. A white youth growing up reading *Boys in the Boat* or watching the 2016 U.S. women's rowing team win the Olympic gold medal can imagine herself as one of the main characters. A Black youth encountering the same sport stories cannot find herself anywhere in the plotline. Amanda recalled that she joined a rowing club *after* she saw the sport referenced on a television show. While she could not recall which show it was, chances are that the characters were white. There was something in the television show that allowed her to see herself in the characters. When she showed up to the first practice, her feelings were reaffirmed by her interactions with coaches and teammates.

When Amanda first joined the team she encountered immediate positive affirmations. Right away her height drew the attention of the coaches. "From the first day of practice I heard, '[You're] going to be good,' [and] 'You have so much potential.' Because I was already huge in seventh grade. And [the coaches] were like, 'Wow, we have so much time to build her into this great athlete.'" Several social processes become disguised and mutated by reducing Amanda's athletic potential to her height. First, Amanda had plentiful opportunities in her community to try multiple sports. These material advantages enabled her to develop and improve her ability regardless of any bodily limitations. Second, she described the totality of her athletic experiences as nearly exclusively white. Her older teammates, mentors, and coaches all shared her racial position. Amanda said she did not think she benefited from these environments: "I don't think [my race] has been to my advantage." But she also never encountered a moment of friction, resistance, or struggle based on her race in sport. Her introduction to rowing was *free from disadvantage*. While Amanda may attribute her decision to row to her height, this choice cannot be disentangled from the racial spacialities she navigated along the way.

When I asked about the racial demographics of their team, rowers said "white." They recounted vivid and strict patterns of racial groupings across sport and position. Noelle and Morgan, both white women growing up on opposite U.S. coasts, stated that they played "white" sports. Noelle described her athletic history as "playing white sports like swimming, water polo, rowing. All very European-dominated sports." Morgan agreed, stating that "rowing is such a white-washed sport. Our entire [college] team [is white]. . . . We're also 75 percent blonde." Noelle went on to explain why she believed rowing was "European-dominated." "It has to do with the body type and stuff like that . . . scientifically, a German girl, versus an African American girl—German girl is probably not going to be the sprinter. You know? When you have someone who's 6'2" and 190 pounds."

A constellation of state efforts to perpetuate the fiction of inherent racial differences emerges in Noelle's quote. The ease through which she links nationality, race, and body type reflects the century-long partnership between academic research and sport that used athletic outcomes to justify white male rule. This "science"—also known as eugenics—traveled from U.S. universities to the Third Reich. The 1936 Nazi Olympic games put Aryan athletic supremacy on display. While the Black American athlete Jesse Owens embarrassed Hitler by dominating the track events, Hitler succeeded overall in wedding bodily discipline, endurance, and work ethic to Aryanness (Brown, 2013). Aryan athletes—including the American *boys in the boat*—dominated endurance events, further retrenching whiteness' monopoly of certain sport forms. Then and now, the Aryan rower becomes visible through its perennial definitional opposite: the Black track athlete. Each racialized athlete enlivens the other and produces the following commonsensical athletic associations: *Someone is a rower because they are not a sprinter. Someone is white because they are not Black. Someone is a sprinter because they are Black. White people cannot be sprinters. Black people cannot be rowers.* This commonsense refrain has the dual purpose of regrounding race in physical, immutable categories of difference that support white supremacist thought and disguising the structural barriers that prohibit Black people from rowing. Both purposes conceal how the state concentrates athletic advantages in white suburban areas.

Track and Field: "You're No Usain Bolt"

Jesse Owens showed the world that Black people could win a white game. He also helped solidify the connection between track and field and Black communities. Eleven people of color—all track and field athletes—participated in this study. Nine identified as Black, two identified as mixed race: one as Latina and white and one as white and Middle Eastern. Middle- and upper-middle-class athletes, across racial groups, tried numerous sports at an early age. White athletes continued to participate in a broad array of athletic activities—including ones associated with Black communities like basketball, football, and track—up to and through high school. White athletes selected their sports based on athletic fit. They believed they had better future opportunities in rowing or cross country than, say, basketball or football (a phenomenon I discuss in greater detail in chapter 4). Black athletes gravitated to track and ended their careers in other sports sooner than white athletes. The primary reason Black athletes gave for choosing track was not athletic ability but racial representation.

LeVar, a Black man who grew up in a white suburb, explained that he avoided all-white sports. LeVar attended a mostly white school. His days were filled with small acts of racism—teachers or peers questioning his hair style—and larger acts—criminal accusations and disproportionate disciplining. Sports let LeVar escape these daily educational harms. LeVar's parents had him try every sport in his suburban neighborhood. But LeVar was searching for one where he could see others like him. "I wasn't going to play water polo. And if I did, I'd probably be the only Black person on the team. . . . I played a lot of sports, and a lot of the teams were in different places. So I've been on basketball teams with all white kids. And for that reason, as a young person, it was like, 'Okay, it can't be that all Black people play basketball.' That probably wasn't the 100 percent correct connection but it led me to the right answer." LeVar's "right answer" is that certain sports, like rowing, are not white—*all* sports are white. White children can play any sport, whereas social and economic barriers restrict sports options for Black children. LeVar's parents researched and found a majority-Black basketball travel team in a neighboring town. His parents would drive upward of forty minutes each way to practice so he could play with people who would not question his race. In high school, LeVar ended this commute. His high school track coach, a Black woman who was also the assistant athletic director, recruited him to join the team. There he found a group of coaches and teammates to whom he could racially relate. LeVar felt emotionally and socially supported and found his athletic success. Participants like LeVar sought out majority-Black sport spaces to find social and cultural affirmation, absent in their majority-white communities.

LeVar's positive experience was complicated by racial slotting. Athletes recounted how their interactions with coaches and teammates informed which sports or positions they joined. Duane recalled how when he first joined track, he was placed in the sprints squad: "The sprint coaches were all Black. They were very typical, old-school, 'You're Black; you [must] run fast.' . . . There's a stereotype attached [to] Black males, like they [think]: 'You're fast, you're strong, you do this, you do that.' There's just typical sports or just typical things you do." Duane resisted this racial slotting and moved toward the majority-white long-distance running.

All five Black women athletes also remembered a coach or athletic mentor pulling them toward running, jumping, or sprinting events. Vera was told that because she has "Black in her," she would be a fast sprinter. Imani recalls seeing the racial divisions even within track, where Black bodies like hers were cordoned into shorter, more explosive events: "And a lot of the distance runners were Caucasian. I [thought], 'Maybe African Americans have really good sprinting genes.'" These initial assessments reflect racial slotting in which sports or events become associated with certain racial groups (Carrington, 2013).

In the 1930s, track was one of the rare racially integrated sports, where individual Black athletes achieved national recognition (Miller, 1998). A convergence of white sport broadcasters noting that Black athletes had "great speed but little stamina" and a burgeoning eugenics movement entrenched the belief that white and Black bodies inherently differed in regard to musculature, bone length, and lung capacity (Miller, 1998, p. 129). This belief influenced coaches' and athletes' decisions, which continually slotted white athletes in endurance and Black athletes in speed events (Miller, 1998). The "science" regarding links between body type and race has long been disproven (Skiba, 2012), most notably through the rising success of African runners in distance events (Miller, 1998). Instead, practices like racial slotting (coaches assigning positions based upon race) and barriers like inadequate access to a range of sporting opportunities in marginalized communities produce racial groupings in sport (Carrington, 2013; Coakley, 2015).

Racial slotting also influenced the athletic trajectories of white athletes in track and field. Several white long-distance runners began in the sprinting events but shifted to longer distances over time. Seamus, a white man, had one such history in the sport. He began running sprints and was better than most kids at his school. But at meets, "I'd get my ass kicked," he recalled. One of his mentors intervened and said to him: "'You're not a sprinter. You're not what you think you are. You're not Usain Bolt.' So that was that. That was the transition . . . and all the sprinters were Black and I was white, and all the distance runners were white. So that was identifying where I should be as a runner. I definitely used that I was skinny and white and short." Seamus encountered one of the rare athletic spaces predominated by Black people: sprinting. By joining the more racially integrated terrain of track and field, Seamus still learned the racial lessons of whiteness. He learned that race is rooted in inherent biological differences that shape athletic success. Importantly, Seamus also learned that his whiteness may preclude him from sprinting but not from track. His mentor guided him into a space in the sport where white people enjoy their segregation and overrepresentation. Coaching decisions like racial slotting protect greater opportunities for white athletes to develop athletic talent.

Josephine, a Black woman who grew up in an upper-middle-class suburb that bordered a major U.S. city, escaped racial slotting because she trained with a private club of mostly Black athletes with a Black coach. The coach still did a physical evaluation, determining she could be a good distance runner. In high school, she joined the school track team. There, white people surrounded her, in classes and in sports. In the majority-white environment, white women became sprinters due to the absence of Black women. There Josephine saw how the physical body had all and nothing to do with racialization. "My friend was a sprinter but she was white, and so if they asked, 'What do you do?' I think my body type gives it away that I'm not a sprinter. But they didn't assume she was a sprinter because she is white. But she is a sprinter. So that's how race got brought up. It wasn't necessarily to me, but it was when I was in the room and there was a comparison happening, because I was Black and she was white. I was a distance runner and she was a sprinter." Josephine's story represents how the racialization process, using bodies as the differentiators, becomes convoluted when the body does not match the stereotype. Her white friend was "built" like a sprinter, meaning she was shorter and more muscular, whereas Josephine is a tall, slender Black woman. Josephine's physical characteristics and athletic performance were not enough to erase her Blackness and place her within the racial hierarchy as a sprinter.

Federal bans on de jure racial segregation did not remedy the centuries of white accumulation of power (Harris, 1993). Instead, people of color encountered a white society that was built to elevate whiteness and protect white rule (Crenshaw, 1988; Du Bois, 1935; Fields, 2001; Harris, 1993; Kurashige, 2008; Ladson-Billings, 1994, 2003; Lassiter, 2012; Leonardo, 2004, 2009; Massey and Denton, 1998; Mills, 2003; Roediger, 2017; Rothstein, 2017; Vaught, 2011, 2017). This dynamic emerges in sport as white athletes can try any sport in their town. Conversely, Black athletes face implicit and explicit forms of racism that preclude their access to most suburban sports. Black participants experienced racial isolation, tokenism, and marginalization in their majority-white communities and schools. Black middle-class families with the economic capital to purchase homes in majority-white areas could not equally access all of their community's benefits. Instead, they turned to a narrower range of sports, searching for racial affirmation.

Gender Segregation on the Sports Path to College

Boys in the Boat is a story about boys and later men dominating the Olympics. Women appear in Brown's (2013) book as men's support staff. They exist as objects of sexual desire and conquest, as cheerleaders, and as mothers. Women athletes emerge in the epilogue. Brown causally notes that when he visits the former 1936 Olympic race course, he now sees "young men and women in racing shells" using the "same racing lines" of the bygone Hitler games (p. 213). In Brown's account, eighty years later women have miraculously arrived on the Olympic stage. He ignores the active struggle and revolution for women to access rowing and the continued gender-based barriers that plague this and every other global sport.

Over a century of feminist activism led to Title IX, which granted state protections against gender discrimination into education (Messner, 2009; Sadker and Sadker, 1994; Suggs, 2005). Title IX states, "No person in the United States shall, on the basis of sex, be excluded from participation in, denied the benefits of, or be subjected to discrimination under any education program or activity receiving Federal financial assistance" (Title IX, 1972, para. 1). This law revolutionized women's access to sport, especially in colleges and universities. But like all dealings with the state, women's athletic access came at a cost. Through the language and implementation of Title IX, *masculinism in the state*, which refers to the "features of the state that signify, enact, sustain, and represent masculine power as a form of dominance" (Brown, 1995, p. 167), expanded. This form of dominance "entails both a general claim to territory and claims to, about, and against specific 'others'" (Brown, 1995, p. 167).

The "progress" offered to women through Title IX still retained men's dominance in sport. The state exercised territorial authority by restricting which feminists and in turn feminist ideals were adopted into law. As discussed in chapter 1, Congress invited white, middle-class, cisgender women to craft Title IX, and in doing so, their articulation of gender and discrimination became codified into law (Mathewson, 1995; Messner, 2011; Suggs, 2005). The resulting law views gender as monolithic and disconnected from other forms of power like racism and capitalism (Crenshaw, 1988). Here, the definitional powers of the state are evident. The state narrowed the terrain of legible claims of gender discrimination. Schools are Title IX compliant when women are represented across campus activities and programs; there is no recourse if the women are all white, cisgender, and middle-class (Crenshaw, 1988; Harris, 1993; Mathewson, 1995). The state also defined gender as biological, oppositional sex categories (Mathewson, 1995; Messner, 2011). This definition prevents legal protections for those whose gender identity or gender experience does not neatly map into these categories. Finally, the state used these narrow definitions of gender to provide narrower solutions for gender inequality. Gender equity largely occurs through separate-but-equal approaches that created gender-segregated K–12 schools, colleges, dormitories, locker rooms, and athletic programs (Grant et al., 2006; Hextrum, 2017b, 2020c; Lorber, 1994; Milner and Braddock, 2016). Gender segregation substantiates male superiority by claiming inherent biological differences exist between men and women, and therefore women never receive equal treatment in the presence of men (Milner and Braddock, 2016; Suggs, 2005).

Separate Is Not Equal

Athletes' earliest memories of physical activity were gender integrated. Participants recalled unstructured play in community parks and school blacktops. Sophia, a white woman who grew up on the East Coast, recalled organizing and creating her own games with neighborhood kids: "I lived in a neighborhood where we had this massive field in the middle of our houses. . . . I would recruit kids and I would bring them all outside and we would play pickup kickball or basketball and we invented games. I would get home from school, grab a quick snack, and everyone would meet outside and we would play until like seven and then we would go in for dinner." Joy and Stella, both white women who lived in rural areas, recalled climbing trees or playing in creeks. Sanya, a white woman from a West Coast suburb, remembered "running around" on the playground and playing tag at recess. In these memories of unstructured play, children drive the activity and exercise their creativity and physicality at will.

Institutions formalize, and in turn gender, children's play. Schools route children's play into formalized and regulated channels, such as physical education, recess games, and after-school sports, eliminating opportunities for youth to design their own physical contests. In these formal settings, youth encountered the institutions' representatives, such as coaches, teachers, and parents, who taught them the right way to play. This "right way" retained a masculine athletic structure.

Many athletes pointed to a memory in PE class as the moment they were told they had athletic potential. PE offers youth a chance to explore their physical aptitude in competition with one another. For men like George and the Physicist, the mile run represented a moment when they were the "best" or "fastest" in the class. For women like Kayla, Chantae, and Josephine, they recalled the mile run as a moment when they were not the best but they had a chance to "beat the boys." Kayla, a mixed-race woman, narrates how her athletic accomplishments compared to those of her male classmates motivated her choice to join the cross country team, her future college sport. "In elementary school I was very tomboyish; I was really into basketball and soccer. I would dress like a boy every day. Play basketball at recess with the boys. I started getting into running [through] the mile [run test] in PE [class]. And I'd be so competitive. I'd have to beat all the boys. Me and my best friend Caroline were like that. We'd compete with each other, compete with all the boys. We could beat all the boys. It was so impressive. It felt so good." She went on to say that she enjoys being a college runner because it provides her an opportunity to push her physical limits. "I love the feeling of just busting out a fast, long run. Cause when you're done and you think back to what you just did, you're like, 'Wow. I just ran 15 miles at 6:30 pace. I'm a beast.' I like that . . . I like the idea of a girl doing something that is considered better than what probably 99 percent of people [can do]. It's annoying to me still that, no matter what, the boys are going to be faster. . . . That bothers me. But, it's just the way it is. But I think as a female athlete, I'm still able to say that I'm better than most people at [running]."

Growing up in the post–Title IX world, Kayla could play sports because of this law. But her inclusion in sport was always compared to or undercut by men's presumed athletic dominance. Kayla identifies as a "tomboy" due to her early athleticism. She even notes she would "dress like a boy" to remain active at recess. Kayla gains affirmation and confidence in her athletic ability not by comparing herself to her best girlfriend Caroline, but because she "beat all the boys" during recess games and the mile run. Kayla, who went on to become a nationally ranked long-distance runner in college, still does not see herself as the best "athlete." Only men can hold such a title. Her success will always be asterisked by a modifier; she is a "female" athlete. In this way, the state has protected men's definitional powers over sport.

Different Sports for Women

While sports are inherently physical contests, these contests still have an arbitrary, social design. Cooky and McDonald (2005) note we could organize sports in a multitude of more equitable ways than gender, such as by height, weight, and ability. But the first grouping that youth who enter sport encounter is not through these characteristics; it is instead through gender. This sends the salient message that gender is *the* defining characteristic for athletic merit (Messner, 2009) and that "young girls are all alike, are physically weaker, and therefore cannot and should not" participate in athletic contests with boys (Cooky and McDonald, 2005, p. 161).

The belief in men's physical superiority led to different and gender-modified sports for women. Women's colleges customized men's sports to accommodate women's supposed inherent physical deficiencies. One example was how women played half-court instead of full-court basketball (Stanley, 1996). These gender-different sport forms persisted after Title IX. In 1974, Little League Baseball created a different version of the game and a separate organization for women: Little League Softball (Travers, 2013). Colleges followed, sponsoring softball programs for women rather than integrating women into men's baseball teams and/or sponsoring women's baseball (Eckstein, 2017). Starting at the youth level, separate leagues and sports with different rules create disparate opportunities for women to develop athletic talent (Milner and Braddock, 2016). Travers (2013) compared the athletic development of three siblings who were Olympic-level softball and professional-level baseball players and found the siblings had minor differences in athletic ability, but their skill levels became varied after experiencing different training regimes that heightened their talent in the masculine and feminine versions of the games. Even though professional baseball is technically open to women athletes, these differences made it difficult for Olympian softball players to successfully try out for and gain a contract in professional baseball.

Different gendered regulations endure across the segregated terrains of all levels of sport competition. The NCAA does not offer the same sports for men and women. Beach volleyball, bowling, field hockey, or softball lack men's teams. Baseball, wrestling, or football lack women's teams. Women now play full-court basketball, but their sport has a shorter distance for a three-point shot, a different shot clock, and a smaller ball. Cross country, track, and rowing at a cursory glance appear the same across gender. In both sports, athletes have similar distances and point systems. But small differences in rules, regulations, and even qualifications reinforce that male bodies are physically superior. In rowing, coxswains, the athletes who steer and lead the boats, can weigh 120 pounds in men's rowing and 110 pounds in women's rowing (USRowing, 2016). In track and field, the NCAA hosts different multievent competitions, the heptathlon for men and the pentathlon for women. The NCAA also allows higher hurdle heights and heavier weights in the throwing events for men (Kleeman and Ikstrums, 2011). There is no physical justification for why coxswains should weigh less, hurdles should be lower, or hammers should be lighter for women. Yet these organizational differences justify male-only spaces and confer the view that men are bigger, faster, and stronger than women (Hextrum, 2020c).

Men's Control of Women's Sport

State-controlled gender segregation has permitted men to retain control and authority over women's sports. Prior to Title IX women led women's sport (Suggs, 2005). In 1972, women coached 90 percent of women's teams (Maatz and Graves, 2012). By 2018, 39 percent of women's teams had female coaches (Lapchick, 2018). Men coached 61 percent of women's teams and 95 percent of men's teams, and men made up 90 percent of athletic directors and 85 percent of university presidents (Lapchick, 2018). Few men's teams are coached by women, and those that are tend to be coed teams such as cross country (Hattery, 2012; Lapchick, 2018). The state enabled and permitted men's coup of women's sport. While Title IX provides women athletes with access to sport, the law offers no such protections for women to work in athletics. This *removal* of state protection for women to retain their authority and leadership positions invited men into women's sports. Physical strength remains the coin of the realm in sports (Dworkin and Wachs, 2009; Messner, 2009; Milner and Braddock, 2016; Pieper, 2016; Travers, 2013). The long-perpetuated state fallacy that all women, including women athletes, are physically inferior to men justified men's takeover of women's sports. Thus, feminist aims to empower women through sport were undercut by partnering with the masculinist state. Women's state benefits preserved men's control of sport.

The gendered coaching structure is a visible way men control women's sports. Women athletes also recalled subtler ways masculine power undercuts their success. The justices in the *Brown* case ruled that state-sponsored segregation could never be equal because segregation communicates the superiority of one group over another. As the state physically removes men athletes from women's athletic teams, it leaves a male footprint behind. Women, who spent their whole lives playing girls-only sports, encountered the specter of boys' and later men's athleticism all along the way.

Savannah, a white woman and the one lower-income athlete who joined a private rowing club, learned she had athletic potential once her scores mirrored those on the "boys' team." "The boys' team was really bad and so it got to the point where my 2K scores started beating some of the other guy's 2K scores, and so I was like, maybe I should just start doing my 2Ks with the men's team.[2] Maybe I'll get better. And every time I'd come out of the erg room, my friend Ryan he'd be like, 'Did you beat my score?' And I'm like, 'Ryan you're the fastest man on the men's team. I'm not going to beat your score; I'm going to beat these guy's score[s].'" Even when men were absent from women's sport, they remained the default standard.

Beating boys on a different team improved Savannah's confidence. She also hedged her own performance by noting that the boys' team was "really bad," referring to how they did not place as high at regional and national competition as her team did. She further hedged by stating that she could not beat the "top" boys. Ranking athletic achievement along gender lines and comparing men and women to one another—even when they no longer directly compete against each other—is one way to continue to reaffirm male supremacy. With no men present, Savannah still measured her athletic success by a male standard.

Captain America, an upper-middle-class white woman, also interpreted her athletic success through male standards. She excelled in many sports, including basketball, swimming, and rowing and at each juncture believed her physical body was the primary reason. She saw her body as an "atypical" female body that she could utilize for her athletic advantage. "There are more males that have athletic capacity than there are females. I was blessed to have my body size and my build that I can use toward sports. And there's not a lot of girls that are naturally built like [me]. And I think that's one of the main reasons why there is such a discrepancy in athletics because of this natural build that most guys are given but not a lot of girls are. That's why I say, at least for me, it was easier. For the majority of women out there, it's not easier." Playing gender-segregated sports taught her that inherent physical differences between men and women account for the athletic "discrepancy." She also learned that her ability came through her physical similarity to men. She did not learn how this athletic discrepancy is cultivated and exaggerated by different rules, training standards, and skill development.

Men's supremacy in sport (and society) is also showcased through their differences from women. Oppositional gender construction—also known as binarism—requires constant reformulation of norms. As women attempt to reach the male standard in sport, the standard evolves. This phenomenon is best illustrated in the recent court case brought by U.S. women's soccer. College athletic departments and professional sports leagues have long justified the bloated budgets and salaries for men's programs by invoking the free market. The logic goes that men's sports have bigger fan bases, bring in more revenue, and therefore deserve greater institutional investments. Of course, this logic disguises the nearly 150 years of investment colleges made to build markets around men's sports. Despite the barriers stacked against them, the U.S. women's soccer team has exceeded every competitive and monetary standard set by (and to advantage) the men's program. The team filed evidence of such in court citing they bring in far more revenue for U.S. soccer than their male counterparts. Despite this, the U.S. men's team receives higher pay (for less work, as the women's team has gone on to postseason competition, winning back-to-back World Cup titles in 2015 and 2019) (Cater, 2020). A judge recently dismissed the women's team claim of gender pay disparity, citing that the women agreed to a different pay structure. The men's superior pay comes down to the bonuses they receive for playing in international competition—a larger and more lucrative market for men's soccer (Cater, 2020). Women's soccer does not have a comparable market, and therefore its players are justifiably paid less. The U.S. women's soccer team shows how the power of definition—in this case setting the standard athletic success—means you can always redefine the terrain of play.

The constant reworking and expanding of male supremacy in sport extends beyond athletic fields. These definitional contests teach men, even those with no sport experience, that they are physically superior to *all* women, even top-level women athletes. Women participants enumerated the times their athleticism was undercut and challenged by men who were not athletes. Vera recalled how her male classmates assumed they would beat her despite her proven records in her sport. "Of course people think, 'Oh women can't be that athletic.' . . . When we had to do track in high school and we had to race, guys were like, 'Oh, Vera runs track; let's see if we can race her.' They just think they're better because they're male. And then when I jump further or when I run faster, they're surprised." In Vera's story, her nonathlete male peers believed they could best her in *her* sport. Through the elevation of male bodies and bonding rituals in male-only sports, nonathlete men can inherit beliefs of their physical supremacy to women (Messner, 2002). No male athletes in the study recalled a nonathlete male (or female athlete) challenging their athleticism. In contrast, for women athletes in the study, no amount of the visible markers of top athletic accolades could inoculate them from gender-based challenges and guarantee their social recognition as *athletes*.

Cutting Men's Teams: The Male Victim

The ever-shifting nature of the male norm in sport took on a beguiling form in the 1980s. As women encroached on men's territory, men recast themselves as victims of women's success. Male athletes were at once invulnerable (and therefore a threat to women) and vulnerable (and therefore needed state protection from women). As supporters of women's sports tried to combat these irreconcilable claims, masculine control of sports expanded.

In 1979 the Office of Civil Rights issued guidelines for how schools could comply with Title IX. Also known as the "Three Prongs of Compliance," the document offers three basic tests the office uses to measure if a school provides adequate, separated athletic opportunities for women. The first prong measures proportionality, or whether a school hosts a similar ratio of men and women athletes to men and women students. Prong 2 offers a grace period for schools attempting to improve gender equity. If a school can demonstrate a history of expanding access to the formerly disenfranchised group and present a plan toward prong 1 or prong 3, then the school is compliant. The third prong measures whether "all needs are met," a vague standard that generally refers to whether all the possible women's sports and/or interests of women in a school or district are offered. (For example, a school can be in compliance even if they have a ratio that favors men, so long as they offer most or all the possible athletic teams for women and can document that no women students want to and can play a sport that is unavailable in the school *and* the governing league.) Rather than adopt prong 3 and ensure that all women's needs were met, the vast majority of schools chose prong 1 (Suggs, 2005; Thelin, 2011). The elevation of men's football and basketball as the primary sources of revenue for university athletic departments led administrators to protect revenue sports at all costs. Schools chose to cut men's sports with the smallest athlete pools and fan bases like wrestling. They simultaneously claimed that they had to cut men's sports to comply with Title IX (Thelin, 2011).

In the 1980s and 1990s, a group of aggrieved male athletes mobilized against Title IX, which culminated in the 2004 federal case *National Wrestling Coaches Association v. U.S. Department of Education* (Messner, 2002; Suggs, 2005). This men's rights movement claimed that Title IX harmed men. The case focused on the small number of men whose sport opportunities were cut as schools complied with Title IX. The state disagreed with the men and reaffirmed Title IX. The court opinion clarified that schools have a right to cut men's sports to comply with the law. While the wrestlers lost the case, they successfully entrenched a cultural narrative that political efforts to support women strip rights from men (Messner, 2002). In this example, the state still uplifts masculinism even when the official state action seems to go in women's favor. By hearing the case and giving men's rights groups a legitimate platform to air their grievances, the state permitted a masculinist narrative to emerge. The case reasserted men's birthright claims to sports and higher education. Men are seen as deserving *all* spots in college sports. Any attempt to provide spots for women is seen as taking something *away* from men.

This narrative has persisted even in the face of women's underrepresentation in all school-sponsored sports programs (as discussed in the previous two chapters). Almost a dozen women participants believed Title IX granted them a greater advantage in athletic recruitment and admission. Monique learned from her peers that Title IX helped her get into college.

> I'm six foot [tall] so that's huge for a woman. . . . All [the] people in my high school judged me that I got into certain places as a woman with Title IX . . . friends would be angry that they didn't get into [Coastal-U] or they didn't get into their Ivy League [of choice]. They're like, "You only got in because of Title IX." Or, "Oh you get a scholarship. I don't have anything." . . . Lots of guys on the men's rowing team [said that]. Maybe they were a little sad that they didn't get a scholarship. But [they shouldn't have cared] because most of them were superrich and drove around in their parents' Porsches.

Monique's quote reflects the complex way narratives surrounding Title IX govern college access. Monique's mostly wealthy, white high school peers "judged" her for getting into college not because of athletics but specifically because of Title IX. This judgment implies that Title IX takes something away from men and gives it to women. In the process, men retain their rightful place in sports and education. Further, Monique learns that men, not women, should use sport for college access. Monique's male teammates made her feel like she received some special benefit not offered to them. In reality, men retain more college roster spots and scholarships than women. Women athletes like Monique internalize these conversations and come to believe that they do not *deserve* to participate in sports in the same way that men do.

The debates among Monique's peers also essentialize the category of women. Women become a singular entity uniformly advantaged by Title IX. Monique's high school and private rowing clubs are in one of the wealthiest counties in the United States—also a majority-white county. The familial, educational, and communal resources her peers possessed primed them for college. Monique noted as much with her retort back to her male peers. Why did they need to worry about getting a college rowing scholarship? They drove around in their parents' Porsches, after all. But Monique does not note the advantages offered to her and her fellow women rowers. Their classification as white by law granted them advantages over women of color. As the next and final section of this chapter discusses, the conflation of "women" and "white middle-class women" ensures only a sliver of women receive Title IX's benefits.

White Women's Sport

Women athletes pursuing the sports path to college received implicit and explicit messages that sports were primarily a masculine activity. Women were told by their white male coaches and peers that they should be grateful of their state-provided opportunities to play sport. Women internalized athletic success defined along a male standard. And women learned that men should lead all sports, even women's sports. While these messages certainly assert male dominance, they also disguise whiteness. Title IX ensured that the schools Monique attended offered sports to girls and women. But Monique did not play school-sponsored sports in high school. Instead, she *chose* to join a private rowing club not subject to Title IX. Further, Monique did not *need* sports as a vehicle for college access; her family, community, and school already provided such vehicles. Finally, Monique did not need an athletic scholarship (though she accepted one). Even though her parents did not own a Porsche, she was far from being economically disadvantaged. Monique, Captain America, Morgan, and the many other women in this book were advantaged in the college-prep process because of Title IX, but it was because of their race and class positions, not their gender.

The 1964 Civil Rights Act and corresponding amendments created separate categories of disenfranchisement such as race, national origin, and sex, under which disenfranchised groups could claim legal protections (U.S. Equal Employment Opportunity Commission, 1964). Religion, race, color, and national origin—other categories of protection—are defined in the Civil Rights Act as separate and distinct from sex. By viewing these categories as separate and distinct rather than interconnected and mutually informing, the state can offer some protections to maintain its legitimacy without redistributing its power. Title IX, as applied to school-sponsored sports programs, reflects this form of state protection.

All facets of Title IX measure whether a school meets the standard of the law by comparing the educational opportunities and experiences across gender. As mentioned above, a school is noncompliant when its ratio of athletic opportunities disproportionately favors men. But the state does not consider race or class when calculating this ratio. Thus, a school can comply with the law by having 100 percent white middle-class athletes.

Title IX does not require schools to host sports. Title IX requires a school to add women's sports only if they already sponsor men's sports. If a school has no sports, then no opportunities need to be provided for women (Mathewson, 1995). Children from low-income families and children of color more often attend schools with few or no sports (Cheslock, 2008; Fields, 2008; Hattery, 2012; Mathewson, 1995; Sabo and Veliz, 2008). Physical education is the primary way that young girls learn sports (Sabo and Veliz, 2008). But 84 percent of girls living in lower-income urban communities do not have physical education at their schools. As I discussed in chapter 2, the athletic opportunities in middle-class suburban areas are multiplied. Suburban children encounter sports in schools *and* in low-cost community-sponsored programs, accelerating their advantages compared to those from lower-income urban regions.

Civil rights protections rely upon citizen reports and legal actions. The Office of Civil Rights is a small bureaucratic agency (and according to Welch Suggs, 2005, is always smaller during Republican administrations) that cannot monitor whether every school actually complies with the law. Instead, the office relies upon citizens to file complaints, and then, depending on the nature and evidence of the complaint, they will investigate. White middle-class women file more Title IX complaints and are more likely to have their complaints addressed than are other groups (Grant et al., 2006; Fields, 2008; Mathewson, 1995). Women of color and/or low-income women are more likely to attend schools that violate Title IX (Mathewson, 1995). Women of color and/or low-income women more often lack the legal and economic resources to file Title IX complaints. The effects ensure white middle-class women—and a few others—benefit from Title IX.

Since 1981, white women have retained anywhere between 70 percent and 87 percent of the total spots on college women's sports teams (Cheslock, 2008). The dominance of white women in sports begins when they are girls. It is worth restating that girls and women occupy the lowest sport participation rates when compared to boys and men across and within every category measured by researchers (Butler and Lopiano, 2003; Cheslock, 2008; Lapchick, 2018; NCAA, 2019, n.d.; Sabo and Veliz, 2008). But women of color, even from middle-income communities, are the least likely group to access sports (Sabo and Veliz, 2008). Even low-income men of color have greater participation opportunities than middle-income women of color (Sabo and Veliz, 2008). Sabo and Veliz's (2008) study included an important comparison. They examined whether children could play *a* sport and if they could play *multiple* sports. As chapter 2 revealed, children who can play multiple sports are more likely to identify one in which they can successfully develop the athletic talent universities desire. Sabo and Veliz (2008) examined youth participation rates in three or more sports. There they found the smallest gender gap in white, upper-middle-income children: 40 percent of boys and 38 percent of girls were involved in three or more sports as youth. But in that same income bracket, they found a discrepancy of almost 20 percent for children of color. Whereas

34 percent of upper-middle-income boys of color are highly involved in sport (just 6 percent behind white boys), only 13 percent of higher-income girls of color are involved in sports (25 percent behind white girls). Another way to put this is that gaps across race are greater than gaps across class and gender. In this sense, Title IX has failed to provide gains for women of color. Even women of color in suburban communities—the areas with the greatest opportunity structure for college sport access—have fewer sports options than white women. These findings indicate why oppression cannot be reduced to one primary cause—race, class, *or* gender. Unique forms of discrimination—as seen through white middle-class women's overrepresentation in college sports—are produced at the intersections of various power structures.

Conclusion

The freedom to *choose* what neighborhood to live in, what school to attend, and what sport to play is a freedom the state unequally extends to Americans. Someone living within or on the fringes of a white middle-class suburb has greater choices for and chances on the sports path to college. State approaches to race and gender segregation illustrate the disparate choices presented to Americans. Segregation constructs walls along the pathway to college that restrict, contain, detour, and end opportunities for the development of athletic talent for white girls and women, boys and men of color, and girls and women of color. Concurrently, segregation ensures that white boys and men retain a wider, more supportive, and more direct route to college via sport.

State support for de facto racial segregation concentrates opportunities to develop athletic talent in white suburban areas. The state relieves today's white population of any culpability for creating, profiting from, and concentrating resources within racially segregated communities. White people in turn retain the benefits of historic racial oppression and are not required to relinquish or redistribute the gains from a white supremacist state. White people living within predominately white communities develop skewed notions of how race and racism operate. One such skewed notion is misunderstanding how they benefit from a white supremacist state. White people learn their athletic options are default opportunities, not advantages. While living in segregation, white people see themselves represented everywhere, in all activities. By seeing themselves as not advantaged and yet everywhere, white athletes in this study unquestionably pursued every sport opportunity in their community. They did not consider whether their race could or should align with an activity. Instead, they chose sport based upon their interest or proclivity. Simultaneously, Black youth suffered implicit and explicit forms of racism inflicted upon them by white community members. These experiences led Black athletes to pursue sports with more athletes of color. Black athletes had only three or four non-white-dominated sports to play; track and field was one of them.

Gender segregation also restricted athletes' choices and reinforced masculine dominance in athletics and beyond. State action, notably Title IX, permitted men to oversee the unequal distribution of resources and opportunities for women to develop as athletes. Men can coach men's *and* women's sports. Men insert themselves into women's sports as the default athletic standard, a standard that women, by virtue of their femininity, cannot achieve. Men's control of sports expands beyond formal athletic spaces. Even nonathlete men believe they are superior to all women athletes.

Women participants recounted how masculine domination shaped their view of athletic success and opportunity. Women learned that athletic success was tied to men's performance. The closer women came to men's scores, the better athletes they were. Further, women were subjected to tests of their ability from nonathlete men, something that never happened in the reverse for men in the study. These sometimes subtle and sometimes not-so-subtle reassertions of male dominance eroded and undermined women's success in sport. Women were denied the opportunity to self-define athletic success and cultivate leadership opportunities. The culmination of these experiences made women feel grateful just to play and therefore satisfied with the fewer, unequal, and male-controlled sport opportunities in their communities.

But not all women could access *women's* sports. The state's varied approach to segregation uniquely discriminates against women of color. Title IX caters to the already-existing social, cultural, and economic patterns of white communities. The law assumes that these communities have the resources to support education and athletic opportunities. If a school offers sports to men, then it must do the same for women. But the law does not redistribute the funding or opportunities from majority-white areas to lower-income communities in which the majority of residents are racial minorities. Instead, communities already with few or no sports opportunities (even for men) remain as they are. Further, the law views gender inaccurately as disconnected from other forms of oppression. As a result, even in resource-rich communities schools can comply with the law by having all-women's athletic programs. Under Title IX, schools are unaccountable to ensure that *all* women can access sports. The state may set the terrain of civic life, but it is up to the people to enact and fortify these boundaries. The next chapter examines how white suburban athletes activate the greater benefits offered to them by the state.

4

Activating Capital

Pay-to-Play Sports

Iceman, a white man who grew up along the U.S.-Canadian border, recalled how ice hockey dominated every facet of his hometown. Hockey provided an athletic and social respite during the long and dreary winter months. Children learned to skate and walk at the same time. Adults socialized through spectating youth, collegiate, and professional hockey matches. Iceman was no different. His siblings played hockey, his dad coached hockey, his friends played hockey, and his friends' dads coached hockey teams. Iceman played in youth leagues, for school teams, and for private clubs—sometimes juggling all at once. He recalled how "from the age of five to twelve, hockey was everything . . . it was just hockey, hockey, hockey. Hockey was a pretty big part of my life. I wasn't excellent, but I was big, and I was pretty fast."

Iceman is not a college hockey player. Iceman is a rower. Participants nostalgically recalled memories of sports that they no longer play. During this point of the interviews, I tried to not interrupt with the obvious question—*Why aren't you a college athlete in that sport?* Eventually, participants' answers to this question emerged. They did not make the cut in their chosen sport, so they selected another with greater opportunities for special admission to college. In Iceman's case, shortly after he enrolled in a private, all-boys high school he realized he was a mediocre hockey player and student. His chances were slim to none to enter an elite college. One day, while hanging out at a friend's house, he noticed paraphernalia from an Ivy League college on the wall. He asked his friend what connection he had to the school. His friend replied, "My brother goes to [Ivy League university]. He got recruited to row there." Iceman recalled saying, "Man, I want to go there. I'm going to start rowing!"

Iceman's race, class, and gender poised him to successfully transition from high school to college. Iceman attended top public and later elite private schools. His mother was a teacher and supplemented his academic curriculum in the home. She also met with his teachers to secure him additional academic resources and hired a private tutor. Iceman saw himself represented across all facets of the educational curriculum. His race, class, and gender were never used to question his abilities. Even with these structural alignments, Iceman still was a "bad student" and believed his academic performance would hinder his college matriculation. "I saw [rowing as] an opportunity to make up for the fact that I was bad student. . . . I remember talking to a [Coastal-U] volleyball player and she was saying, 'I'm basically just here because it's a means to an end.' You didn't do very well in high school, so you did much better at something else—you found a way to get around the whole 'having good grades' thing, to get into a top-tier university, to get a better job." By high school Iceman knew that despite his social advantages, he might not receive admission to college. He could have continued along his path at a prestigious, all-boys private school and could likely have matriculated into a university. But he felt his academic record would deny him access to his preferred university. To maintain his social status, Iceman activated his privilege by taking specific and intentional actions. Iceman used his advantages to chase a near guarantee for university access: college rowing.

Iceman had the *choice* to row, a choice unavailable to most people who are not white, not middle- or upper-class, and not located on the coasts. The state facilitated his choice to row through the tactics of *formal* laws and regulations that created his suburbs and schools, *relational* partnerships with white community members to concentrate resources within their boundaries, and *removal* by preventing lower-income and racial minorities from accessing these same resources. Collectively these state actions provided Iceman with disproportionate opportunities compared to most American youth. He had abundant options to choose from, rowing being one of them. Rowing provided a secure route for Iceman because he is one of a select few who can access the sport.

The constellation of state tactics facilitated the moment in which Iceman could *choose* to row. But Iceman still had to make that choice to activate his advantage. This nuance is the crux of Bourdieusian reproductive theory. The transmission of advantage lacks guarantee. If advantaged groups made a different choice—in Iceman's case to not row and to enter college admissions as a subpar white, middle-class, male student—reproduction would take a different course. Agentic actions by individuals are necessary to secure broader reproductive effects. The state, in partnership with privileged groups and private entities, facilitates the transmission of advantages as it rewards individuals who do (Bourdieu, 2011; Calarco, 2014, 2018; Kaufman, 2005; Lareau, 2011, 2015).

Iceman was induced to row because he saw the potential benefit—elite college admissions—outweighed any costs to him and his family like intensive time commitments, bodily injury, and steep club membership dues. The investments needed for the transmission of advantage also obscure the transaction. As Iceman *chooses* to row, he accrues personal and financial hardship along the way. In the American meritocracy, the costs people endure justify the outsized rewards they receive if they succeed in their endeavors. Meritocracy also implies both equal opportunities to play the game and that the winners are evenly and fairly judged. The first half of the book examined how the state secures unequal opportunities to advantage white suburban communities. Here, I begin to explore how the markers of merit employed by universities are arbitrary and disguise the transmission of advantage.

Special athletic admission permits high school athletes like Iceman to use their athletic talent to enter college through a different portal. In Iceman's case, his rowing abilities, not his academic record, secured him college access. Assigning outsized value to an individual's characteristics, experiences, values, or dispositions that align with the state's interest is a process of *symbolic violence* that maintains existing power relations (Bourdieu and Passeron, 1977). Leisure practices like rowing are *symbolic* because they are imbued with meaning that extends beyond the act of pulling an oar through the water. Elevating rowing—a sport associated with elite white communities—is an act of state perpetuated *violence* when the state rewards those who row at the expense and exclusion of most Americans. These acts of violence are disguised when the public comes to see markers of merit as neutral and objective rather than arbitrary and elitist (Bourdieu, 2011; Bourdieu and Passeron, 1977). Thus, when Iceman is accepted to Coastal-U, his success seems meritorious, not engineered.

In this chapter, I discuss two arbitrary criteria that colleges value as athletic merit: participation in exclusive sports or events and membership in pay-to-play clubs. Within white suburban communities, knowledge circulated that colleges rewarded these two tactics with special admission. In turn, members of these communities, like Iceman, pursued them to activate their advantage. By valuing exclusive sports and clubs, universities reinvest in neoliberal state tactics. Exclusive and private sports have displaced formerly public community and school-sponsored teams (Coakley, 2011a). As advantaged groups turn away from public resources and invest toward private opportunities for *better* products (like "better" sports teams), the state justifies its public divestment by citing the poor quality of the public realm (Fabricant and Fine, 2015; Harvey, 2005). These actions exacerbate disparities as the few public sports programs offered in lower-income communities are displaced, while white suburban communities retain their public and private benefits. Thus, universities commit *symbolic violence* by valuing participation in exclusive sports and pay-to-play clubs in their admission process. These markers of merit are false in their design but real in their harmful unequal distribution of resources and opportunities to succeed in the United States.

Sport for Some, Not for All

As discussed in chapter 2, the state helped contain opportunities to develop athletic talent within white suburban communities. These neighborhoods have disproportionate access to low-cost community sports and school-sponsored sports that align with those offered by universities. Sport is also an endemic part of social life in these communities (DeLuca, 2013; DeLuca and Andrews, 2016; Messner, 2009; Stirrup et al., 2015). With a wide array of sports opportunities and youth playing sports, these communities developed a knowledge system and exchange process about how to improve athletic performance. Participants learned through their own personal experience trying different sports, through watching older teammates navigate the recruitment process, through parents conferring notes among each other, and through coaches with vast experience in the industry that certain sports, or subspecialties within a sport like a particular event in track and field, yielded better odds at being recruited to college. Only those capable of navigating the barriers can participate.

Laura, a white woman from the East Coast, framed her parents' influence on her athletic as follows: "My Mom went to Harvard and my Dad went to Stanford. Thank god I row." Implied in her statement is the knowledge that Laura would not have replicated her parents' educational attainment without rowing. The sport granted Laura access to an elite university, not identical to but closely aligned with her parents' degrees. Like Iceman, Laura saw rowing as a chance to secure a coveted spot at an elite college. Laura's community taught her how to pursue certain exclusive opportunities within rowing to develop an athletic portfolio colleges desire.

Laura, like many white middle- and upper-class college athletes, already was primed with a college-prep habitus. Laura grew up a few states south of Iceman in an East Coast town of about twenty thousand residents, 93 percent of whom are white. The median family income from the area is nearly $215,000. Laura described her town as "affluent" and home to the nation's "one percent," its wealthiest citizens. Her hometown hugs the Long Island Sound and offers over two-hundred acres of city sponsored park land, including beaches, fields, and hiking trails. One park even has paddle tennis courts—a game similar to tennis but played on a smaller court with solid rackets. An indoor club house, fitted with air conditioning, area rugs, couches, and flat screen televisions, abuts the paddle tennis courts. The parks department also sponsors summer concerts, movie nights, and festivals for the community. Each May, for the past thirty years, the town has hosted a model boat regatta. Regatta participants can either build their own boat, or purchase one, and race around the town's pond. In 2019, the city council's most pressing civic issues included notifying the public about preventing tick and mosquito borne illnesses; updating commuters about an ongoing bridge-infrastructure upgrade; and a calling for volunteers to assist with maintaining one of the town's six revolutionary and civil war cemeteries.

Laura's community also sponsors the top public high school in the state (150th in the nation). Laura, along with 98 percent of her classmates, graduated, and 74 percent of her class took Advanced Placement courses. Laura described her high school as a place where students showcased their privilege. "People dress like it, and they drive Jeeps. It was all about how you were perceived by other people." While her high school does not publish a college-going rate, Laura was convinced "everyone" attended college post-graduation. "Everyone went to college. 100 percent of my grade went to some sort of college, whether it was community [college], or maybe one or two enrolled in the army but they had plans to go to college."

Laura's access to abundant public recreational facilities, festivals, and college-prep curricula comes through the state tactic of *removal*, or stripping these rights and resources from other communities. Her town, schools, and facilities were all guarded and policed to prevent outsiders from entry. But the residents could freely enjoy and utilize the community resources at their will. They faced no consequences or reconciliation for the benefits they accrued at the expense of, and harm to, others. This opulence and affluence directly aligned with admission to elite universities. Most of her classmates attended Ivy League or top private and public universities. When I asked how her classmates accessed these universities, she replied, "Usually kids would get recruited [for sports], or their parents had enough connections where they could get them into a good school, or they were smart enough that they could get in themselves. It was a combination of things." For Laura, her "combination of things" was to pursue an even more exclusionary route. The resources and assets in her community already exploited various systems of scarcity. Her community hoarded academic resources, ensuring that neighboring communities did not have equivalent funding structures, curricula, or teachers. Her community hoarded athletic resources, ensuring that neighboring areas did not have the same number or quality of free public parks and athletic venues. Her community exploited the scarcity built into elite college admissions, priming its members to obtain the few coveted spots offered in each admission cycle. Even with these numerous easements, Laura's community created yet another exclusionary avenue: rowing.

Laura played lots of sports growing up. At a young age she did gymnastics and swimming. By elementary school she played club soccer, basketball, and lacrosse. By high school she settled on soccer and track (the high jump event). Her public school had one of the top lacrosse teams in the nation. Laura told me that all the starters on the lacrosse team received admission to Division I teams at top universities. It was a common occurrence at her school for high school athletes to use their athletic talent in lieu of academic credentials to gain access to a top university. She knew that colleges offered this exceptional route for athletes. She also knew that she would not get recruited in soccer or track. She did not think she had the skills, ability, or interest to put in the extra hours needed to improve her athletic credentials in these sports. At the end of her freshman year one of her classmates, who rowed, told her to come out for the team because rowing offered a path to college. In her final year of high school, out of the nine seniors, three, including herself, accepted admission to Coastal-U. "That's pretty cool," she told me.

Laura joined the private rowing club in her area, which was run by the junior national rowing team coach, who charged approximately five thousand dollars per year in membership dues. This club had a record of sending athletes to Division I programs. "All the girls in my club had gone to a D-I program," Laura explained. "I sort of knew, coming on to the team, [that] I would row in college." Laura also remembered how her coach instilled in the rowers that they all could become college athletes. Laura recalled her coach telling the team, "I want all of you to be good enough to row in a D-I program. So in order for you to do that, you need to do this to get there." Laura went on to explain that "this" entailed developing physical talent through intense time commitments, physical conditioning, and weight loss regimes and cultivating social relationships with college coaches by using strategies like attending college and national team camps (discussed in the next section). Laura's choice to pursue rowing and join this private club paid off: she received exceptional admission and scholarship offers to Ivy Leagues and top public universities. She selected Coastal-U.

Laura's community taught her that certain sports, or subspecialties within a sport, yielded better odds at being recruited to college. Even in resource-rich communities, some sports were more popular and competitive than others. Laura, like Captain America, Noelle, Monique, and Morgan, for instance, all started out in swimming. They could join this sport because they came from communities with the infrastructure to provide pools, private swim clubs, and coaches with knowledge of the sport. But each hopeful athlete came to realize that swimming offered a much narrower route to college. The amount of swimmers at the youth level compared to the high school level created a competitive environment that these women believed they could not ascend through. In contrast, rowing, which also requires particular physical, cultural, and social infrastructure, is even rarer than swimming. Chapter 2 described the mismatch between the availability of rowing at the high school level compared to the college level. This mismatch becomes an exploitable resource for those who can access elite, private rowing clubs.

Exclusive Events

The seemingly public accessibility of track and field ("all you need is a pair of shoes") may excuse it from scarcity. High schools across the United States host track programs that require far less infrastructure than rowing. Yet track athletes learned that certain events required more resources and facilitated greater college access. London's story represents how athletes who can access the exclusivity built within track can create greater odds for themselves in college recruitment.

London, a mixed-raced middle-class woman, recalled how as a child she enjoyed the freedom of running. As she aged, she picked up team sports, namely volleyball, and took a hiatus from track. She was drawn back to the sport as high school approached and as she began thinking about college. London attended a sports-focused private Catholic high school where over 10 percent of the graduating class was recruited to college for sports; her family knew sports provided preferential access to college. In coming back to track, she had less success than she had enjoyed in her youth. London characterized herself as an "average" sprinter, jumper, and long-distance runner.

Assessing her future in the sport, she decided to specialize in triple jump. Her primary rationale for this decision was the lack of competition. "I was trying to find my niche in high school. And we didn't have any triple jumpers. And there was also a jump coach who thought I'd be really good at it, and so that's when I committed to triple jump." As the main triple jumper on the team, London stood out because there was no one else to outshine her. While she had some initial success in the sport, she still did not rise to the state level. London sought out guidance and support from a family friend who ultimately counseled her in how to best be recruited to college as a track athlete: "We had a family friend who shaped a lot of my [athletic recruitment] during my junior year and senior year. And he was also a track dad. He knew my mom, and his son was on the track team. And he was like, 'Why don't you try the heptathlon? You're pretty good at all these events but not top at all these events.'"

Through her social connections forged through her enrollment in private high school and private track clubs, London learned how to pursue a less competitive event and better increase her odds at recruitment. Only two states have public schools with heptathlon. The scarcity of the event automatically advantages athletes like London in recruitment. As London recalled, her community taught her how to find a "niche," or an area to stand out compared to her peers, to increase her recruitment odds. The standards for merit were also lower. London did just one heptathlon before she received admission to Coastal-U. She lacked "objective" merits in her chosen niche. Instead, as chapter 6 shows, London created proxies for her merit to convince colleges she could be a successful heptathlete.

When athletes like Iceman, Laura, and London pursue sports or events with fewer competitors, they activate their privilege. As chapter 2 discussed, white suburbs created exclusive sport offerings available to some and denied to others. Because of this, members of these communities can exploit this scarcity by pursuing a sport or event with fewer athletes. This scarcity permits those with access to become standout athletes with fewer competitors along the way. As Monique said in the introduction, she never believed she was the best athlete; she believed she simply had the opportunity to row—an opportunity denied to so many others. Purposefully selecting restrictive sports like rowing or events like heptathlon grants athletes an early strategic advantage on the sports path to college. But selecting a rare sport is insufficient. The next step requires athletes to invest in privatized clubs and coaches.

Accelerating Advantage: Club Sports and Private Coaching

Attending a high school with a rowing program certainly increases one's odds of becoming a college rower. But rowing for a high school team is not required to become a college rower. Colleges need not restrict their recruiting pool to school-sponsored programs. Colleges can recruit athletes who play for private sports clubs. The privatized model of developing athletic talent offers additional ways for those with access to resource-rich communities to secure and protect their advantage.

Privatized sports have displaced free and community-driven athletic programs that are less specialized and competitive (Coakley, 2011a, 2015; Hoff and Mitchell, 2006; Messner, 2009; Sabo and Veliz, 2008; Zdroik and Veliz, 2016). Private sports clubs, or pay-to-play teams, are not directly subsidized by communities or schools and have higher entry fees. As discussed in the introduction, neoliberalism allows private markets to proliferate within and alongside state-run mobility institutions. Aspiring college athletes are more likely to develop the athletic talent colleges want through private sports teams than through high school programs (Eckstein, 2017). Just like paying to take classes to improve one's SAT scores, paying for private sports clubs improves one's athletic ability.

Middle- and upper-middle-class families can evaluate their community's sport offerings and supplement where needed. Study participants supplemented their high school sports by joining private athletic clubs and hiring private coaches. Thirty-six of the forty-seven participants joined private, fee-based club sports throughout their athletic careers. Prior to high school, private clubs were commonly referred to as "travel" or "all-star" teams, in which the advanced players in recreational leagues could continue their sports at a higher, more competitive level and for more months of the year. These competitive teams required greater financial and time contributions from families, including paying for travel costs, additional uniforms, club memberships, and equipment. The middle-class participants benefited early on from community-subsidized low-cost sports, and they later paid for additional opportunities to further their advantages. Participants sought additional opportunities in two ways. In the first instance, participants joined club programs when their schools did not offer their sport. In the second instance, participants were already involved in a school sport but wanted additional training or expertise to increase their athletic ability. To do so, they joined a private club or hired a private coach. These economic investments furthered the cumulative advantage already built into resource-rich communities.

Private Boat Clubs

Access to rowing, in most cases, flowed through private boat clubs. While sports like basketball, soccer, and football have elaborate, expensive, and extensive private club opportunities that exist alongside school programs, rowing mostly exists within private clubs. In this sense, aspiring college rowers supplement the athletic opportunities available at their high schools by leaving their schools altogether. Of the twenty-four rowers in the study, only one joined a public school team. Four others picked up rowing through their private boarding schools, and the rest accessed the sport through private clubs. The lack of public opportunities to row means participants need financial resources to join the sport. As Casey, a white middle-class woman, aptly summarized, she became a rower because her family could afford private club fees: "We had the money for me to row. And it is a very expensive sport. I'm really lucky that my parents could afford to send me [to a club program]."

The cost of private crew clubs varied by region but in all cases required family financial contributions. The average membership for the top ten U.S. junior rowing programs was $2,674 per year. The cheapest club, located in Upstate New York, cost $1,300 per year. The priciest club was in a neighboring state, Connecticut, and charged $3,900 per year. Whereas taxpayer dollars subsidize the costs of facilities and equipment for recreational and school teams, private clubs raise these funds primarily through membership fees. Private rowing clubs raise funds to pay for coaches' salaries, the real estate of the boat club, the permits to row on public waterways, and the equipment, including boats, oars, and ergometers. Rowing has two types, sweeping (one oar per rower) and sculling (two oars per rower), which require different equipment. In sweep rowing, the common events are the pair (two-person boat), the four (four-person boat), and the eight (eight-person boat). The cost of an eight, the predominant boat in U.S. racing, ranges from $40,000 to $65,000. This cost excludes the oars, which cost between $200 and $300 each. In sculling, the common events are the single scull (one-person boat), the double (two-person boat), and the quad (four-person boat). Sculling boats are also costly, with a new single scull priced around

$12,000, a double about $14,000, and a quad around $27,000 (pricing estimates came from Pocock, the American manufacturer for rowing equipment).

Three rowers in the study bought a single scull to enhance their training. Camilla, a white woman from the West Coast, said her father purchased her a higher quality boat than available through the club when she became more serious about rowing. Having her own boat gave her more opportunities to train. She did not need the club's permission to take the boat out on the water, to take the boat to races, or to compete with her teammates. In addition to the cost of the boats they buy, rowers must also pay their private clubs to store their boats. Fees to store a boat can be an extra $60 per month.

Membership and equipment fees were just the first of many costs accrued by rowers. Private boat clubs can also require donations through money or volunteer hours. One club in the study fined rowers up to $200 if they did not complete the required volunteer hours. Clubs also had rigorous handbooks detailing the appropriate clothing, behavior, and appearance for the sport. All clubs required participants to purchase uniforms for the sport. For instance, a New York Rowing Club required all athletes to have a uniform for the fall and spring. In addition, it offered pricing for "recommended" athletic gear. Purchasing their required and recommended gear cost $507.43 per person.

Rowing clubs promote the fact that they offer need-based athletic scholarships. How clubs distribute scholarships is less clear. One East Coast rowing club has the following requirements to be considered for a scholarship: the athlete must submit their parents' tax returns, write an essay, and, if selected, complete weekly volunteer hours doing maintenance for the club, including cleaning the boat house. Clubs also post contingencies around the scholarships, including coaches' discretion, attendance, and athletic performance. As one California Rowing club explains, "The Scholarship Committee grants aid based on financial need, positive attitude, and volunteer participation. All grants are subject to certification by a coach that the rower had good attendance and a positive attitude the prior semester." There are no guarantees that private clubs will give out a scholarship or that someone in need who would want to row would receive one. Those two factors alone suggest that private clubs do not provide equal or enough opportunities to all who may want to participate. But even those who beat the odds and receive a scholarship are subjected to a categorically different rowing experience than those who can pay their own way. Their inclusion in the program is at the behest of the coach and whether they can align with characteristics that are raced, classed, and gendered such as having a "positive attitude." If a scholarship athlete is required to clean the boathouse after practice while the rest of the team heads home to rest, recover, or begin their homework, they might easily develop a "negative attitude."

The rowing clubs the study participants belonged to did not advertise how they awarded financial-need scholarships. The study's college rowers offered consistent memories of junior rowing. Most described their teammates as "well-off" and "white." Morgan, whose team rowed on a section of the Erie Canal, was the only participant who remembered their private club discussing the high costs of the sport. After her New York rowing club earned a spot at the junior national championships, some of her teammates said they could not afford the trip. Travel costs are one of the many expenses not covered by membership fees. The team spent the year trying to win enough races to qualify for club nationals. Morgan had never considered her team might forgo the trip for financial reasons. During the meeting, the team chose to drive, over flying, the nearly thousand miles, to cut costs. After this team conversation, her program became much more explicit about the costs involved in rowing. The team website now lists the races and locations in advance, recommends that families book travel early, and suggests food to eat on the road. Morgan felt this transparency allows families to better control the costs, whereas before the club made the travel decisions and billed members.

Only one of the twenty-five rowers in the study received a junior rowing scholarship. Savannah, a white woman who grew up in California, came from an artistic family with few college attendees. She played recreational soccer growing up—her parents and siblings remain baffled that she became a college athlete—deviating from her family culture. In high school, one of Savannah's friends came up to her "out of the blue" and said, "Hey, you're really tall; you should come to a [crew] practice." Savannah knew nothing about the sport. She thought it was canoeing or kayaking. Savannah told me that this interaction left her "really confused. I didn't know what [crew] was. I'd never been in a boat before." Savannah attended the first practice and performed well on the erg—often a first test given to rowers to assess their basic strength and athleticism. After her first practice, she remembered telling her mom, "That was so much fun. I'm so invigorated, and I'm so energetic, and I'm so excited about this new thing!" Despite her enthusiasm, Savannah knew right away that she could not continue in the sport. She did not return to practice the next day because her mom could not afford the club dues.

Luckily for Savannah, her friend persisted and tracked her down at school. She mentioned to Savannah that the rowing coach kept asking about her. Savannah hesitated and confessed to the friend that she could not afford to row. Savannah's friend mentioned that her club had scholarships and that she should return to practice and ask the coach if she was eligible for one. The coach decided that Savannah's athletic potential outweighed her lack of funds and offered her a scholarship. Savannah's club funded her throughout the rest of her high school rowing career. At times, the club could not cover all her costs, including a stint on the junior national team. This forced Savannah to seek out donations—from her school, community, and extended family—and host fundraising events like car washes to complete her rowing experience. Spending her free time hustling

for funds to pay for her rowing races is just one example of the extra labor scholarships athletes endure that is not required of those who can pay their way.
These barriers are reflected in who ultimately is represented in club sport spaces.

Savannah was one of three working-class study participants. She accessed
rowing because she lived on the fringes of a wealthy white suburb in which the
sport was located. As she was the lone person on her team who needed financial assistance, the team could subsidize her participation. She also tapped into
the wealth within the larger community by raising money to fund her travel.
Savannah was the rare exception for whom sports did provide upward mobility. The rest of Savannah's teammates purchased spots in a private rowing club
to accelerate their already-advantaged college-going opportunities.

Private Track Clubs

Initially track appears more accessible than rowing. Whereas rowing is accessed
mostly through private clubs in a few select regions, track is the second most
featured American sport offered by high schools in all fifty states and Washington, D.C. Nearly 17,000 high schools across the United States sponsor track
and field programs, with 600,097 men and 488,592 women participating in the
sport (NFHS, 2019). That is 241 times the amount of U.S. high school rowers.
Said differently, three in every twenty public high schools have a track program.
But the availability of high school programs did not limit participants' investment in private club opportunities. USA Track and Field, the governing body
for the sport, has over 2,000 private club memberships for those willing to pay
a little extra to participate in the sport.

Many aspiring college track athletes recalled how they joined private clubs
to supplement their school programs. Three in twenty high schools may have
a track program, but not all track programs host all events. The primary reason study participants joined private clubs or hired private coaches was to gain
expertise in events not offered at their school. The broad view of high school
access to track captures whether schools sponsor an outdoor track program or
a cross country team. But the sport is richly complex. Track has at least seven
specialties requiring different training, knowledge, and expertise: sprints, jumps
(long, triple, high, and pole vault), throws (hammer, javelin, shot put, discus,
and weight), middle distance, long distance, relays, and hurdles.

The costs for club track memberships are more diffuse than those for rowing. I researched track programs in comparable areas to the rowing clubs and
found the cost for membership ranging between $100 and $960 per year. But
the costs accumulated beyond dues. Athletes purchased gear like uniforms and
multiple pairs and types of track shoes and spikes. The required clothing costs
for one California track club totaled $155.96 (excluding shoe costs), in addition
to membership dues of $960 per year (Marin Waves, 2016). Track participants
explained that shoes were an essential cost in their sport. All participants needed

at least one pair of shoes and one pair of track spikes. Each averaged around $100 per pair. Long-distance runners can go through a pair of shoes each month. In addition, the shoe and spike type vary per event. Even among events involving jumping, the shoe varies. LeVar remembers changing his spikes three times at a meet between jumping and sprinting events.

Chantae, like Savannah, was one of the few working-class students who became a college athlete. A Black woman, Chantae grew up in a "bad neighborhood." She characterized her elementary schools as "an all-Black school in a little ghetto neighborhood." Chantae said that growing up "I was never around any white people. All I saw was Mexicans and Blacks all my life." Her caregivers wanted her to find "positive things" she would "actually enjoy" to keep her "off the streets" and out of trouble. They also wanted to switch her to a different school. Chantae lived on the periphery of a white school district. Somehow— Chantae does not remember how—she transferred to a different school. Chantae started sixth grade in an "all-white school" in "a better neighborhood." This school had a track program, which she joined.

Chantae started off "doing everything" in track. She competed in all events shorter than 400 meters. By high school, Chantae's turnover had slowed. (Turnover refers to the speed at which your feet touch and push off the track. This equates to the frequency of strides someone can take in a given time interval. Someone who can take more strides per second has a better chance of running a faster time.) Chante's high school coach recommended she try the sequence of the triple jump—"hop-step-jump"—which requires speed, strength, balance, and coordination to master. Chantae liked the movements and wanted to continue in the event. But her public school coach lacked the skills to train her. To continue in the event, she had to leave the public realm and join a private club.

Chantae's family decided to pool their limited resources to fund her club track career. Even still, her family's precarious finances meant she could not consistently participate. "My mom does hair, so her money was really inconsistent. One week she'll have a good week when everyone comes in and gets their hair done. And then other weeks, she wouldn't. During club season, you have to pay for [the club]. And pay for your way to the meet. And have money to spend [at the meet]. They didn't give me anything. So it kinda influenced it. But, for the most part she always got it done." The institutional requirements of club sports assume that participants have the financial means to invest in their athletic futures. This assumption strips resources from the public sphere— as even those with limited means take their monies out of public school sports and toward private options—and reproduces economic inequality. Those with financial means purchase the skills and expertise guarded within the private realm. As Chantae notes, she did not receive financial assistance or scholarships to pay for her additional costs. Unlike Savannah, Chantae's community members could not subsidize these additional costs. Chantae did not host a carwash or go door to door soliciting donations. Instead, when her family could not afford the club dues or the travel costs, Chantae missed practice or a meet. She believed these inconsistencies hurt her athletic development.

In other cases, track athletes supplemented their school programs by hiring private coaches. Private coaching for all kinds of youth sports has grown since the early 2000s (Bick, 2007). Track coaching is offered between $50 and $100 per hour in most regions (Bick, 2007; Marin Waves, 2016). Malcolm, a Black man who grew up in a majority-white suburban area, believed his private coach secured his college running career.

Malcolm entered the sports path to college at a young age. By seventh grade he competed in club track, quickly specializing in the long jump. His older sister also had early success in the long jump, and their family decided to invest in a coach for the two young athletes. Their club and his school lacked effective coaching in this area, offering up a sprints coach to help them with the long jump. After two years with a private coach, Malcolm became one of the nation's top junior long jumpers. He and his sister endured a grueling schedule training with a private coach and the high school program. They spent Monday through Friday with their high school team and after practice did individual workouts prescribed by their private coach. On Saturday and Sunday, the siblings commuted forty-five minutes to train with their private coach in person. Their private coach came to all their track meets, and even in college he acted as Malcolm's mentor. Looking back on his youth sports, Malcolm recalled that he trained like a "professional." "It's always been me and my sister and coach. We've trained like professionals. He was a professional long jumper. He trained us like professional long jumpers."

The public narratives around track—*all you need is a pair of shoes*—portray track as widely accessible. Malcolm's shoes did not provide him professional training. Instead, Malcolm employed similar tactics as the rowers, seeking out privatized, exclusive athletic opportunities to further his advantage. His family had the financial resources to pay for a private coach, who offered him the knowledge and expertise to become a top national long jumper. In this way, Malcolm furthered his advantages by looking beyond his community. If he had just trained with his high school track team, he might not have become such a high-ranked runner. The *removal* of athletic opportunities from public spaces like schools motivates those with means, like Malcolm, to take their monies elsewhere. This decision further erodes confidence that the public can provide adequate training for athletes and therefore justifies potential future state divestments (Fabricant and Fine, 2015; Harvey, 2005). Since private clubs and coaches have steep entry requirements and are not widely available, those who can access these resources are automatically advantaged. Malcolm could become a standout long jumper because opportunities to do so are infrequent. Using the private sector to supplement athletic opportunities furthers the advantage of resource-rich communities with plentiful recreational and school sports.

Conclusion

Suburban communities use their higher tax bases to construct public parks and host recreational sports. Youth growing up in these areas have greater access to low-cost, safe, and higher-quality opportunities to develop athletic talent. These broad alignments grant immediate advantages to suburban residents. Yet speaking to athletes who successfully navigated collegiate recruitment revealed how suburban youth competed against one another to create and secure ever more exclusive opportunities to develop athletic talent. At each rung of education, children and young adults face a barrage of assessments designed in ways to favor those of elite white communities. Individuals like Iceman, by virtue of where they are born, whom their parents are, what they look like, and the resources embedded in their communities, are advantaged in these assessments. Still, Iceman fought for the scarce and coveted spots at top universities. This struggle to retain middle-class standing leads individuals like Iceman to pursue innovative ways to maintain their standing. As other scholars have noted (e.g., Lareau, 2015; McDonough, 1997), this race to remain in the middle class also creates a sense of entitlement to college access that creates even greater scarcity throughout university admissions.

Schools take center stage in these power struggles because the state has vested them with the authority to define, authenticate, and reward merit (Bourdieu and Passeron, 1977). Elites use their social standing to influence the organization and outcomes of schooling (e.g., Apple, 2004; Bourdieu, 2011; Bourdieu and Passeron, 1977; Calarco, 2018; Khan, 2012). Colleges could select their incoming class in infinite ways. It is no accident that the processes and assessments universities use align with the skills, dispositions, and resources concentrated in white suburban communities (Bowen and Bok, 1998; Davies and Guppy, 1997; Guinier, 2015; Johnson, 2014; Stevens, 2009; Weis et al., 2014). Elites using their influence to select and assign value to certain cultural materials to retain their power is *symbolic violence* (Bourdieu and Passeron, 1977). The knowledge and strategies used by white suburban communities to gain an edge in college admissions are legitimated when universities mark these efforts as meritorious and therefore deserving of exclusive access. Strategies valued in athletic admissions include pursuing rare sports like rowing and purchasing exclusive club memberships. When universities value these strategies instead of cultural habits that are more common in disenfranchised areas, they signify the former as *deserving* of college access. Thus, athletic merit is a form of symbolic violence.

Marking privatized resources as valued and meritorious in college admissions furthers the divestment of public athletic opportunities. This accelerates the distance between advantaged and disadvantaged communities as the state can credibly claim that publicly funded opportunities are not worth investing in (Brown, 2005, 2019; Coakley, 2011a; Fabricant and Fine, 2015; Harvey, 2005; Vaught, 2017; Weis et al., 2014). The transmission of privilege occurs when white suburban families *choose* to pursue private and elite sports. Education researchers have long tracked how white middle-class families' flight from public schools decreased state funding and educational outcomes in the public schools. Conversely, when white middle-class families stay in the public schools and invest dollars and labor to improve the schools, the public schooling experience improves (Baker and Corcoran, 2012; Fabricant and Fine, 2015; McLaren, 2007; Weis et al., 2014). So long as white suburban families keep pursuing private sports for college admissions advantages, public athletic programs will dwindle.

The pursuit for novel ways to secure advantage reveals the arbitrariness of how institutions define merit. The public common sense assumes that athleticism is an objective, easily measured disposition. But what constitutes athleticism? Who defines athleticism? And how is athleticism measured? In applying these questions to college admissions, it becomes clear that no universal definition of athleticism exists. In fact, stories presented in this chapter and the forthcoming ones show how athletes with little knowledge or experience in their sport were admitted to college as athletes. In these cases, the *gentleman amateur* remerges. When the NCAA required athletes certify their status as gentlemen, it affirmed traits detached from athleticism. Gentleman invoked character, morality, and discipline—all attributes that elite white men monopolized. Gentleman did not invoke whether someone could perform an athletic skill. Today's college athletic admission process still measures and rewards criteria detached from athletic skill. Coaches can assess an athlete's extrinsic associations (e.g., affiliation with a private club) and intrinsic attributes (e.g., are they a "good fit" for the team—discussed in chapter 6). These merit assessments are not intuitive. Instead, athletes *learn* through their social networks how best to position themselves in the athletic recruitment process. This is the topic explored in the next chapter.

5

A Guide

Socializing Future
College Athletes

Malcolm, a Black man who grew up in a white suburb, is a second-generation college athlete. His father, now a physician, competed in college track. Malcolm called him a "track guy" who knew "since day 1" how to raise his children to become college athletes. Malcolm and his sister received college admission and scholarships for their track accomplishments. Malcolm understood why people may attribute his track success to "genes." He knew track required "raw physical talent." But Malcolm vehemently rejected the notion that "natural talent" could propel someone to college. "People think Usain Bolt is the fastest man in the world because he has the fastest-man-in-the-world genes. I honestly don't think so. I think there's somebody on the block somewhere that can probably run faster than Usain Bolt if they got the same coaching and the same technique.... I don't think the world sees that. I think they're like, 'Oh he's just some God, so he can do it.' No, [Bolt] put his time in.... You have to put your time in regardless of what sport it is. People don't understand that." Both of Malcolm's parents grew up "on the block"—an urban area where the state's *removal* practices transferred resources from their neighborhoods toward white suburban areas. Malcolm's parents were the rare exceptions who excelled in spite of state tactics. They graduated from college and became professionals. With their newfound economic success, they moved to a white suburban community. Their neighborhood offered plentiful safe, low-cost sports.

Malcolm is a credible narrator regarding what it takes to become a world-class athlete. Malcolm and his sister trained with coaches who competed in the Olympics. Malcolm and his sister completed Junior Olympics programs prior to college. Malcolm earned a college scholarship for track and is an all-American long jumper and a hopeful future Olympic competitor. Malcolm has firsthand experience developing the athletic talent akin to Usain Bolt—eight-time Olympic gold medal winner (in 2008, 2012, and 2016). Malcolm correctly diagnoses how media coverage mystifies how individuals become athletes. When viewers watch Bolt breaking world records, they do not see *how* Bolt accrued the physical capital to best the standards set by legitimating institutions like the Olympics.

Physical capital refers to the "social formation of bodies," a process that infuses "symbolic value" into athletic feats (Shilling, 1991, p. 654). Physical capital reinforces hierarchies as not all bodies or athletic feats are afforded the same symbolic value in our culture (Shilling, 1991). In Malcolm's example, "somebody on the block" has the physicality to become an Olympian but lacks the opportunity to shape their talent into a form recognized by athletic organizations. Institutions like Olympic training centers legitimate the unequal social value assigned to capital by associating them with winnowing mechanisms and merit tests. These processes present the accumulation of symbolic and material capital as objective and fair rather than as arbitrary and elitist (Bourdieu and Passeron, 1977). While we are led to believe that Usain Bolt's individual talents propelled him upward, Malcolm observed that someone becomes the fastest man through communal resources to develop physical capital. The processes that elevate one form of physical capital over others and that guard and restrict access to the elevated form reproduce unequal chances for athletic achievement.

Developing physical capital requires access to certain forms of social capital or socializers like parents, teammates, and coaches who facilitate and instruct an athlete's skill development. Here, the *relational* dimension of the state once again emerges. The state relies upon people to ensure reproduction. In Malcolm's case, he could have trained in his school and recreational leagues, which were already far superior to those in neighboring communities. Instead, his father chose to intervene. Malcolm's father used his cultural knowledge or sense of the "rules of the game" (Lareau, 2015, p. 3) of how athletic admission operates. He then invested his economic resources to develop his children into college athletes.

Malcolm later described the additional labor his father put in to help him and his sister improve their athletic performance. He strategically enrolled Malcolm in certain club track programs with the best coaches. He later found a private coach to help Malcolm in his specialized event (long jump). And he critiqued Malcolm's performance. "Even at track practice, [Dad] was there. After track practice when I got home. Before track practice. On the weekends, he worked me. Did extra workouts. So it's technique. Because I got all that technical work [to do]. . . . That's the thing about being great in track . . . you got to work your form." Malcolm's father could have invested his money, time, and knowledge into his public school team and improved the athletic experience for many young athletes. Instead, he used his financial resources to purchase private club and coaching opportunities for Malcolm. It is understandable why Malcolm's family, as the rare individuals who escaped the state's assault on Black communities, would protect their current social standing. But doing so still supports the state's efforts to harm Black communities. Malcolm's father assisted the neoliberal state's project of transferring formerly public goods into the private realm by investing his resources in the private sphere rather than the public (Fabricant and Fine, 2015). The transfer of resources from the public to private restricts the potential pool of athletes. Instead of sharing knowledge and resources with a larger number of track hopefuls at the public schools, he concentrated them in Malcolm and his sister.

Malcolm's story also indicates how obtaining the physical capital universities desire requires an immersive and consistent exposure to sport socialization. He became a top athlete through his social interactions across varied settings—including communities, families, schools, and sports—to cultivate specific skills, characteristics, and performance. As discussed in the book's introduction, this socialization occurs over an extended period to *"produce a durable training"* (Bourdieu and Passeron, 1977, p. 31). Importantly, this durable training does not neatly emerge through a preprogrammed template. The extended period and varied relationships needed to develop physical capital produce individuals with seemingly disparate and contradictory profiles. Iceman—whose story anchored the previous chapter—and Malcolm came from oppositional racial, familial, and community groups. Iceman had no family ties to college sports, began as a hockey player and later transferred to his college sport rowing, and attended an elite all-boys private school. Malcolm had generational ties to college sports, started and ended his athletic career in track, and attended public schools. Power reproduction does not unfold in neat, predictable iterations. If it did, it would be too easy to contest and disrupt (Bourdieu, 2011). Instead, the slight variations in when, where, how, and who becomes a college athlete secure reproduction.

In this chapter, I describe the underlying commonalities in college athletes' varied approaches to securing physical capital. I describe the *social capital*, or central relationships, that creates the physical capital universities desire. Caregivers, coaches, and teammates socialize athletes to develop the characteristics preferred during recruitment. No single relationship is the driving factor for collegiate recruitment. Instead, interactions among caregivers, coaches, and teammates are critical for athletes to develop the athletic talent universities desire.

Caregivers

Attending school in the United States is compulsory, but playing sports is not. The voluntary nature of athletics means that caregivers must live in a community with the option for their youth to play sports. As discussed throughout the book, this first condition automatically eliminates many youth from the sports path to college. The voluntary nature of athletics also means that those who live in communities with sports *choose* to play them. In the study, families with knowledge of athletics as a route to higher education strategically enrolled their children in sports, financially invested in their athletic futures, and invested time into their development as athletes. Fourteen participants, Malcolm included, came from families where one or more of the caregivers had personal experience or knowledge of the sports path to college. For other participants, their families learned of the path because such knowledge circulated within their communities. In the latter instance, families subsequently began to research, invest, and support their children's athletic interests. Both versions required caregivers to invest in their children's athletic future.

Caregivers Start the Path

A high school student whose caregivers attended college has a much higher likelihood of attending higher education than someone who would be the first in their family to do so (Pascarella et al., 2004; Stephens et al., 2014). Because of this, I believed most participants would be second-generation college athletes. Instead, a caregiver's athletic history was much less relevant than their college experience. Of participants' caregivers, 85 percent attended college, whereas 25 percent played post–high school sports. Nine participants gleefully discussed how little their parents knew about sports. They relished being the family expert on the subject.

Of the fourteen participants who came from families who knew of, and strategically placed them on the sports path to college, most were white. This finding also diverges from existing literature that proposes Black families are more likely than white families to view sports as a mobility vehicle (Beamon, 2010; Curry and Jiobu, 1984; Edwards, 1979, 2000; Harris, 1994). Black and white families similarly invested in their children's sporting success.

Erwin, a white rower, is one example of a college athlete whose family did not predesign a sports path to college. Instead, special admissions found them. Erwin's parents attended college and pursued careers related to their degrees.

Their social networks were filled with other college graduates, many of whom were raising their children for university admission. Erwin's earliest childhood memories are laced with messaging about college access. He recalled that in early elementary school his parents were already speaking to him about preparing for his college application and which activities he should join to appear "well-rounded" on his application. Along with achieving high grades, his parents expected him to play sports, join clubs, and complete community service to prepare him for college admission.

Erwin played various sports but was mediocre at all. His older brother, though, excelled in one extracurricular activity: fencing. Erwin's mother befriended some of the other fencers' mothers during the drop-off and pickup periods of practice. She learned from these moms that some were strategically enrolling their offspring in fencing and other sports like rowing to gain preferential access to elite colleges. When I asked Erwin how he first began rowing he said, "I got signed up for rowing"—meaning his mother enrolled him on a rowing team. At the time, he knew nothing about the sport. "I thought [rowing] was when you [row] a kayak down waterfalls. And I was like, 'Where's the place where we can do that in [the tristate area]?'"

Erwin did not take to the sport immediately. He initially resented the long time commitments, grueling workouts, and disciplinary structure of the team. But his father required he stick with the sport he started. His high school coach had experience creating winning programs, and as Erwin continued to attend practice and immerse himself in the team, he slowly improved. By his junior year he competed in national-level competitions. Once again, his family intervened: His father, employed as an investigative journalist, used his personal connections and research skills to learn about college athletic recruitment. He studied the tactics employed by those who succeeded and learned several strategies that help prospective athletes through recruitment. Throughout his junior year, Erwin's father taught him how to speak to authority figures, helped him create a rowing résumé, took him to regattas attended by college coaches, and introduced him to them. At the time, Erwin resented the formal manner in which his father encouraged him to interact with the coaches. He did an impression for me of how he would talk in a "professional" voice. He dropped his voice low and spoke in punctuated syllables and said, "Oh, coach, good afternoon, [Erwin] here." He was relieved when Coastal-U offered him admission. He remembered thinking, "Thank god [Coastal-U] recruited me"—otherwise he would not have attended an elite college.

The manifestations of the state Erwin encountered, including his suburban communities, public schools, and public school sports teams, gave him the skills, knowledge, and disposition desired in university admission. But his story also represents how people act to retain their advantages. Erwin's parents socialized him to attend college to retain his middle-class standing. Through connecting with others also seeking to secure and retain their advantages, Erwin's mother learned the cultural knowledge to give Erwin an edge in college admissions. She could have ignored these insights and let Erwin compete in the classroom against his middle-class peers. Instead, she enrolled him on a rowing team to increase his chances. There, Erwin's teammates and coaches taught him the physical and technical competencies of rowing. His father also intervened and studied how he could get his son recruited. Thus, Erwin became a rower and later a college athlete through his family's strategic invocation of community socialization and networks.

The "Accidental" College Athlete

Erwin's story also represents how his parents' original strategy—enrolling their children at an early age in extracurricular activities to enhance their college admission prospects—coincidentally aligned with the necessary steps required to become a college athlete. Through enrolling their children in extracurricular activities, Erwin's family developed a network of other parents who taught them about additional college acceptance strategies. Further, by playing sports most of his life prior to high school, Erwin was probably better positioned to pick up a sport like rowing than if he had never done a sport before. Additionally, Erwin's immersion in white middle-class communities allowed him to develop the traits to "properly" approach college coaches—who represent institutions that reflect and perpetuate white middle-class values. While each participant had unique details, mishaps, trajectories, and flukes that landed them a college offer, collectively their narratives showed how the parenting practices already employed in white middle-class communities develop college-going adults. These details *conveniently* align with the required skills, dispositions, and knowledge required in athletic recruitment.

Most participants first joined sports because their caregivers believed athletic participation provided the holistic development for children to prepare them for college. Sports are now an endemic part of white suburban parenting (e.g., Andrews, 1999; DeLuca and Andrews, 2016; Messner, 2009; Stefansen et al., 2018; Stirrup et al., 2015). Parents in these communities control the types of sports offered and the values, skills, and dispositions cultivated in these sports. DeLuca and Andrews (2016) found that swimming clubs enable white middle-class parents to transmit class and race values that prepare their children to navigate social hierarchies such as competition, work ethic, and goal setting. Participants reported how their parents encouraged sports participation because it could offer a sense of community, teach social habits like obeying authority, competition, and goal setting, and build "character" by tolerating loss and failure. As I discuss later in this and the subsequent chapter, these are the same characteristics that college coaches—many of whom also arose from white middle-class communities—desire in college athletes.

In the book's introduction, I also discussed how neoliberalism has altered community-sponsored sports. Middle-class parents who enroll their children in sports to cultivate a middle-class lifestyle encounter an expensive, exclusive, and hierarchical system. The winnowing mechanisms within youth sports mean parents pay a steep price for their child's athletic advancement. Along the way, parents encounter the sports path to college. George, a white man from a coastal town, offers one such example.

George described his family as "laid-back" members of a beach community. He characterized his town as "chill" where "no one is uptight," where people can "kinda do [their] own thing" and things operate at a "slow pace." He grew up across from a park and a mile from the beach. His parents encouraged him to enjoy the outdoors and play with other kids in the area. They also signed him up for the local recreation leagues. He played tee-ball, soccer, and basketball all by the age of six.

George quickly developed a passion for basketball. He recalls, even when he was as young at six years old, crying if they lost a game and yelling at the referees if he received a bad call. He wanted to spend as much time playing the sport and improving his skills as he could. At times his parents tried to tone down his athletic passions, reminding him that the scores of games are irrelevant. George felt his parents were supportive of his interests and said he could quit sports at any time. By thirteen George had joined an all-star travel basketball team that practiced six days per week, often from six to eight o'clock at night, and traveled across the Southwest for tournaments. The travel often required that George miss school and his parents take off work on Fridays. It was around this time that George felt his parents' attitudes toward sports shift. As early as George could remember, his parents said school should be his top priority. But their actions soon betrayed their philosophy.

> Sometimes we wouldn't get back [from basketball tournaments] until late Sunday night. And then I would cram to do all the homework. I remember one time we had this huge project due in eighth grade ... [and] there was this tournament and I was freaking out, like "I'm not going to be back in time, I'm not going to be able to finish it." I get back and I start working on it. And my mom was like, "Yeah, you're not going to school tomorrow." [laughs] It was like worth half your grade in eighth grade. So it was like, "Yeah, you'll just go half-day. When's it due?" I was like, "It's due at one o'clock." She's like, "Yeah we can have it done before one." I remember all my teammates rolled into school at the same time [laughs]. We're like, "Alright, none of us got it done, this is great."

In this scenario, George and his mom knew he had a big project due. They chose to skip school, not the tournament, to finish the assignment. By virtue of her race and class position, George's mother was afforded the option by the school system to make such a decision on behalf of her child. Truancy officers were not sent to George's door when he did not show for his compulsory school day. Instead, George's mom was permitted by the school to keep him home and finish the project. The school and George's parents compromised on their own rules to enable the neoliberal model of athletic participation. They forgave school attendance in order for George to pursue sports. As George went deeper along the sports path to college, his parents became greater enablers of his athletic success.

After joining the cross country team to stay in shape for basketball season, George realized he had greater chances of success in running than in basketball. By high school he turned his whole focus toward running. George said he would often go to bed by six o'clock after track practice and wake up the next morning to do his homework or try to fit it in during recess or other class periods. In his junior year of high school George was elected captain of his cross country team. He disapproved of his coach's training strategy and said as much to him. The coach kicked George off the team for his disobedience. When he came home that night, George's first action was to research how to do an interdistrict school transfer. If he could not compete for his own school's team, he would go to another school. He also called his friends on different programs to evaluate which school to move to. He even had his parents' blessing. His parents were there for him every step of the way. They helped him find the paperwork to file for a transfer. Right before George switched schools, his coach apologized and let him back on the team but revoked his captaincy.

Even though George's parents did not initially intend for George to pursue the sports path to college, he would not have been able to become a college athlete without their help. George's family stumbled upon the sports path, but once they were on it they engaged in all the required activities and investments to ensure that George could make it to the finish line. George's passion for basketball led them to find an elite team and pay the requisite membership dues, tournament fees, and travel costs. In supporting George's interests, they even drew upon their knowledge of how to navigate the school system, finding ways to gain permission for him to miss compulsory school days to travel to tournaments or to make up his assignments. Importantly, the school system positively responded to George's parents' actions. They received the benefit of the doubt that they could make appropriate decisions for George, such as removing him from school to finish an assignment. These are just some examples of the "hidden entry requirements" (Bourdieu, 1978, p. 838) of time, labor, and resources that parents and caregivers must invest in to ascend through youth sports.

The Toll: Required Athletic Resources

The elevated symbolic value attached to some parenting styles is one way legitimating institutions achieve reproduction. Another is by attaching capital requirements. Pierre Bourdieu (2011) combined the words "social" and "capital" to convey this. Thus, social capital—one's access to particular socializers and social networks—has economic costs and benefits associated with it. In George's case, his parents could socialize him in ways that would best navigate the constraints that occur when combining elite athletics and academics because they had the economic capital to invest in his athletic future. In previous chapters, I discussed the financial resources needed to develop the physical capital universities desire, including costly club dues, travel, equipment, and coaches. In addition to these costs, participants and their families invested another form of economic capital: time.

George's parents had high-paying and flexible employment that allowed both of them to travel to all his games. George also engaged in sports year-round, practicing upward of six hours per day during the summer months. My findings resonate with existing research. Athletes and their families had leisure time to invest in sport (Bourdieu, 1978; Coakley, 2015; DeLuca and Andrews, 2016; Messner, 2009). Through economic capital, participants built physical capital by improving their athleticism.

Michael Messner's (2009) ethnography of youth soccer describes the "pipeline" of the gendered division of labor that structures youth sports. Community-sponsored sports keep their costs low because they rely upon parental volunteer labor. The head coach of a given team may be paid a nominal salary, but the assistant coaches and other adults who help run the program are volunteers. It is up to the head coach to recruit this volunteer labor force. Messner found that head coaches recruit a "team parent," almost always a "team mom," to do the miscellaneous work associated with today's youth sports, such as creating team banners, organizing snacks for the games, coordinating travel, and coordinating awards. Messner observed how volunteer labor mapped onto gender-segregated divisions of labor in the home and workforce. Men received the default assumption that they could and should be the public-facing leaders of the team who coached sports, whereas the miscellaneous domestic responsibilities fell to women. These patterns of domestic labor also flowed from suburban lifestyles: those in suburban communities are more likely to have one parent, typically a woman, in flexible employment or working as a full-time parent (Messner, 2009).

Study participants observed similar patterns of gendered division of labor that shepherded their sports experience. CM, whose mother was a former college- and Olympic-level track athlete, did not coach her children's sports teams or help with their training or conditioning or even discuss their performances. Instead, she handled the "social aspects" of the program and was a "team mom." CM's father, who had no experience in sports, helped his children through injuries, created training and nutrition plans for them, and scrutinized their athletic performance. This division of labor was common. Women and mothers took on the primary tasks of transporting athletes from game to game and doing the domestic responsibilities for the teams. Participants recalled that these practices continued through high school. Taylor, a white woman whose own mother had been a college track athlete, was the primary caregiver in her home and did not have paid employment. Her mother worked alongside the mothers of Taylor's cross country and track teammates to create cultural experiences that transcended the actual training involved in the sport. Taylor recalled that her team had "secret sisters" before every race, meaning teammates would give each other small presents before they competed. The team moms also ran a booster club and raised funds for both the girls' and boys' cross country and track teams. The booster club hosted barbecues and pasta dinner nights to bring the team together and raise additional donations. Taylor did not know exactly what the money supported but remembered that the events were "fun" and gave the team something to look forward to after running endless laps around the track. Taylor described how it felt to be so supported in her athletic pursuits: "And on my team we were all just white, privileged. Our moms did everything for us. Especially the top girls. We were totally little babies. . . . I don't think any people's moms worked, really. Maybe. That's so bad thinking about it. . . . And so yeah, I felt very lucky." Taylor felt "lucky" because she came from a family with the financial resources to support her running career.

Taylor became aware of her privileged status by observing why some of her teammates quit the sport:

> I remember there was this one guy. He was on the team and he was really fast. He was Mexican. He was really fast. But then his mom couldn't drive him to practice or something. . . . It was so sad because he was so good but he just couldn't come. And I remember we were captains my senior year. And we had to lead practice because coaches aren't allowed to for a couple weeks. And these girls would come. And there was this Hispanic girl who—she didn't have running shoes. There was one or two of them. They had on Converse or something. And we were like, "Okay, everyone needs to have running shoes." But it's hard to be like, "you have to go buy them," because they're expensive. Yeah, it's just sad because it's definitely not always equal.

The "Mexican" boy and "Hispanic" girls were displaced from Taylor's team not because of their physical potential but because they did not have the necessary maternal and financial support systems. Taylor's high school team, like most youth and high school sports, required the unpaid time and labor of parental volunteers for their children to play sports. Sports demanded, at minimum, that youth have daily transportation to and from practice—which occurs outside the normal bounds of the school day and school-provided transportation— a "hidden entry requirement" inaccessible to many youth. Immersed in this environment, Taylor reenacted the same requirements and chastised two of her potential teammates for skipping practice and lacking the adequate gear.

Taylor, whose parents were track athletes, never thought about appropriate running gear because her parents always provided her with such items. These requirements had the intended effect. Even though Taylor recalled she did have racial diversity in her community and her school, her cross country team was simply a "bunch of privileged white girls."

Taylor was lucky in another sense. Taylor's father provided the income that supported her family's upper-middle-class lifestyle. Taylor's mother provided the unpaid domestic labor for her home and athletic teams. This meant Taylor's time was free from employment or domestic responsibilities. Her parents' labor gave her the free time needed to invest in sports. One of the more striking features of participants' life histories is how few held jobs or child care responsibilities. None contributed to their family incomes. Iceman worked in high school, but, as he explains, employment was for individual growth, not economic need. "Along with playing a sport, we all had to have a summer job. . . . I would wake up at four forty-five to row, and then I had to go to work, and then I had to go to a practice or a game in the afternoon. And the workdays were really long. And I wanted to row and play hockey. I [told] my Dad, 'I can't do this. I need to row. I really want to play hockey. And I don't have to work.' And he was like, 'Yes you do. You've just got to be tough.'" Iceman's time working construction for his father was laborious, but it was not performed out of economic need. As he pointed out, the family did not need the income from his employment. His family could financially support his sports participation and private school tuition during this time.

Another feature of Iceman's life and the lives of other participants is that none included contributions to the domestic responsibilities of the home. A few did symbolic chores, but none were primary caregivers. The freedom from domestic or economic employment allowed participants to dedicate time and energy to high-level sports participation. Those who became college athletes, therefore, accessed dividends from at least three forms of social capital to pay the toll of the sports path. First, their socializers could pay the direct costs of elite sports, such as membership fees, private coaching, and equipment. Second, the socializers could cover the indirect costs, investing their time into transporting, coaching, and attending athletic practices. Finally, socializers relieved youth of economic or domestic responsibilities so they could focus on sports. Yet even these three cost layers were insufficient. To develop the athletic talent universities desire, youth went beyond their families. Coaches provided the specific socialization into the athletic ways of being universities desire.

Coaches

One of the largest differences between students on the sports path to college and their non-sport-focused peers is their relationship to coaches. Coaches with knowledge of the athletic training styles and demands of college sports can better prepare their athletes for recruitment. Just like an Advanced Placement high school course promises to train students for college-level curricula, certain coaches promise to train athletes for college-level teams. In turn, athletes connected to such coaches can point to their training as evidence that they are ready for college. Yet the maldistribution of opportunities to develop athletic talent also reflects a maldistribution of coaching expertise. Not all high school or club programs have coaches who can train athletes in the physical and technical aspects required in college sports. Thus, college recruitment advantages those who can access *particular* coaching expertise.

"Pushing Your Limits": Cultivating Athletic Stamina

Throughout a lifetime of learning several sports, participants recounted how the athletic environment adapted and changed their physiques. The physical conditioning of sports is one such "durable training" (in Bourdieusian language) that reshapes individuals to fit the social and cultural athletic environment. While caregivers provided the resources for athletes to commit to sports, coaches created the curricula that shaped youth into eligible college athletes.

Coaches with knowledge of college-level athletic demands created strenuous workout regimes. These regimes mimicked the hours of commitment, training volume, and physical intensity offered in college. Participants vividly recalled the physical and mental shock they endured when switching from recreational sports teams to competitive club programs designed to prepare athletes for college. Many remembered hobbling around high school within the first few weeks of joining the team, their muscles sore, exhausted, and in shock from the new athletic load. Cooper, a white woman from the West Coast, decided to try rowing after her neighbor recommended it. Cooper did not think too much about the decision. She had already played seven other sports and saw this as "another one to put under my belt." The training load was like no other sport she had done. "This was the first sport where I was completely obliterated at the end of practice, like I can't do anything, I need to go to bed. I would stay up and do whatever I needed to do. . . . I was so sore my first week. . . . [I remember] sitting in science class and I couldn't move my muscles I was so sore. My dad had to drive to [the school to] give me aspirin." Cooper still remembers the physical shock and lasting pain of her first week of rowing. In hindsight, this pain signified to athletes the coaching style would produce results.

High school coaches also reenacted collegiate athletic teams by increasing the time commitment. At the youth level, seasonal sports took place in the fall, winter, spring, *or* summer. If a participant played "year-round" sports, they did multiple sports during different seasons, such as playing soccer in the fall, basketball in the winter, track in the spring, and swimming in the summer. At the high school level, "year-round" meant playing the same sport all year. High

Table 5.1
Average practice time prior to college

Sport	Year-round youth sports (%)	Year-round high school sports (%)	Double-day workouts (%)	Hourly practice time per week
Girls' cross country/ track and field	67	80	20	15.45
Boys' cross country/ track and field	92	83	33	17.79
Girls' crew	56	78	44	17.47
Boys' crew	71	71	43	17.50
Total	68	79	36	17.10

school sports that mirrored college commitments required camps, retreats, or practices throughout the summer. Most of the cross country runners received training schedules that they could complete either on their own or with the team at a specific time. Along with running five days a week in the summer, CM's high school track program hosted a Mammoth Camp in the California mountains. For club sports like rowing, the participants either continued to row with their club or tried out for the junior national team. With large, and often financially costly, summer commitments, high school athletes' "time off" was a brief reprieve in December. As Taylor recalled, even if there was no mandatory practice during winter break, "it was always expected that you do stuff on your own."

Another tactic to increase commitment was to hold "double-days" or twice daily practices. Double-days involve waking up earlier than other students to train before school, followed by a second practice session after school. As table 5.1 represents, the average practice commitment per sport during the school year was about seventeen hours. Further, sixteen participants invested twenty hours or more each week practicing for their sport. This excludes time spent commuting to practice or competing at meets. Rowing and track competitions could last twelve hours and took place most spring weekends.

Coaches with knowledge of college training regimes also instituted cross-training sessions. Athletes performed weight training, conditioning sessions, and even alternative athletic activities like swimming or yoga to improve their fitness while protecting their bodies from overuse injuries. Sanya, a white woman and one of three working-class study participants, due to her proximity to a suburb, attended one of the wealthiest public schools in the United States. She described her high school track program's cross-training routine.

We'd have long practices. [Coach] was very technique oriented. I remember there was a lot of drills and specific exercises to strengthen—he was all about the weight room. . . . We'd start practice at one forty-five [with] a never-ending meeting. We'd always joke about how long his meetings were 'cause he'd have some inspirational speech before every day of practice. Between the technical stuff, the weight room, the post-practice talk [where] the coach about [recapped our workouts] it wasn't [until] six thirty that you were going home. It was long. When I got older we would do morning practices. Like aqua jogging in the morning. And that would be from like six to seven.

Her track practices lasted nearly five hours every day, with a combination of meetings, technique work, and physical conditioning. Her coach used the school's plentiful resources. His athletes used the weight room to develop their fitness and the pool to relieve the pressure on their joints.

Sanya was new to this intensive athletic regime. She began high school with a different coach with minimal track and field knowledge. Sanya attended shorter and less specialized practices with no ties to college preparation. Shortly after she joined the team, the school hired a new coach who instituted the tactics recounted above. Sanya was skeptical at first. "Our new coach [brought] specific workouts [and] it shifted [how] we approached practice. At first I totally rejected him. But then I realized we were getting more results. And so I started really embracing him. And we had a close relationship. It almost felt like college. You'd kinda get nervous before practice: 'is this a big workout today?' As opposed to before [I] didn't even think twice about practice.... He was definitely a huge part of why I improved so much and why I started looking at the sport in a different light." Many participants reiterated Sanya's sentiments. They believed their most successful high school coaches were those who replicated the college training style and standards. In this way, high school coaches cultivated a habitus mirroring college-level athletics. Athletes within these environments developed the physical capital that aligned with college athletics.

Kalie, a white woman who attended a private school and joined a private rowing club, explains how her high school habitus improved her college recruitment chances: "We [practiced] year-round. Which is crazy. Most kids do their sport for one season. When you tell [college coaches] you're [practicing year-round] and how much you're doing [at practice], they're like, 'Whoa. You're a pretty committed high school kid to be able to [row] that long.' Freshman year in high school and you're committing six days a week all year to something shows you're pretty dedicated [to your sport]." Kalie believed that her coach's training regime set her apart from other potential athletes. A university coach could confidently assume that someone from this program, because they trained like college athletes, could endure college-level rowing.

In addition to required practice and competitions, thirty-two participants did optional workouts. This included aerobic conditioning, weight lifting, and skill development. Casey, a white woman and member of an exclusive rowing club known for producing college athletes, described the time investment for required and optional rowing practices: "We trained six days a week, for three hours, required. And you had extra work on your own. . . . I would come two hours early, do practice, stay an hour later. Literally, I was there for six hours [per practice] my senior year." Casey's rowing commitment indicates how college standards influence high school sports. The NCAA limits college training sessions to twenty hours per week. Study participants recounted that their coaches maneuvered around this rule through "volandatory" workouts—saying that practice was "voluntary" when in fact it was mandatory. If athletes missed a volandatory workout, they could face consequences. Casey was attenuated to volandatory practices in high school. Her coach created "extra work" that would help improve her performance. While this work was not technically required, she did it because her coach encouraged her to do so.

High school programs that require practice year-round twice per day and "voluntary" extra conditioning mirror the training style instituted by college coaches. College athletic training schedules require athletes to practice twice per day, practice year round, train through injury, put in "voluntary" work, and elevate their athletic participation above all other life pursuits (Adler and Adler, 1991; Beamon, 2008; Coakley, 2015; Eckstein, 2017; Grenardo, 2016; Hawkins, 2013; Hextrum, 2017a, 2020b; Jayakumar and Comeaux, 2016). The social, physical, and psychological harms associated with pursuing athletics in such a way are well documented (Adler and Adler, 1991; Beamon, 2008; Coakley, 2011a, 2011b; Grenardo, 2016; Hawkins, 2013). This harm makes the endeavor no less exclusive. As discussed in previous chapters, participants accessed coaches in their resource-rich communities and private clubs who mirrored college programs.

The Technician

The maldistribution of opportunities to row in high school compared to college has led many college programs to fill their rosters with current college students who have never rowed before. Some college rowers, like myself, learn the sport in college. This phenomenon misconstrues rowing as an untechnical, easy-to-learn sport. All sports, including rowing, require technical knowledge. Kalie is a coxswain, a position in rowing that closely resembles the coaching role. She recalled how her first year of rowing she had a novice coach—someone who was also in their first year of coaching. The coach did not teach her how to become a coxswain and instead gave her a boat and a microphone and set her on the water. Kalie recalled how the "first three weeks" of rowing she just "told stories in the boat." She remembered thinking, "Cool, I have a microphone, people have to listen to me. I have an audience." To put this story in a more familiar context, a coxswain telling stories to rowers is akin to a quarterback performing a stand-up routine in the huddle.

The next year, Kalie moved up in age level and received a new coach. Her new coach was a veteran of the sport and spent his summers coaching the junior national rowing team. The coach gave her metaphors to think about her role as a coxswain and begin to develop her skills.

> My high school coach told me, "You can be a cheerleader, you can be an airplane pilot, or you can be a commander. Those three styles are different, and different [boats] will want different things. Maybe last year the boat needed you to be an airplane pilot. But this year, they need you to be motivating and [be a cheerleader]." When my coach started talking like that it was like, "Oh, I get that." You have to have in your repertoire different styles of things so that you can figure out what the boat needs.

Seven years later, Kalie spoke as an expert in the sport, detailing how she assessed a boat's needs and the varied tasks she must simultaneously execute as a coxswain. In this description she gives a sense of the complexity involved in rowing:

> [First] I make sure that the [rowers'] stroke rate is effective and powerful.... We could go at forty [strokes per minute], but is that really going to be faster than a thirty-four? From there, I go to the technique side of things, looking at whether [a rower] is slow off the catch. [In this role] you have to be kind of a mini-coach. And then there's the [boat feel] side of it where the boat isn't working together and [the rowers'] timing is out of sync. And [then I have to] establish a race plan so they know what's going on, so the rowers know what to expect.... Basically you're the brain. Let them do all the physical stuff, turn off their heads, so you can do it all for them. [For the rower-coxswain relationship to succeed] you have to make sure your rowers trust what you're saying ... or they [won't] listen to you.... And [all the while] I'm steering [the boat] because if you don't steer straight you basically lose a race for your boat.

This passage reflects Kalie's transformation from a novice coxswain to an expert. Kalie entered rowing as an extroverted performer excited that she had a captive audience who could listen to her stories. Years later, practicing year-round under the tutelage of her expert coach, she learned how to develop multiple coxswaining styles; assess the speed, power, technique, and overall effectiveness of a crew; translate her assessment into tangible feedback to improve the rhythm, flow, power, and speed of a crew; develop trusting relationships with rowers so they listened and executed her commands; and all the while steer a delicate vessel through water. Even in Kalie's elite private rowing club, she still encountered the difference between a coach with knowledge of the sport and a coach without. The scarcity of rowing programs and rowers means fewer people understand this sport. Further, not all rowers want (or need) to become coaches.

With all the complexity involved in rowing, the sport reduces to two positions: a rower and a coxswain. In contrast, track and field has various events, and not all track programs host all events. Not all schools have the technical knowledge set required for the field events like triple jump, pole vault, and high jump. Hosting a track "program" could simply mean having a place to run. This is far from the equipment and expertise needed to produce successful athletes in multiple events. For instance, while track is available at three in twenty U.S. public high schools, only forty-four public schools host the heptathlon—an event in which women track athletes compete in seven events (NFHS, 2019). As yet another example of gender disparity, sixty-four public high schools host the decathlon—an event in which men track athletes compete in ten events (NFHS, 2019). The inconsistency of events offered across track programs forces athletes to search elsewhere for coaching expertise.

When Chantae—the only participant who was Black *and* working-class in the study—started her freshman year of high school, her sprinting times slowed. Her coach recommended she try jumping events instead. She tried the triple jump and immediately liked the rhythm and skill involved in the event. Triple jump is also far less popular and available than the 100-meter dash. Triple jump involves "a lot of technique," Chantae explained. "For triple, you can do the majority of the things good, but it's the little things that are going to take you way further." The first two years, her high school coach taught her the basics of the event. But "he wasn't really a good coach. He kinda just stood out there while we're doing everything. He wasn't really coaching us." Chantae turned to a private club to improve. Those coaches helped her develop a routine to "practice more consistently." They gave her a weight training regime and supplemental summer workouts.

Still, the private club lacked a triple jump specialist. Chantae needed to find a coach with the technical expertise to take her from good to great in her event. Chantae's mom worked overtime, scheduling extra hair appointments to pay for a private triple jump coach. Chantae explained the technical details of her event that required specialized expertise. Before she could do so, she asked me for a pen and paper. "Long jump is just one jump. [Draws a half circle on a piece of paper.] Triple jump is a hop, a step—and that's on the track—and then a jump into the sandpit. [Draws out three semicircles.] [Triple jump] is three phases. You have to [keep] your mind and body connected to make your body do what you need to do. You have to make your body get at the right angles and hold those angles [while simultaneously being] quick through all the transitions [through the phases of the jump]."

Both Chantae and Kalie recounted how their coach's knowledge transformed them from good to great athletic prospects. Accessing coaches with this knowledge is never guaranteed. Neither athlete initially had a coach with the skills to train her in her requisite position. Kalie graduated into such a program, provided by her private, elite rowing club. Chantae used her family's limited discretionary funds to purchase this additional access. In both cases, the technical expertise resided outside the public school system and instead in privatized, paid-for, supplemental athletic activities.

The Mentor

The sports path to college remains a voluntary route to higher education. Many talented high school athletes cannot access the resources to translate their athleticism into college access. Even if they know sports can get them to college, they may not know the necessary steps. High school, club, and private coaches play an instrumental role in helping athletes transition to college. Coaches provided the vision and the knowledge of how students could convert their athletic abilities into college access. Particularly for study participants whose families were not heavily involved in their sport, the coach stepped in to provide the vision and the means. Fifteen participants acknowledged that they would not have known it was even possible to participate in intercollegiate athletics if their coach had not intervened.

Sophia, a white woman, grew up on the East Coast close to an Ivy League college. She never imagined she would be an intercollegiate athlete, let alone participate on one of the top college teams in the nation. Her parents were the first in their families to go to college and instilled in Sophia that "college was always where I was going. I never considered not going to college." They focused on her academic curriculum, ensuring she did her homework, played viola, and enrolled in honors classes. She was confident that she would go to *a* college, but "everyone's goal" at her high school was to attend an Ivy League college, and it was Sophia's goal too. One day she saw a flyer at her school that advertised a rowing club affiliated with the local Ivy League university. This connection piqued her interest.

Her parents were indifferent to sport. Sophia did not play organized sports. Her main form of physical activity was playing tag or hide-and-go-seek with the other neighborhood kids. When she mentioned the rowing club to her parents, her dad did a little internet research. He came across an article that discussed the legacy of rowing at Ivy League colleges and how high school students could use the sport for college access. He shared the article with Sophia. "If my dad had never mentioned anything to me, I never would have done it." The spark of knowledge that rowing could provide Ivy League admission ignited Sophia's interest in the sports path to college. But she was still a long way away from developing the talent needed.

Sophia's parents financially supported her by paying for the club membership, new athletic clothing, and travel costs, including a competition in

London. Two years in, the team hired a new coach. The coach set the standard that the whole team could become college rowers. "After this new coach came, he really revamped the whole program and was having one-on-one meetings with rowers about rowing in college. . . . The number of people who committed to rowing in college definitely increased after he came 'cause he put much more of an emphasis on it. And also, our team was just, way better after he came, [which made it more likely] we could get recruited. Prior to that there were significantly less [people from our club team who rowed in college] and now everyone does." Sophia's coach normalized the concept that athletes from the program go on to participate in college sport by first telling them it was a realistic goal. He did that through repeated meetings, encouragement, and ramping up athletic commitments. During her junior year, her coach taught her which colleges had the best rowing programs, how to approach college coaches at local races and through emails, and how to create an athletic résumé that highlighted her accomplishments. She concluded that of all her other relationships, her "coach helped me the most" with athletic recruitment.

Sophia's parents, school, and community prepped her for college. Her parents moved to a middle-class community with top-ranked schools in the backyard of one of the top three ranked universities in the world. They raised her with the means, vision, and supplemental activities that enhance one's college-going prospects. Her siblings attended college, two in the local area, but not Ivy League universities. She focused on extracurriculars, like viola, that her family believed would help her become a "well-rounded" college applicant. But none of these activities provided her with the extraordinary guarantee of access to a top university. Rowing provided one such route. For students already on a college-going trajectory, coaches enhanced their prospects. Coaches with the knowledge of college athletic training and the skills to imitate it did so. Athletes with access to these elite programs developed a further refined and attenuated habitus that positioned them for an athletic route to college. For instance, Sophia also learned that simply rowing is not enough. She experienced two different coaching regimes. The first provided her the physical conditioning, technical expertise, and vision to become a college athlete. Her second coach's training regime mirrored that of a college program, and with his guidance and vision, she was able to translate this into a well-packaged application to the nebulous college athletic recruitment process.

Athletic Talent: No "I" in Team

Caregivers and coaches provide the infrastructure and knowledge to guide athletes on the path to college. But the *durable training* to form a habitus requires total immersion in a culture (Bourdieu, 2011; Bourdieu and Passeron, 1977). This total immersion involves peer cultures that normalize a certain college-going habitus (McDonough, 1997; Weis. et al., 2014; Willis, 1977). Participants' primary peer culture came through their teammates. Teammates built college-prep cultures by helping one another develop the vision that they could become college athletes, complete rigorous training regimes, gain the technical skills, and learn the ins and outs of college recruitment.

Some clichés do hold true. One that did so in my study was that "there is no I in team." Developing athletic talent is a collective effort. Participants' caregivers provided the vision and means for athletes to train. Their coaches offered skill instruction and exacting training standards. But their teammates offered a unique form of support. Teammates collaborated and offered one another the psychological, social, and physical dimensions necessary to become an elite athlete.

Reggie, a white man and international college student, recalled the difference between training for the single scull, an individual event, and training for a collective eight-person boat event: "[Training with teammates involves] drawing energy off of others, pushing with others, working together toward a goal. Rather than [the] alienation felt in the single. [When I'm in a single] I can turn around [and end a workout] and no one would care, no one would worry. Whereas in an eight you gotta work together, work as a team, not let each other down. Like it's easier to wake up in the morning, [laughs] [because your teammates] are getting you out of bed, literally." Reggie felt "alienation," or being apart, isolated, and alone, when he trained by himself for an individual event. In contrast, training with his team added motivation, accountability, and purpose to his training. His teammates even granted him the reason to leave the comfort of his bed in the wee hours of the morning.

Athletes also recounted the specific ways that teammates improved their performance. In rowing and track, coaches cultivated competitive environments, often ranking the athletes against one another and setting increasingly high standards for achievement. Through this internal competition, athletes strove to best their teammates and reach ever higher to meet their coaches' demands.

Monique explained how her coach's training standards seeped into her optional workouts and rowing goals. She recalled how one year her "three friends" and teammates sought a spot on the junior national team. To make the cut, they needed to complete an individual 2,000-meter race on an ergometer under a certain time. The four friends trained together outside of required practice hours and completed several versions of this test to try to make the junior national team standard. But the competition among each other was even fiercer than the drive to make the team: "I pull[ed] a 7:18 erg. And then my friend goes and she pulls 0.2 slower than me. So she decides to do another one, and she pulls 7:10, and then I get pissed off and I pull 7:08. And then she gets pissed off and then, does another erg, and then I get another erg and I beat her. And then she stops and I was like, 'Yes!' That was crazy competitive. I don't think I'm even that competitive anymore." Through their internal competition, Monique and her friends made the junior national team standard and bested the time by over ten seconds. They, not their coach, set the stakes of this competition through which they collectively improved.

Monique's memory also indicates how teammates created norms and cultures outside the coach's purview. In Monique's case, the team encouraged one another to work out beyond the formal training schedule. These extra workouts improved Monique and her team's performance.

The immersion in the college-prep athletic culture extended beyond formal practice hours. As Erwin ascended in rowing, he learned from his teammates that success required a unilateral focus on the sport, even outside of practice. He described his high school teammates as "type-A personalities," or the kinds of people that "obsess" over every little detail. "I call them lifestyle rowers," he told me, or rowers who reorganize their lives with rowing at the center. "[A teammate of mine] would get up every morning and do an hour on the erg [rowing machine], before school, in high school. And then do school. He used to walk down the hallways [Erwin makes the rowing motion], like this. He used to row down the hallway to work on the motion. And sit in front of the mirror so he could see his shoulder." When Erwin joined the team, he had much to learn about the technique of the sport. His teammate who rowed behind him was a surrogate coach, telling Erwin how to improve his form. Erwin recalled that his teammate would spend his free time watching "every rowing video in the world." He would come to practice and say, "We need to row more like the 1979 German women's lightweight double, from the third world cup." Erwin's novice response was, "What's the [rowing] World Cup?"

When Erwin first joined the team, he suffered a family tragedy. Most mornings he attended practice and tried to "survive" the workout with minimal effort. But immersion in this team culture changed his approach to the sport. He began to do extra workouts and to research the sport. His efforts improved his performance as he led this team to compete in junior rowing at U.S. nationals. As he summarized, "It all worked out I guess." The "it" he refers to is that half of his boat went on to row at Ivy League colleges; Erwin joined an elite public school team.

One of the skills participants' teammates taught one another was how to prepare for practice. Early on, athletes saw preparation as arriving a few minutes early and warming up before practice. As they matured in the sport, athletes learned that preparation for the next practice should occur at all hours of the day. Teammates created and perpetuated this culture, which many referred to as the "twenty-four/seven athlete lifestyle" in which they used all hours of the day and night to improve their athletic performance. Terrance, a white man who was part of one such team, explains:

TERRANCE: [Teammates] help you be more of a twenty-four-hour athlete. If you're good friends with everybody on the team, then you tend to hang out with people on the team and you tend to make better choices because everyone on the team wants to succeed and you know everybody wants the same thing. They have the same goals . . . it just helps you do all the right little things.

KH: What do you mean by the "twenty-four-hour athlete"?

TERRANCE: It's just doing all the right things to make sure that your body is ready to compete—eating right, sleeping right, hydrating, not doing too much exercise outside of practice—all the little things that wear you down but you don't really pay attention to.

Terrance's description of the twenty-four-hour athlete epitomizes the formation of a habitus. Athletic talent is not achieved in limited repetition or trial and error. Rather, it reflects a lifetime investment of material and symbolic resources. Teammates are one such resource through which individuals can enhance their own abilities through collective advancement. Within a team, individuals continuously attempt, rework, refine, and attenuate their abilities, drawing strength from each other throughout the process. Terrance reminds us that the work of a team, and of developing athletic talent, does not end once the rowers arrive at the dock or the runners exit the track. The habits of a college-prep athlete cultivated within college-prep athletic programs extended into all facets of the athlete's life.

Conclusion

The capital requirements imposed on potential college athletes reinvigorate the *gentleman amateur*. While not all college athletes are elite white men, their journeys to college traverse elite, white, masculine terrains. They developed physical capital through exclusive athletic communities such as private sports and coaches. These settings were exclusive as advantaged groups enacted barriers to entry.

Only those with the capital to enter into and pay the additional hidden costs—like time and transportation—could continue on. These costs were also symbolic and favored the disposition, knowledge, and skill cultivated in white suburban communities. Black families like Malcolm's needed experiential knowledge of the sports path to college and needed to act early and strategically to stay on course. White families like George's and Erwin's could enter at any point and received deferential treatment along the way. Physical capital also required gendered investments, as women more often than men did the unpaid and undervalued labor needed to develop their children's physical capital. College athletes need not all be elite white men to enliven the *gentleman amateur*. Instead, colleges require that athletes develop physical capital by engaging in practices that legitimate whiteness, elitism, and masculinity.

The relational power of the state also emerged through socialization. Physical capital requires *durable training* across settings. In this way, the interlacing of social life becomes apparent. The demands in one setting must be reinforced and accommodated in another. The college-level training regimes required by high school coaches necessitated labor and time by caregivers. Caregivers reinforced these demands by supporting their athletes through them. Teammates provided the community infrastructure that enabled participants to reach for high levels of athletic achievements. Teammates set increasingly higher standards for one another, completed the work side by side to stave off alienation, and created twenty-four/seven athlete lifestyles. By supporting one another through the rigorous demands of athletic achievement, teammates activated the physical capital.

The elaborate support systems that produce and facilitate the transfer of physical capital demonstrate how athletic talent becomes a scarce, unequally distributed resource. When athletes like Usain Bolt perform on a global stage, their talents are reduced to individual attributes like inherent speed or work ethic. The inner workings of the state guide Bolt's athletic performance. The state—in partnership with communities, private entities, and individuals—elevates certain forms of athleticism over others. Capital requirements guard the elevated forms of athleticism. Capital ensures "somebody from the block" has fewer athletic chances than "somebody from the burbs." As suburbanites reinvest their resources into their communities over others, they increase the symbolic and material value associated with the elevated forms of capital. In turn, they elongate the distance someone "from the block" must travel to achieve mobility. The next chapter explores the moment of selection, or how college admissions practices *choose* athletes from the burbs and not the block.

6

The Offer Letter

Athletic Talent Secures
Preferential College Access

One participant chose her team nickname—Captain America—as her pseud-onym. I warned her that this choice might identify her to future readers. She was unfazed and proceeded with her decision. Captain America's college coach gave her this nickname after she represented the United States and won a gold medal at the under-23 world rowing championships. Captain America, a white woman from the Mountain West, is rare even among Division I athletes: she has won national and international championships. I asked if winning one felt better than winning the other: "It's weird, you're not the first person to ask me that," she replied. She said she felt more pressure to win the world champion-ships to "not let my country down or give America a bad name for rowing," but found greater significance in winning the NCAA championship. Captain America spent ten months per year training with her college teammates and only one month training with the national team. Her investment of time and relationship building with her Coastal-U teammates gave the NCAA victory greater significance. She believed that neither victory fundamentally altered her sense of self—"I don't identify as a world champion or a national champion." Instead, she believes these accomplishments increased her "confidence in what I can do in the sport."

The athletic victories Captain America won for Coastal-U and the United States bolster exceptional athletic admissions. Her championships suggest that special athletic admissions identify the best athletes regardless of their social positions. In reality, the state uplifted Captain America above other youth. She developed athletic talent through the state's interlacing of property, law, community, leisure, schools, and capital. All previous chapters discussed how the state, in partnership with advantaged groups, concentrates economic, social, cultural, and physical capital in suburban communities. Members of these communities preserve and extend their advantage by seeking out exclusive enclaves and novel forms to best each other in the race to elite colleges. Growing up in a suburb versus a low-income urban area leads to a markedly different upbringing. Recall the life histories recounted by two high-profile athletes: Jenny Simpson and Caylin Moore. In narrating her journey to the Olympics, Simpson never mentioned that she struggled to find food or safe housing or that she watched her friends and family members die from gun violence. The state *removed* these harms from her majority-white suburb and contained them in Moore's majority-Black inner city.

Colleges justify the radically different life experiences Americans like Simpson and Moore endure by valuing and rewarding the practices, capitals, and dispositions of suburban areas. Schools, as extensions of the state, are empowered to transform embodied forms of symbolic capitals into markers of "cultural competence" like academic qualifications, which are afforded "conventional, constant, legally guaranteed value" in our society (Bourdieu and Passeron, 1977, p. 50). These academic qualifications grant access to better employment, housing, health care, safety, and schools. Legitimating institutions, like colleges, present the unequal distribution of social goods as fair and just. College graduates are seen as having earned their degrees and corresponding social rewards. In reality, schools provide a smoother path into and through their winnowing mechanisms for those with the symbolic capital deemed valuable by elites and the state. By earning a college degree, symbolic capitals are exchanged into an economic form—a college degree that someone can use for greater social rewards like employment and housing. Special athletic admission is one such legitimating institution. Special admission permits athletes to convert the capitals they accrued in white suburban areas into a universally recognized good: a college acceptance letter.

The ease of or difficulty with accruing and converting capital is the basis of reproduction. Rewarding athletes with a universally recognized measure of competency—athletic admission—disguises the *formal*, *relational*, and *removal* state tactics that concentrate capital in suburban areas. When Coastal-U advertises Captain America's national and international medals, her success becomes a fair outcome of a just admissions system. The public does not see a system designed in unequal and arbitrary ways to validate and uplift the capitals and dispositions of white suburban areas. The public accepts inequality built across groups, communities, schools, and sports when it seems like athletes like Captain America earned their achievements. This chapter explores the unjust and subjective policies, procedures, and practices within special admission that favor white suburban athletes.

Deregulation: Admission Advantage through an Absentee State

Colleges use two methods of bureaucratic state power (Brown, 1995)—expressed through layers of organization and policies couched as neutral and objective—to preserve existing social hierarchies through admissions. First, higher education institutions create standard, publicly available applications through which any person can apply to their institution. Presenting college admission as universally available to anyone who can fill out the forms belies the underlying capital exchanges required to traverse educational bureaucracies. As a hopeful college student encounters the admission form, they face numerous and onerous tasks. Capital requirements—resources, skills, connections, and knowledge needed to best present oneself as a successful applicant—underlie each task. With over 4,300 higher education institutions in the United States (Moody, 2019), students cannot apply to all colleges. Students' perception of which colleges they can apply to (and get into) and the burdensome rules of admission, like prerequisites, recommendation letters, essays, and deadlines, winnow the applicant pool (Buchman et al., 2010; Espenshade and Radford, 2009; Guinier, 2015; McDonough, 1997; Weis et al., 2014). White, middle-class high school students are more likely to apply to a broad range of institutions, whereas low-income students of color and first-generation college students are more likely to apply to low-cost regional institutions (Buchman et al., 2010; Espenshade and Radford, 2009; Guinier, 2015; Weis et al., 2014). This interactional effect produces academic undermatching as highly qualified students do not matriculate to top-ranked universities (Bowen and Bok, 1998; Weis et al., 2014).

After a student applies to college, college admission officers subject their application to several review stages. This leads to the second way college admission maintains existing hierarchies. These reviews favor applicants with the informal knowledge of how to tailor their college selection process and admission materials to meet the undisclosed norms and behaviors (Davies and Guppy, 1997; Espenshade and Radford, 2009; Guinier, 2015; Khan, 2012; Lareau, 2015; McDonough, 1997; Rivera, 2016; Shamash, 2018; Stevens, 2009; Weis et al., 2014). Together, the formal and informal rules students navigate in college admissions legitimate existing social order.

The bureaucratic power embedded in college admissions manifests itself differently within athletic admissions. Athletic departments lack publicly available admission portals and trained admission officers reviewing all the possible applicants. Like with all forms of state power, the absence of bureaucratic layers does not mean the absence of the state. The vacuum of regulation has empowered coaches and athletic administrators to define, run, and operate special admissions for college athletes. Most institutions permit coaches to drive the process and generate lists of whom they want on their team (Shulman and Bowen, 2001; Smith, 2019). If an applicant's name is placed on this list, they have far greater admission odds than they would have through the standard process (Shulman and Bowen, 2001; Smith, 2019). Athletic departments say they need this deference and autonomy to secure the best athletes to fill their rosters (Shulman and Bowen, 2001; Sperber, 2000). These differences enable athletic departments to offer easier, exceptional, and semiguaranteed college access to those students whom college coaches endorse.

The absence of formal regulations and admission channels invites in the winners of the class and race struggles occurring in suburban communities. Athletes like Captain America use athletic admission to accelerate their advantages. The structural alignment in Captain America's background poised her to go to college, but not necessarily a prestigious school. As she explains, rowing provided her an "easier" route than most of her elite high school peers had to replicate her social status. "Athletics is such a good outlet if you're trying to get into a school. . . . The process for me was so easy. . . . I [was] done with the recruiting process before everybody [finished applying to college]. And in my head I [thought]: 'Haha suckers. Look what rowing [has] done for me. Now you have to go through normal people processes.'" In Captain America's case, if she labored through the "normal people process," a top university may have admitted her. Yet her sport enabled her to skip this process and ensured the intergenerational transfer of privilege.

The state used its *formal* governing powers to grant regulatory authority to the NCAA over college sports. The NCAA has used its regulatory powers to oversee academic criteria for college admission. Over several decades, the NCAA has instituted national academic minimums for college athletes. All potential athletes must reach an academic minimum for college recruitment. Today's standards reflect over a century of compromise within the NCAA regulatory body of how much autonomy to grant individual universities in governing their athletic programs (Smith, 2011). To pass the NCAA eligibility certification, athletes must maintain a 2.0 high school GPA in thirteen core courses and must have a combined SAT score of 700 (NCAA, 2016). The eligibility standards also include a sliding scale for GPA and SAT scores. If someone has a GPA higher than 2.0, they could earn a lower SAT score, and vice versa.

The NCAA allows universities to determine their own admission policy—even one that allows recruited athletes to have grades and test scores below those required in a particular university's admission process—so long as it adheres to this academic floor. Coastal-U has a highly competitive undergraduate admissions process. The acceptance rate for the 2016 class was 17 percent, with an average unweighted high school GPA of 3.90 (weighted 4.42) and a combined average SAT score of 2125. A faculty committee oversees Coastal-U's athletic admissions. Coastal-U's policy permits three hundred athletes per admission cycle as "special talent" applicants. The policy includes tiers of admits within these three hundred slots. If an applicant reaches the academic criterion of a 3.0 high school GPA in fifteen core courses, they are recommended for admission with no further review. This standard is well below the average Coastal-U admitted student. If an athlete does not reach the institutional minimum, then they undergo further review in consultation with the director of admissions, the director of academic support, and the admissions committee. The committee ultimately makes the final determination. During data collection, this policy permitted the committee to admit, in one admission cycle, 60 percent of athletes who did not reach institutional minimum criteria. The policy has since been revised. Currently, Coastal-U policy allows the committee to admit, in one admission cycle, 20 percent of athletes who do not reach institutional minimum criteria.

Athletic admissions have few regulations and minimums compared to the standard process. The recruitment process begins when an athlete registers with the NCAA and certifies their amateur eligibility (NCAA, 2017). The certification process targets an athlete's compensation (amateurism) and whether they meet minimal academic standards (NCAA, 2017). So long as an athlete passes initial certification, universities retain discretion for any other evaluative criteria in admitting student athletes (NCAA, 2017; Smith, 2011). Universities have designed admission processes that defer to coaches to evaluate athletic talent (Hextrum, 2017a, 2018, 2019a, 2020a; Shulman and Bowen, 2001; Smith, 2011). The state can also achieve social control outside of direct regulations (Brown, 1995). Deregulation, or the removal of state rules, permits individuals to enact the state's will in its absence. Special athletic admissions represent this form of state power.

The deregulated nature of athletic admissions permits most of the academic and athletic assessments to occur through informal contacts between hopeful college athletes and college recruiters. Study participants interacted with college coaches over several months, or in some cases years. Each point of contact represented a potential moment for assessment and evaluation. The numerous structural barriers described throughout this book prevent *most* youth from ever having the opportunity to speak with a college coach. Those who make it to this phase encounter a nebulous and subjective recruitment process that creates further hurdles to entry.

Athletes recalled different and inconsistent standards for college recruitment. Only twelve participants were told that they must meet an athletic standard for acceptance. Instead, athletes were told different benchmarks for admissions. Some women's rowers were told they needed to break 7:30 on a

2,000-meter ergometer test, whereas others were told 7:20 and one was told 8:00. Some track athletes were told they needed to run, jump, or throw in a certain time or distance, whereas others were told to "keep up the good work."

The inconsistencies in how athletic merit is defined and judged represent *symbolic violence* (Bourdieu and Passeron, 1977). The state empowers institutions to name, evaluate, and reward merit. The result is an uneven distribution of valued social goods—in this case special university admissions. Elites have used their influence over institutions like higher education to align the merit tests with their interests (Bowles and Gintis, 1976; Davies and Guppy, 1997; Demerath, 2009; Dixon-Román, 2017; Kaufman, 2005; Khan, 2012; Lareau, 2011, 2015; Piketty, 2014; Rivera, 2016; Weis et al., 2014). Thus, these merit tests consolidate access to valued social goods. Without publicly available definitions of merit (e.g., no SAT equivalent exists for athletic admissions), athletic merit arises through interaction and performance. Hopeful recruits present themselves as important team contributors. Coaches signify which behaviors are acceptable for college admission by the athletes they choose. A hopeful athlete requires access to specific forms of economic, social, cultural, and physical capital to successfully exhibit athletic merit. Therefore, special admission requires dynamic interaction between bureaucratic power, symbolic violence, merit assessments, and merit performance (portrayed in table 6.1). This process enlivens the *gentleman amateur* and concentrates valued social goods in suburban communities.

Physical Capital: Uniting Status, Athleticism, and Access

Each previous chapter documented the entrenched and prolific barriers that restrict access to the athletic merit universities value. Captain America's case is no different. She accrued athletic accolades prior to and during college because she had privileged access to scarce resources. Captain America's parents were physicians and raised her in a town that was 97.3 percent white, with a median family income of $111,901. She attended private schools and played in private club sports, including rowing. The athleticism she displayed to college recruiters is a form of *physical capital*, or bodily performances that reflect one's social position (Shilling, 1991). As Monique said in the introduction, evaluating whether someone can contribute to a college rowing program more aptly measures whether someone has the *opportunity* to row.

Not all high school rowers and track and field athletes become college athletes. Those who can matriculate to college sports do not always activate their opportunity. While there may be as many reasons as there are high school seniors for why someone does not activate this opportunity, here I focus on *how* physical capital becomes legible to college recruiters. Study participants embedded in communities with knowledge of athletic recruitment created supplemental

Table 6.1
Special admission: Legitimating white suburbia's capitals

Capital	Regulation	Action	Confirmation
Physical	1. Colleges can profit from pay-to-play development camps; colleges cannot grant need-based aid to attend these camps 2. No time limit on when an athlete should start college	1. Athletes who attend colleges' pay-to-play camps increase their physical and social capitals 2. Athletes not admitted in first round take gap years to improve their chances	1. Coaches conflate camp attendance with merit and admit athletes accordingly 2. Coaches recruit athletes who take a gap year
Social	1. Rules permit networking across Olympic, college, high school, and youth planes	1. Athletes use their social capital (e.g., coach's reputation) as merit	1. College coaches solicit and accept recommendations from youth coaches
Cultural	1. No standardized application form 2. Limit on the number of official campus visits but no limit on the number of unofficial campus visits 3. Rules permit current college athletes to weigh in on the selection process 4. No formal criteria for rewarding scholarships	1. Athletes create their own portfolios to showcase their merit 2. Athletes with the funds, knowledge, social capital take unofficial visits 3. Athletes package themselves to align with college team 4. Athletes negotiate scholarships	1. Coaches solicit, evaluate, and accept athletic portfolios 2. Coaches solicit and reward athletes who take unofficial visits 3. Coaches admit athletes who align with their team standards 4. Coaches give scholarships to those who negotiate

strategies to accumulate and later display universities' desired physical capital. These supplemental strategies made athletes stand out in a crowded field and secured their recruitment. Here I offer two representative examples: pay-to-play sports camps and the gap year.

Maneuver the Camps System

Selecting an exclusive sport or event was the first strategic move for study participants to ease their path to college via sport. Athletes learned that the next stage would entail accruing markers of competency to draw coaches' attention.

Previous chapters discussed how access to private clubs and reputable coaches could serve as markers of merit. Within these exclusive spaces, athletes learned that these affiliations might be insufficient. They learned another way to improve their recruitment chances: attend university and national team camps. These camps are costly, selective, and prestigious and promise to transform campers into recruitable athletes.

Taylor's first "memory" of running was riding in a jogging stroller pushed by her mother. This story reflects the centrality of running in their family. Taylor—introduced in chapter 5—already had the familial and community knowledge to enter the sports path to college. Her parents met as college track athletes. Her wealthy suburb had abundant sport opportunities. Her parents supplemented her community resources and paid for private clubs and gym memberships. They even trained alongside her. Her high school had a history of shepherding runners to the college level. In reflecting upon what central experiences enabled her to become a college-level runner, Taylor kept return-ing to one experience: attending a university-sponsored track and field camp.

Taylor learned about the camp from her teammate's older brother, who ran track at a prestigious university. The camp simulated college life: campers stayed in the dorms, ate at the dining hall, interacted with current college athletes, did multiple workouts per day, and attended seminars on improving their ath-letic ability. The camps gave Taylor the vision and tools to pursue a route to col-lege via track.

> [I learned] how you can be a college runner [and] how you can be one of the leaders on your team. . . . I remember [a coach] talking about the qualities of a runner. There's hard work, competitiveness, and then talent. . . . [He'd have us ask ourselves] which one do you think you have? Are you really competitive? Do you have a lot of talent? Or do you work really hard? [And] if you're not so talented, but you're really competitive, [then emphasize your competitiveness]. And I had never really thought about that. . . . I realized [at camp] that a lot of people pick this path [athletic recruitment]. . . . I think that camp really turned me around. Especially in my head—having that vision [that], it's totally doable.

Taylor turned to the privatized camp system—not to her public high school track team—to gain the knowledge and skills to navigate recruitment. At these camps, athletes learned the traits college coaches want. They also developed rela-tionships with current coaches and athletes. The camp taught Taylor the insider knowledge necessary to improve as a runner, pursue college athletic recruitment, and package herself appropriately to college coaches.

Concentrating access to valued social resources behind capital barriers restricts the pool of potential college athletes. The NCAA narrows the pool even more by regulating camp discounts. Universities can offer reduced camp fees only for "objective criteria" available to all registrants, such as registering for the camp by a certain date (NCAA, 2017, p. 140). The NCAA excludes financial need or hardship as an objective criterion worthy of a discount. The NCAA's camp regulations grant athletes like Taylor recruiting advantages. Her family could afford $1,000 for a weeklong camp. Camps study participants attended ranged from $595 to $1,145 (excluding travel expenses) for a three-day camp.

The NCAA restricts nonrevenue athletes to seven face-to-face athletic evaluations with college coaches (NCAA, 2017, p. 104). Yet camps are excluded from this limit. College coaches can evaluate and train prospective college athletes at these camps so long as they are open to "any and all entrants" (NCAA, 2017, p. 140). Athletes who can pay for these camps can enhance their odds by spending a week with coaches developing their skills and showcasing their improvement. In this way, camps can also function as extended tryouts for athletes to display their skills to future recruiters. Camp attendance promises to transform an unknown athlete into a legible and desirable candidate for admission.

The NCAA also permits college coaches to work at private youth camps. Coastal-U coaches spend the summers working for youth development teams sponsored by the national team and use this opportunity to identify athletes. These national team camps are also fee based and confer merit. College coaches are permitted unlimited contact with national team coaches and can even request referrals for potential athletes from them. Furthermore, college coaches can coach for the national team, including development camps, where they can coach, mentor, and evaluate potential recruits (NCAA bylaws 13.12.2.3.8 and 17.2.8.1.2.2). Attaching greater athletic opportunity to fee-based university camps reconfigures the *gentleman amateur* in the present day. The elitism encoded into college sports remains as the knowledge, skills, and connections needed for athletic merit are guarded behind costly camp dues.

Laura's recruitment experience showcases how the NCAA's deregulation of privatized athletic camps enables privileged groups to accelerate their advantages. Laura, whose story was introduced in chapter 4, is the daughter of Harvard and Stanford graduates and joined rowing to replicate her family's and community's social standing. Laura's private rowing club coach worked for the U.S. rowing team. Laura joined rowing, and this club, to enhance her college-prep opportunities. But these actions had yet to secure her advantage. By her junior year, Laura suffered multiple injuries and was not a high school starter. Despite her spotty athletic record, her coach encouraged her to try out for the junior national team. Selection began with a 2,000-meter race on the ergometer. When she arrived at the junior national team camp, she realized her time was the "slowest of the group" of thirty rowers. In reflecting on how she was selected, Laura opined, "I think they chose athletes that they thought had a lot of potential."

The "they" Laura is referring to is the selection committee. Laura's club coach was an influential member on the committee. Laura made the "slowest" group of junior national teams, also known as the high performance camp. Laura never made the junior national team boat, but her affiliation with the team boosted her confidence and recruitment prospects. Another committee member, and a coach of the national team, worked for Coastal-U. During Laura's first summer at junior nationals, Coastal-U's coach watched her row and spoke with Laura's high school coach about her potential. Laura was offered a chance to attend Coastal-U before her recruiting process even began: "That's probably how I ended up at [Coastal-U], because I met [the Coastal-U coach] at [junior nationals] and he was like, 'You should come to [Coastal-U].'" Laura's story illustrates the discretion and manipulation permitted in markers of athletic merit. Through paying to row at a prestigious club, Laura began her journey to college as an athlete. But she still had to accrue certain markers of merit. One such marker came through attending national team camps—a process aided by her high school coach. The camp connected her to her future college coach. Laura effectively purchased social connections through her private club and national team attendance that secured her college admission advantage.

Twenty-one participants attended a national team training camp. These camps allow athletes to develop athletic résumés they send to coaches during athletic recruitment (Hextrum, 2020a). The degrees of national team participation vary widely—depending on the age and skill levels of the athletes when they attend—but all required payment. USRowing requires junior national hopefuls to attend a one-day identification camp, costing $50 to enter, excluding travel (USRowing offers ten to twelve camps per year across the country). If an athlete performs well, they are invited to a "selection camp," a two-phase process for coaches to solidify the junior national team. Phase I is a two-week overnight camp costing $3,290 (USRowing Juniors, 2018). Top athletes in phase I are invited to phase II of national team selection, which costs $2,050, to finalize lineups for junior nationals. If athletes show potential but not enough to compete at Junior Worlds, they attend the less-competitive Canada-U.S.-Mexico championship camp, which costs $2,890. If selected for the national team, athletes must pay to compete: "Yes, athletes who make the team will be required to pay a fee to cover the cost of food, lodging, airfare, and all other expenses associated with attending the World Rowing Junior Championships" (USRowing, 2018, para. 10). An athlete who completes the selection process will have paid $5,390 in camp fees alone, excluding travel and other participation costs.

These camp costs disqualify those without the individual, familial, or communal means. Savannah, the one working-class participant who attended a national team camp, hesitated when she was invited. She initially declined because she could not afford the camp fees. But her club coach convinced her they would find the money somewhere, as he believed—rightly so—the camp could secure her college recruitment. It took Savannah months to raise the funds, which she did by asking for donations from her school, rowing club, and extended family. Savannah is one of the rare exceptions who made it through the costly camp system. Her presence on the junior national team and later college team represents that reproduction is not absolute. As a white woman in good academic and athletic standing, she was an accepted member of a white middle-class community (Savannah recalled that the local newspaper did a story about her, citing the high grades she maintained even while competing year-round for a rowing program). Her working-class status did not fully exclude her from rowing. Her fundraising efforts were fruitful, as the institutions in her resource-rich community provided her the means necessary to attend the camp.

Savannah matriculated to college in spite of her economic background. Exceptional stories like Savannah's validate society's winnowing mechanisms as fair and just. Savannah's access to an exclusive sport and even more exclusive camp demonstrates that economic barriers are surmountable. Colleges that use private club and camp affiliations as markers of merit can then credibly claim these criteria are universally accessible. Savannah's story disguises at least two ways athletic admissions transfer privilege to advantaged groups. First, Savannah's admission obscures how the deregulated camp system and merit assessments concentrate the knowledge, skills, and connections needed for successful recruitment in privatized, exclusive spheres. When colleges conflate camp attendance with merit, they restrict college access to those who traverse these elite terrains. Second, Savannah's admission conceals how she endured a markedly different selection process than her middle-class peers. Savannah's peers did not go through such tenuous conditions to receive athletic admissions. Her admission bypassed the sharp opportunity disparities in college recruitment. Instead, all athletes seem to have earned their way to college, just like Savannah.

The Gap Year

The NCAA restricts collegiate participation to four seasons of competition to be completed within five years (NCAA bylaw 12.8). The five-year count begins once someone is enrolled full-time at a "collegiate institution" (NCAA, 2017, p. 79). The NCAA recognizes various situations that exempt athletes from this five-year limit, such as Olympic or military participation and pregnancy. Unlike international competitions such as the under-23 championships, the NCAA does not restrict athletic participation based upon one's age. In Division I athletics, the NCAA requests athletes enroll in a collegiate institution one calendar year from their high school graduation. Put another way, despite the frequency of athletes directly matriculating from high school to college (as thirty-nine of this study's participants did), doing so is not a requirement. Hopeful college athletes can spend an additional post–high school year honing their skills, developing their résumés, and forming connections, all in an effort to improve recruitment. Six of the eight participants who did not matriculate directly to college engaged in such activities. These six participants were all white and middle- or upper-middle-class. Their decision to pursue additional enrichment opportunities reflects the entitlement imbued in white middle-class habitus, as discussed in chapters 4 and 5. In contrast, Duane and Chantae, both Black with precarious financial standings, encountered bureaucratic systems that prevented their direct matriculation. The same opaque and contradictory recruitment regulations that enabled white middle-class aspiring athletes to activate and further their advantages ensnared Duane and Chantae and created a more difficult path for their transition to college.

Four international athletes, all rowers, took a gap year to focus on rowing. Through word of mouth from family, friends, or teammates, they learned they could enhance their athletic résumés by delaying college for a year. During their gap years two held part-time jobs in pubs and restaurants, and one took courses at a local college. Steve did neither and exclusively focused on rowing. He lived with his parents (and did not pay rent) and commuted to a nearby internationally renowned rowing club. In reflecting on this time in his life, he made an insightful pun, referring to it as a "nap year." In between morning and afternoon training sessions, Steve had "so much time to do whatever I wanted. I could just sleep. It was like a nap year [laughs]. I took so many naps. It was brilliant." Steve cheekily characterized this year as a time of rest because he had no such time in high school or later in college. Rest is a currency in athletics that improves one's focus and performance. Without work or school, Steve could focus on rowing and rest in between training sessions, arriving at each practice refreshed and primed for peak performance. During his nap year, Steve improved his rowing times and won several prestigious races. But his affiliation with an exclusive club secured his recruitment.

Steve spent most of his youth as a competitive swimmer. In high school, he made it to the youth British nationals and came in fifth in the breaststroke. During the event, he posted his fastest time and highest national ranking to date. But his performance was inadequate. He failed to place on the junior national team. In his home country of Britain, the national team, not colleges, represents the next level of competition beyond high school. Shortly after, Steve faced a monthlong illness that removed him from training and school. The cumulative disappointments and his time away made him reconsider his sport. When Steve recovered, he quit swimming. Concurrently, one of his friends, who was a year older, earned a spot on the British junior national team for rowing. Just like Iceman, Steve felt that if his friend could succeed in this sport, so could he. Steve found a local rowing club and saw immediate results. He believed that his "big lungs and big heart" from swimming gave him an advantage.

Steve also joined rowing to pursue admission to an elite university. The same friend who joined the junior national team was recruited to an Ivy League school for rowing. As Steve's swimming career subsided, so did his high school exam period. He realized his grades and test scores would not place him in a top British university. "I didn't get good enough grades to go to Oxford or Cambridge.... I could get into a decent university but not the best. And I knew that if I tried to get recruited to an American university, I would go to the best university and the best rowing program, if I got good enough at rowing. That's where the gap year took me. [I applied to] the best club in England, where the Olympians go. [This club] was really good for recruiting purposes." Steve pursued a gap year because, in his short rowing career, he had yet to gain the attention of American recruiters. His high school club was "tiny"—a dozen people. The team never placed at nationals and had no reputation for producing college or Olympic athletes. In assessing his high school academic and athletic performance, Steve decided to invest more time in sport and pursue athletic recruitment.

"Choosing" to take a gap year requires much more than individual determination. Steve was one of three participants (the others were Reggie and Will) who rowed at this prestigious club on the River Thames and were later recruited to Coastal-U. The club's application process was rigorous. The rowing club is nearly two hundred years old and is world-renowned for training national team members, future Olympians, and college-level athletes. Monetary contributions and athletic feats cannot guarantee entry. To be considered, an athlete must be nominated by a current club member and complete an application, including multiple letters of reference from their previous rowing clubs, a physical assessment, and a personal essay. All three agreed that their time at the club and their recommendations from the club coaches were key to being recruited and receiving scholarships to U.S. college rowing programs.

The British club is located on the stretch of water used for the Henley Regatta, a British rowing race dating back to 1839. The race no longer adheres to amateur principles, and crews around the world come to compete to win the coveted Grand Challenge Cup. The regatta features a winnowing process of dual races—only two boats compete against each other at once—to determine the final two competitors. As Steve explained, Henley takes place on his British club's "home territory," where they trained daily. When crews around the world come to event, they immediately learn of the British club. The race attracts thousands of spectators, including college recruiters. Racing at Henley, for this club, is an invaluable résumé line.

International students—like Will, Steve, and Reggie—undergo different admission scrutiny at Coastal-U. As a public university, Coastal-U must adhere to state mandates that regulate the ratio of international to domestic students. International athletes, therefore, face stricter athletic benchmarks for recruitment. This is part of why Will, Steve, and Reggie took a gap year. All three were in contact with Ivy League and elite public university coaches at the start of their recruitment. They were told they needed to complete a 2,000-meter ergometer test in a set time, while supervised by their coach, to receive special admission. With the additional months, Olympic training partners, and expert coaches, Steve and Reggie reached and exceeded the time standard. With their connection to a prestigious club, race experience at Henley, and an acceptable time on an ergometer test, Steve and Reggie secured the markers of merit that would appease the Coastal-U coaches. But Will struggled to complete the ergometer test in the proper amount of time. Like Laura, Will leaned on his connections to a renowned coach to counteract his athletic performance.

Prior to joining the British rowing club, Will attended boarding school in Australia, rowed for a top program, and obtained admission at his top-choice Australian university. During his time in boarding school, Ivy League universities recruited several of Will's rowing teammates. Will's mother attended university abroad, and Will developed this dream for himself. He saw rowing as a route to an American university. Will learned from Reggie—whom he knew through high school rowing—that taking a gap year to train could improve his recruitment chances. Will joined Reggie and journeyed to England. The Coastal-U coaches were interested in Will but said he must drop his time. After a few months at the British club, he had yet to meet their standard. The Coastal-U coach ceased contact with him. Will then used the British club's coach to gain back favor with Coastal-U: "The [English] coach was like, 'Will, he won our seat racing. He's doing really well on this, blah blah blah.' [Steve] was already going, this English bloke who was there. He got in. And said I was doing really, really well, blah blah. I was like, 'Ah, thanks.' And then [Coastal-University Coach] was like, 'Okay, you can come.'" If Coastal-U had not recruited Will, he would have returned to Australia and enrolled in a reputable university. He did not need *special* admission for college access. Will's time at an elite Australian boarding school and an esteemed British club imbued him with the entitlement for greater college access. After activating each of his markers of privilege, Will still failed to reach the athletic markers set by the coach. Will's story shows how bureaucratic regulations and actors can bend in ways to grant greater advantages to certain groups. In Will's case, Coastal-U's coach discarded his own athletic standards and permitted Will to submit proxies for athletic merit. Coastal-U permitted Will to use his British club's name, his British coach's recommendation, and even his teammate's performance as evidence that Will could succeed at Coastal-U. Selecting athletes from an elite British rowing club with historic ties to the advent of amateurism links U.S. college access to the cultural ideals of masculinity, whiteness, and elitism. The state reinvests in these power relationships by conferring elite admission on those like Will who can demonstrate their proximity to and alignment with the *gentleman amateur.*

This same bureaucratic easement afforded to members of the British rowing club was not offered to Black study participants. Chantae and Duane are both Black and came from lower-income communities without prestigious clubs, coaches, or races. They had to achieve state rankings in their events before they received recruitment offers. Even with offer letters in hand, their fate as college athletes had yet to be sealed. NCAA regulations permit universities to require athletes to sign binding contracts to accept an admission or scholarship offer. If an athlete tries to break this contract and go elsewhere, they can lose a year of athletic eligibility or college playing time. But athletes are not protected if the university breaks the contract. During Duane's senior year, he signed a letter of intent to attend a university in the Southwest. In August, as he prepared to move to a new state and begin college, he learned the athletic department "lost" his letter and that therefore his application never made it through the admission process. Despite a clerical error on their part, the school did not honor their side of the contract. The school revoked Duane's spot on the team, his admission, and his scholarship.

The bureaucratic net of educational requirements also ensnared Chantae. Shortly after she accepted her offer to Coastal-U, she failed her second year of Spanish. Chantae's special admission to Coastal-U allowed her to have a lower GPA and SAT score than most applicants but still required she complete a "college preparatory" curriculum, including two years of a foreign language. Even though Chantae failed Spanish, she still graduated from high school. Chantae's high school graduation requirements misaligned with the college enrollment requirements. Therefore, she could not enroll at Coastal-U that fall.

Duane and Chantae later joined the Coastal-U team and became exceptions to the reproductive forces. They did so through the help of "cultural guides," or upwardly mobile individuals who intervened and helped them navigate the "rules of the game" of dominant institutions (Lareau, 2015, p. 3). Two coaches at Coastal-U mediated their admission process and taught Duane and Chantae how to enroll in community college to retain (in Duane's case) and gain (in Chantae's case) the required athletic/academic minimums. Both athletes saw their coaches as "heroes" who arrived at important crossroads in their lives.

Duane and Chantae went through the same college sports bureaucracies as the rowers. But Duane and Chantae were subjected to different contours of bureaucratic state power. As members of dominant communities, the rowers approached bureaucracies with entitlement and used multiple strategies to retain their social standing. They used their economic capital—time and money—to pursue gap years and obtain athletic merit markers. Their affiliation with prestigious clubs became "evidence" that they could contribute to Coastal-U's team. In contrast, Duane and Chantae, as members of subordinated groups, had to overperform in a highly competitive high school track context and become top-ranked athletes in their respective events to be recruited. Further, bureaucratic power still disrupted their merit markers. They faced an obstinate bureaucracy that cast them out. Duane and Chantae received special admission through a chance alignment with college coaches who went beyond their job duties.

Social Capital: Connections Grant Admission

Duane, Chantae, and the international rowers' stories of athletic recruitment reflect how social relationships facilitate college access. Social capital theory assumes that social connections—such as those between Will, his teammates, and his coach—translate into future favors, actions, and opportunities (Bourdieu, 2011). The outcomes of these favors, actions, and opportunities rely upon how the reputations of these social connections are viewed by confirming institutions, such as higher education (Bourdieu, 2011). In Will's case, the reputation of those around him and the willingness of his coach to call in a favor on his behalf secured his athletic recruitment. Coastal-U validated the worth of Will's social connections by offering him a valued good—admission to a prestigious university. Athletes like Will can use these high-value social relationships to maintain their social standing through admission to an elite American university.

Disparate Regulations of Social Contact

The NCAA has 162 rules regulating college coaches' interactions with high school athletes. Few regulations exist for contact between recruiting agents—members of the high school athletic community, such as camp, high school, private, and club coaches who can speak on behalf of athletes—and college recruiters. The hyperregulation of athlete/college contacts increases the importance of recruiting agents. Colleges offer no standard template, solicitation, or request for a potential athlete to submit recommendations on their athletic performance. In this absence, a proliferation of contacts between and across the college recruitment planes emerge.

As chapter 5 discussed, nearly all study participants acknowledged their coaches as important figures in their athletic development, teaching them the skills and knowledge needed to improve in their sport. Coaches with high athletic reputational status contributed to athletes' college admission journeys in another sense. Fourteen participants believed they lacked the athletic merit to become college athletes. Instead, one positive word from a coach on their behalf translated into college admission.

Social capital assumes that not all reputations are afforded the same value by institutions. Such is the case for coach recommendations. Certain high school and club coaches develop reputations within their sporting communities for producing and mentoring successful athletes. A recommendation from one of these coaches could translate into admission. CM's family—her mother and older sisters competed in national and international races—taught her which track coaches had reputational currency. CM's family ensured that she attended a high school with such a program. As CM explained, coaches develop a reputation through producing athletes who win races and matriculate to college. "The people that end up being [recruited] are the ones who have those notable high school coaches where everyone knows their name, because they're doing well. . . . They always had great kids. . . . There are those schools where their coach is great and their kids are great. They had that, almost-collegiate mindset where they were pushing their kids with the ultimate goal of being college level." In CM's assessment, top high school coaches developed a positive reputation because they trained athletes with a "collegiate mindset." When colleges admit athletes trained by high-status high school coaches, they validate the coaches' reputation for producing college athletes. Athletes flock to these programs because of their reputations. With limited time and resources to recruit, colleges look within these high-status programs, over others, to identify athletes for their rosters. Lost in this cyclic reproduction is whether athletes from these programs are truly more talented than those coached by less-prestigious individuals. Instead, athletes from prestigious programs are assumed to possess more talent because of their proximity to high-status coaches.

Being on a top team does not secure recruitment. Coaches also have to actively intervene and use their reputations to sway recruiters. This was the case for Will. His affiliation with an exclusive British club connected him with college coaches but did not manifest in admission until his coach intervened and convinced recruiters to admit him. Likewise, Kalie's recruitment experience shows how successfully recruited athletes used their coach's reputation to stand out in recruitment. If this was insufficient, coaches intervened on an athlete's behalf and used their reputational capital with colleges to secure their athletes a spot on college team. Coaches took such measures because their own social capital increased as they transitioned more and more high school athletes to the college level.

When I asked Kalie if her family's financial status ever influenced her sports participation, she replied, "My dad's a lawyer; we're fine." She went on to explain that her family had the resources to send her to private schools, pay for her private sport club memberships, and send her to sport development camps. Before settling on her college sport, rowing, Kalie played soccer and gymnastics and was a cheerleader. Like many of the rowers, Kalie joined the sport after a friend at her private high school recommended she join the team. She knew nothing of the sport except that it occurred on water. "Being in the water is huge [for my family]," Kalie explained. Her father and grandfather were in the navy, and she grew up "boating since I was two days old. We go sailing every summer, we go on speedboats." When presented with the opportunity to do a water sport, Kalie recalled this family connection to aquatics and decided to attend the first practice.

Two years later, Kalie became the top coxswain for the program. As a sophomore she was in charge of leading the top boat. Her crew had won most of their regional races and placed at nationals. Still, it had yet to occur to Kalie that she could leverage her rowing career for college access. At the time, Kalie was considering attending a regional university. She had a passion for animals and knew the local university had a strong veterinary program. She also knew that veterinary medicine is a competitive field and that her high school grades could prevent her from matriculating into the program. "I was an average high school student. 3.3, like fine—above a B. And so, I wasn't expecting myself to go to an amazing school." Kalie's high school coach intervened and gave her the vision and means to become a college rower.

The Coastal-U rowing coaches worked for the national team and were once college athletes. Their long history in the sport gave them a wealth of high school and club contacts to draw upon. Several of the rowers and track athletes, including Kalie, had high school coaches who had gone to college with or worked alongside the Coastal-U coaches.

Kalie's coach spent his summers working for the national team alongside the Coastal-U coaches. Each year he helped athletes from his club team transcend to college and national terrains. He had intimate knowledge of and experience with athletic recruitment. One important piece of knowledge he had is that he could recommend athletes for admission and that college coaches would accept his recommendation. As Kalie explained, her coach "has good pull with coaches around the country; if he says a kid is good, coaches are going to listen." Kalie believed that her coach's recommendation was particularly important in her case. As she explained to me, coxswains lack any sort of objective measures that other athletes have. She could submit race results, but often wins are attributed to athletes. She could submit tapes of herself coxswaining a race, but again no set criteria exist for how to evaluate her tone and tempo. "[My] coach's recommendation was huge, right? Especially with a coxswain. [My] coach saying, 'Hey, this girl is doing a good job,' I think is a big deal."

Kalie's case also shows how college athletic recruitment mends the gaps and inconsistencies in power reproduction. Kalie used her coach's recommendation to earn admission and a scholarship to Coastal-U. As Kalie put it, her coach helped her "get into schools that I wouldn't have been able to get into." Without rowing, Kalie acknowledged, "I would never have gotten into [Coastal-U]. . . . [Rowing] definitely opened the doors academically to places I wouldn't be able to go." Kalie's high school academic performance did not neatly mirror her privilege. Her high school performance disqualified her from admission to top universities. But athletic recruitment provided Kalie an institutional avenue to rectify this mismatch and maintain her social standing. Without regulations monitoring and preventing contact, her coach built his reputation through working for the national team and placing high school athletes on college teams. Further, with no clear measures of athletic merit, a coach's reputation became evidence of Kalie's athletic potential. Put differently, Kalie's social capital transformed her physical capital into a form valued and recognized in athletic recruitment. This transformation indicates how athletic merit is undergirded by subjective criteria borne through interactions among suburban community members, private clubs, bureaucratic regulations (or lack thereof), and college coaches.

Imperfect Alignment: Last-Minute Addition

Upward mobility stories—the exceptions to the rule—like Savannah's help secure public support for special admission. Another is through the imperfections built within the process. Not all members of advantaged groups secure their privilege or, more aptly, secure what they feel entitled to because of their privilege. These slight uncertainties in how advantage is conferred legitimate institutions, like higher education, that secure the intergenerational transfer of privilege.

Coastal-U's athlete admission policy begins with a rationale for its existence. The university "recognizes the practical needs for efficiency and expediency, especially since the campus is competing with other colleges and universities for top student athletes." The "practical needs" justify an alternative admission timeline for athletes. Coastal-U's standard admission process requires applicants to submit their materials almost a year prior to the start of classes. In contrast, the school has a rolling admissions policy for athletes. Several study athletes were admitted as late as the week prior to the start of classes, an impossible feat for a student applying in the standard admission process.

Sophia was one such athlete who joined the Coastal-U rowing team shortly before the fall term. She spent the first eighteen years of her life dreaming about attending her local Ivy League university. Her mother was an alumnus of the university. Many of her classmates matriculated there. Sophia's rowing club trained on the campus, and she spoke to the Ivy League's rowing coaches regularly. Sophia worked with her high school counselors to match her academic curriculum with the university's standards. She retook the SAT several times to improve her score. As Sophia recounted these details, I kept wondering, "Why is she at Coastal-U?" Finally, we got to that point of the story in our interview.

"It's a sad story," she started. The story is "sad" because Sophia placed all her efforts toward her chosen Ivy League. She even turned down an offer to row at Stanford, telling the coaches she planned to attend this Ivy League instead. In late spring of her senior year, Sophia received her rejection letter from the Ivy League team. She tried to earn her offer back to Stanford, but they had given her spot to someone else. She was devastated. Sophia could have enrolled in her local community or state college. Instead, she chose to live at home and retake the SAT. She would reapply to the Ivy League, this time as a regular student.

In April of her senior year, she was recounting her tragic state to one of her high school teammates, then a rower at Coastal-U. Her teammate told Sophia she should talk to the Coastal-U coaches. Her teammate explained that Coastal-U had a flexible admission cycle compared to Ivy League universities. Sophia contacted the Coastal-U coaches. The coaches had yet to use up their admissions spots. Based on Sophia's coach and teammate recommendation, they offered her a last-minute spot on the team. A few months later Sophia arrived at Coastal-U.

Recruitment narratives like Sophia's show how college coaches recruit from insular and exclusive high school and club programs. Laura recalled that all nine of the high school seniors on her rowing team received exceptional admission to college, three of whom (including herself) accepted offers at Coastal-U. Similarly, Kalie had several teammates who matriculated to Coastal-U. Amanda, who learned from an older teammate how to highlight her strengths, said the class above her sent three rowers to Coastal-U. Typically, researchers point to the ways benchmarks and minimums restrict access to institutions. Athletic recruitment shows how the *absence* of criteria also narrows opportunity. Without making the admission process widely available, knowledge of recruitment remains concentrated in social networks. By recruiting athletes from these networks, colleges validate these relationships and knowledge, further entrenching the alignment.

Admission to an exclusive college transforms the symbolic and immaterial dimensions of one's habitus into material and objective forms of "cultural competence" that are universally recognized (Bourdieu and Passeron, 1977, p. 50). But cultural reproduction is not *guaranteed*. Unlike the tactics displayed in Operation Varsity Blues, in which Rick Singer's clients paid for direct access to spots on Ivy League athletic teams, Sophia was not guaranteed access. She represents one of the cases that do not perfectly align in intergenerational reproduction. However, for Sophia, the "sad story" of her loss of status and prestige ended with her landing at an elite university, just not the one she dreamed of.

In this way, reproduction may not be a direct, guaranteed route, but it still has predictable outcomes.

Cultural Capital: Navigating the Nebulous Athletic Admission Standards and Processes

The recommender represents social capital. The content of the recommendation—what a coach or teammate says about a potential athlete—is cultural capital. When a high school coach references attributes about an athlete—such as they are "college-ready," a "hard worker," or a "team player"—the coach invokes cultural capital. Cultural capital represents one's attitudes, behaviors, preferences, and values. These attributes are linked to one's social standing and occur in embodied (accumulated within the body and cannot be delegated to someone else) and objectified (existing within objects like an athletic championship or a college acceptance letter) ways. When universities admit athletes who display certain cultural capital over others, the institutions validate the athletes' enactments. Here, I discuss several of the most common representations of cultural capital that universities valued in recruitment.

Marketing Campaigns: "Fake It Till You Make It!"

Without publicly available standards for recruitment or a process for athlete admissions, study participants created their own methods to catch recruiters' attention. Athletes learned through their socialization networks how to translate their athletic histories into marketable materials. Athletes recalled three common strategies to gain coaches' attention, to navigate the recruitment process, and to secure admission. First, athletes learned to be proactive and not wait for coaches to make contact. Second, they learned they should build portfolios of their athletic achievements and submit these (even when unsolicited) to college recruiters. Third, athletes learned to craft narratives that made them more desirable. These three strategies reflect cultural capital, or embodied skills, dispositions, and knowledge. When coaches accept the materials submitted on behalf of athletes, they validate these cultural capitals, such as the skill to market oneself, as measures of merit.

Study participants first initiated recruitment by sending emails of interest to coaches. Athletes did not conceive of the idea or write the email themselves. Coaches, teammates, or parents helped draft the initial emails. CM learned from her older sisters (who were successfully recruited to college as track athletes) and her high school coach (who placed athletes each year on college teams) that she should approach colleges first. In her initial emails, she requested additional information about their programs. Receiving information about a program was not CM's actual goal. Rather, the email connected CM with coaches and placed her on their recruitment radar. The email started the conversation between CM and college programs. CM's email started with the line, "I'd really love to talk to you about the possibility of maybe going to your school." She then listed her recent athletic achievements. Her sisters gave her another important piece of advice: in all interactions with coaches, convince them that their program is your top choice. CM concluded her emails by stating as much.

During these initial encounters, athletes learned to package their athletic achievements. They wrote narratives and compiled pieces of evidence to highlight their strengths and disguise their weaknesses. The Physicist explained how he caught the attention of college recruiters. "The coaches weren't really clamoring after me." But that did not stop him from approaching the top schools. In the fall of his senior year, he "really started actively pursuing coaches." In his emails he asked coaches "what they looked for in an athlete." If they responded, he tailored his responses accordingly. If they did not, he sent them materials and a story that showcased his skills. He would send them "my stats" and a "highlight video" he made of his best races. He saw this process as "testing the water" to see "what was out there for me based on what I'd done at that point." In packaging his strengths, he used his scores across various events to highlight his potential. He wrote to coaches and explained, "I was a good middle-distance runner with the potential to be a good long-distance runner." The Physicist used the discretion within athletic admissions to convince recruiters that he could make up his speed deficit with his breadth of skill. By offering admission to the Physicist, the Coastal-U recruiters excused this shortfall and legitimated his marketing skills.

Athletes created elaborate portfolios containing their athletic histories of all times, scores, meets, and regattas attended, national team appearances, names of teammates who were recruited to college, and media coverage. They could list such achievements because of their membership in exclusive communities. For instance, Captain America sent weekly updates to coaches with her most recent 2,000-meter ergometer score, her club team's race results, and news mentions or awards for her achievements. She had these accomplishments because her family purchased private club memberships, paid regatta fees, and paid for her to attend the national team development camp.

In an admission world with amorphous and irregular standards, athletes marketed their past and *potential* merit. Stella is one such participant who was admitted as an athlete with no prior experience in her sport. Stella was a strong kayaker—a sport not sponsored by the NCAA. She heard through her kayaking teammates that college rowing coaches recruited athletes for athleticism, not direct athletic experience. I asked how she translated "athleticism" during the admission process. Stella explained that she viewed the recruiting as "fake it till you make it." To her this meant pretending to be "a big deal—even though I wasn't—I had to make it seem like I was." She did this through one clever marketing tool. "One of my [kayaking] coaches, she went to the Olympics a lot. So she wrote me a letter, and I put an Olympic letterhead on it. It looked really cool." The Coastal-U coaches were intrigued by Stella's potential and invited her to visit campus. Stella brought the coaches a box of chocolates when she visited. She believed these personal touches offset her inexperience.

When schools admit athletes who submit unsolicited narratives, dossiers, or chocolates, they validate the actions, skills, and characteristics of athletes with certain forms of cultural capital or those who meet normative standards of acceptability. The original amateur regulations used dispositional requirements—*gentlemanliness*—to prevent anyone who was not white, elite, or male from participating in college sports. These dispositional requirements did not measure athletic skill. The value colleges place on certain forms of cultural capital, such as marketing materials, reconstructs the arbitrary and restrictive enrollment criteria of past eras in the present moment. Three athletes—Stella, Goose, and Noelle—had little or no experience in their sport but received admission. No people of color received such benefits.

Campus Visits: Time to "Sell Yourself"

Study participants deployed these marketing tactics to gain campus visits. Campus visits provided even more chances for an athlete to prove their admission case. The NCAA (2017) permits two types of campus visits: an "official visit," in which the university pays for an athlete to tour the campus, and an "unofficial visit," in which the athlete pays to tour the campus (p. 86). The NCAA has fifty-five rules related to official visits, including limiting athletes to visiting five universities; limiting the visit length to forty-eight hours; limiting the cost of food, housing, transportation, and entertainment; limiting family involvement; and limiting contact between athletes and university representatives. In contrast, the NCAA has twenty-four regulations on unofficial visits, eighteen of which restrict how much an institution can spend on an athlete during their visit. Prospective athletes can pay their own way to visit any college, meet with as many coaches as are available, and visit the same campus or coach multiple times. Unofficial visits granted athletes multiple opportunities to impress college coaches and secure athletic recruitment. Thus, the unofficial visit advantages students with financial means, knowledge, and social connections. Of the three low-income students in the study, one did an unofficial visit because she lived close to a university. Even then, her recruiting process unfolded through the regulated channels, as she went on two university-sponsored visits.

Students arranged unofficial visits by using the skills, knowledge, and connections outlined above. Often, an unofficial visit began with an email asking for permission to visit the campus and meet the coaches. Those who took unofficial visits were surprised by the offer of admission during these informal conversations. Merlin, Imani, Terrance, London, and Josephine all received admission during their unofficial visit. The advantages these well-connected and well-funded individuals had expanded during the scholarship negotiation process.

Universities also requested that athletes make unofficial visits. Unofficial visits save athletic departments money and paperwork. Merlin, a white middle-class man, was one such athlete who was asked by a Coastal-U recruiter to make an unofficial campus visit. His recruitment story unfolded after: "The coach added me on Facebook. And then we just got to talking, and he's like, 'Oh, you should come on an unofficial' and so I went on an unofficial." Merlin then drove eight hours to Coastal-U, paying for food, gas, and lodging for his unofficial visit. His investment yielded a return: a few months later, Coastal-U offered him admission as a track athlete.

Unofficial visits require hopeful college athletes to invest economic capital—time and money. Five participants traveled across the country, one athlete traveled internationally, and one athlete traveled to over twenty schools. Family members often accompanied athletes on unofficial visits, meaning their immediate social networks also had flexible employment and/or time to dedicate to these trips. For instance, Josephine, a Black runner, grew up with affluent self-employed parents whose jobs were demanding but afforded them the flexibility to take time off to support her athletic and academic activities. During recruitment, her parents attended all her college meetings.

Unofficial visits also required money. Josephine, Kalie, and London, who are all from the West Coast, had their parents sponsor a weeklong trip to East Coast schools. Along the way, they met with coaches and toured programs, marketing themselves and assessing the schools. Morgan and Laura, who are from the East Coast, did the opposite, traveling west with their parents to market themselves and assess schools. The airfare alone on a bicoastal trip would cost upward of a thousand dollars for an athlete and one parent.

Campus visits are valuable because they provide athletes a chance to secure admission. The interpersonal interactions between potential college athletes and college coaches during these visits demonstrate how coaches recognized and validated the cultural capital associated with white suburban areas. London's story of recruitment offers one illustration.

As a freshman in high school, London was on the cover of an issue of a free local magazine. She included this article in her athletic portfolio, along with her high school transcripts, athletic résumé, statement of interest, statement of athletic goals and potential, and coach's recommendations. During London's junior year of high school, her family sponsored her college trips along both U.S. coasts, during which she unofficially met with twenty prospective track coaches. Before she visited each school, she looked up the coach's contact information, sent them her athletic portfolio, and requested an unofficial visit to their campus. London was injured at the time and had not yet posted any college-level scores. Through these visits, she learned that "the whole recruiting process was a whole lesson on how to sell yourself [and explain] why you are better than the person who's trying to compete for your spot."

Her last unofficial visit was to Coastal-U. She was nervous because of the school's reputation and thought she had little chance of gaining admission. Once on campus, London treated her meetings with coaches as opportunities to further market her strengths to the staff. "[The Coastal-U coaches] sat me down for a two-hour interview. . . . And I talked the whole time. Debate [Club] definitely helped me . . . to be comfortable with public speaking." I asked her to clarify what she discussed in the interview, and she shared the following:

> They'd ask me about my training. And so I would tell them, like a [typical] day, or my training. . . . They'll ask you about other stuff you're doing [outside of sport]. I talked about debate. Or I'd talk about how the independence of being a track athlete transfers over to my school and academic life. So I'd just purposefully weave in who I was into my answers. And I don't think that everyone does that. But I just sort of knew that I had to. . . . And at the end of the interview they were like, "Okay, we want to give you something. . . . We'll mark your application for you if you want to come here."

London believed she intuited the recruiting process. In reality, however, she had experience and coaching that likely assisted her access. School debate taught her the skills of argument and persuasion. Furthermore, Coastal-U was her twentieth college visit. At that point she had extensive interview practice and feedback. She described various rejections that took place during other unofficial visits and how she asked for feedback on what to change in her interactions with coaches. Thus, through her socialization and her socioeconomic resources, she learned what the coaches wanted—a confident athlete with a strong work ethic who can balance the rigors of competitive athletic and academic programs.

For many of the athletes, like Merlin, Imani, Terrance, and Josephine, coaches offered university admission during their unofficial visits. Unofficial visits provide a large advantage for families with resources, social connections, and knowledge of the recruiting process. Regulations permit athletes' families to pay for unlimited trips around the country and unlimited trips to a given university, permitting them limitless chances to impress college coaches. Of the three low-income study participants, one took an unofficial visit because she lived close to the university. When Coastal-U offered athletes like London admission, they validated the cultural capital she displayed. London was offered admission not because she displayed an immense, unique, or unprecedented level of athletic merit. Instead, the university rewarded her for presenting her skills in a favorable way.

Exclusion over Excellence: Team Fit

At the time of our interviews, athletes had successfully transitioned from hopeful recruits to current college team members. They were now experiencing the socialization into life as college athletes and into the specific practices of their teams and sport environments. Part of this socialization process required them to host and evaluate potential recruits. When a potential athlete takes an official or unofficial visit, they stay with a member of the current team. This is one of the many unpaid labor obligations placed on college athletes.

NCAA regulations allow athletic departments to require college athletes to host recruits when they visit campus (NCAA, 2017). Hosting recruits does not count toward the twenty-hour limit of official athletic responsibilities. By hosting a recruit, a college athlete is deputized as an official representative of the university. The Coastal-U athletic department handbook—a document of department rules that all athletes must agree to obey to join the organization—reminds athletes it is their responsibility to host recruits and comport themselves in an appropriate manner while doing so. "While serving as a student host, you represent your team and [Coastal-U]. Therefore, appropriate conduct within institutional, [conference], and NCAA guidelines is expected and required of you. As a student host, you must represent the University and Athletic Department in a positive manner and conduct yourself responsibly and ethically."

As student hosts, athletes exposed recruits to the student athlete experience. College athletes took recruits to practice, to class, to meals, and on campus tours. College athletes also socialized with recruits and answered their questions about Coastal-U or collegiate athlete life generally. College athletes knew that they represented the university during all aspects of the visit and that they should never speak ill of their team, department, or college. They also knew that recruits could soon become their college teammates. So they wanted to be honest with them and offer a realistic account of the time, labor, and difficulty of collegiate athlete life.

George, a track athlete, explains the message he tried to convey to recruits. "I usually go with: 'It's going to be the most rewarding four to five years of your life. If you can get through going to school here and being an athlete here, nothing after that will be more challenging.'" Malcolm, one of George's teammates, offered a similar account: "[I tell recruits]: It's going to be a constant struggle. There's not a single part of these four years that are going to be easy, athletically or academically, and you have to be ready for it. Because if you're not ready for it, you will suffer, academically and athletically." George and Malcolm gave these "honest" accounts to ensure their future teammates would be ready for the realities required by their team. When college athletes interact with recruits, they are assessing whether and how these individuals can contribute to their teams. Malcolm went on to say that when he evaluates a recruit, he considers whether the person will view the collegiate athletic experiences as a "challenge" and a "competition" and yet feel confident that "[they'll] be able to do [it]."

The institutional regulations and coaching practices invite current college athletes to evaluate potential athletes. Current athletes cannot access a recruit's application materials, like their grades, test scores, or athletic histories. Instead, they are asked to assess "team fit," or the extent to which a recruit might "mesh" or "gel" with the team culture. In recalling their own experience with recruitment, athletes remembered how important team fit was in earning a spot on the team. As current athletes, they perpetuated this same standard in evaluating recruits. When most nonrevenue college athletes are white and middle-class, team fit connotes the extent to which one aligns with this race/class position.

Josephine, an upper-middle-class Black woman, recalled the intrinsic characteristics that she was subjected to during recruitment and the standards she now places on future recruits. She also emphasized the role team members have in evaluating potential recruits.

> [Recruitment] has to do with team dynamic and if [you] fit into the energy of the team. I was really lucky that I did. And I was lucky that my recruiters liked me. It is what it is. The team ultimately decides [who can join the team]. [Recently] we had an amazing top runner. But she just didn't fit with our team. And we told the coaches, "This is an amazing runner, but she just doesn't really sit well with us. There's something that's not right." And they didn't take her. . . . It doesn't matter as much how great you are now. . . . [Recruitment] is about if you sit well with the team because that's everything.

Josephine's account reveals how recruitment considers the cultural capital alignment between the team and the potential recruit. The characteristics she lists, including whether the team "likes" someone or if the person "fits" in with the "team dynamic," represent whether embodied, intrinsic characteristics in a recruit are agreeable to the evaluators. In Josephine's account, these characteristics superseded one's athletic scores. Current athletes can reject a recruit—even one who is an "amazing" athlete—if they do not align with the team.

Josephine's team is majority-white and middle-class. Her Blackness did not immediately disqualify her from fitting in with the team because after a lifetime in her white suburban community, Josephine learned how to assimilate to white norms, behaviors, and ways of being. She recalled how she went to a talk at Coastal-U hosted by the African American studies department and how it was one of the first times in her schooling experience when she was not the minority. She said she could finally "breathe" and let her guard down in a way that she never could in a previous environment, including her current athletic team. But a lifetime in white environments has also trained Josephine how to impose these standards. Josephine has now become an extension of the university, holding future athletes to the cultural capital requirements that align with white middle-class communities.

Rowing offers a starker example of how these cultural capital assessments exclude and perpetuate homogeneity. During the study, nearly all 120 Coastal-U rowers were white. In her narrative, Noelle described the ambiguous criteria for team membership that may have contributed to the team's demographics. Noelle, a middle-class white woman, joined a rowing club in the fall of her senior year of high school. She was one of twenty-one participants coached to join a sport for college access. The coach of her private rowing club was a former college teammate of Coastal-U's current coach. They maintained a close friendship, and the Coastal-U coach often took Noelle's coach's recommendations for college athletes. Noelle had rowed for a few weeks when her recruiting process began. She made up for her skill deficit through a highlight reel. "I had no erg scores, nothing to go off of. [The Coastal-U coach] actually asked me to send him a video because I had so little. . . . And I sent him a video and he was like, 'This looks good.'" After receiving Noelle's coach's recommendation and reviewing the video, the Coastal-U coach invited Noelle to visit the campus.

Reflecting afterward, she believed her recruiting trip to Coastal-U sealed her fate—that she was a "good fit" for the team. She explained how recruiting was also one of the reasons why her team was so successful: "[Our coaches] did a good job recruiting. Even if you're a top athlete, [Coach] is not going to invite you to the team or recruit you if she doesn't think that you're going to mesh well with the girls." Coastal-U's rowing team was overwhelmingly white and middle-class, which likely improved Noelle's odds for being recruited since she had little athletic merit. Subjective measures like team cohesion allow those with knowledge of how to navigate the system to actively pursue rowing and modify their behavior accordingly.

One of the defining characteristics of whiteness is monoculturalism. Diane Gusa (2010) positions higher education, particularly predominately white institutions and predominately white spaces within institutions, as central to achieving monoculturalism. Monoculturalism elevates one way of knowing, being, working, and experiencing the world while eradicating all others. Eradication occurs by demanding that all members conform to one worldview, behavior, and set of norms. Whiteness permeates higher education by presenting the "normal" cultural behaviors as conforming to "white standards of decorum" (Gusa, 2010, p. 471). Any behavior that deviates from the white standards is devalued, punished, and marginalized. White people in this environment do not have to give anything up as they already align with what is required of them. In contrast, Black people, like Josephine, must conform or face rejection.

When athletic departments, coaches, and athletes require potential applicants to "fit," "mesh," or "gel" with the team, they (re-)create monoculturalism. While the state produced antidiscrimination legislation that permits (limited) entry of women of color and white women and men of color into college sports, monoculturalism is one tool to reinvigorate the *gentleman amateur* in the presence of more diverse athletes. Athletes of color must conform to white standards of behavior, decorum, and culture. Women athletes must conform to a narrow form of white femininity—one that requires their subordination to men. Although special admission provides advantages to women athletes—particularly white women—their advantage is undercut as their athleticism remains devalued compared to men, is controlled by mostly men coaches, and is less likely to lead to leadership positions in sport. The recruitment process is the first attempt to ensure that those admitted adhere to these norms, values, and ways of being. Conformity as a measure of merit can exclude even those with outstanding feats of athleticism (as Josephine witnessed) or include those with little or no experience in the sport (as Stella and Noelle experienced). Tying conformity to a valued and universally recognized good—in this case admission to an elite university—reflects how athletic recruitment functions as a legitimating institution. The state support for athletic recruitment makes it possible to secure a spot at an elite university for those who can conform. By rewarding the symbolic forms of capital more often present in white suburban areas, the state validates and elevates this form of cultural capital above all others.

Athletic Scholarships: Confirming Capital

In addition to special admission, athletic recruitment offers another valuable good in capital transmission and conversion. Universities can offer monetary rewards—athletic scholarships—to lure recruits and further validate the capital they displayed. There are limited regulations on how universities offer scholarships. White suburban athletes stepped into this deregulated zone and secured scholarships as their knowledge, skills, and dispositions aligned with the subjective and obtuse standards emitted by athletic representatives.

The NCAA has twenty-four bylaws related to athletic scholarship offers. The organization limits how much a school can award an athlete, how the funds are used, how many scholarships a given sport can offer, and when a coach can offer a scholarship. As discussed in chapter 1, several of these regulations may change through ongoing lawsuits. So far, these lawsuits have targeted revenue sports. The NCAA differently regulates scholarship allocations across sports, with two classifications: head count and equivalency. Revenue sports are head-count sports (as are gymnastics, tennis, and volleyball). In these sports, scholarships function as all-or-nothing rewards. A coach can offer either a full scholarship or nothing to an athlete. In equivalency sports, which include all other NCAA teams, coaches can divvy up scholarships. Women's rowing has a maximum of twenty scholarships at any given time available for freshmen through fifth-year seniors. The team can have twenty women on full scholarship or can divide up those twenty scholarships into parcels, giving a few women full funding while others receive as little as $500 each semester. Each university creates their own policy for allocating funds in equivalency sports.

The NCAA does not regulate *how* schools reward athletic merit through scholarship offers. This *removal* of state oversight transfers privilege to advantaged groups. Schools are not required to consider an applicant's financial need (or lack thereof) when awarding an athletic scholarship. Schools did not automatically offer study participants athletic aid. Instead, participants negotiated compensation. More commonly, athletes who did not need the funding asked for and successfully received it. Twenty-five athletes, including the wealthiest person in the study, Laura, displayed the cultural capital to negotiate scholarships. A common tactic to secure an aid package was to use offers from one school against another. This worked for seven participants. Captain America learned that a future college athlete should never accept her first offer. "Recruiting is so weird. It's like a betting game. Like, 'Well this college can give me this. What can you give me?' I definitely used my rowing abilities as a leverage to put myself out there for colleges to see what they could offer me." When the Coastal-U coaches approached her, she presented a list of schools that offered her full scholarships and was able to convince Coastal-U to offer her one as well. For another eight participants, the game of chicken did not end in their favor. Eight participants turned down a full scholarship to another institution, one they perceived as not as prestigious as Coastal-U. Coaches told four of these students they could earn a scholarship if they performed well in college. Anthony, once such athlete, took out debt to attend Coastal-U instead of accepting a full ride to another institution. He hoped to earn a full scholarship within the first two years at university to ease his debt load. I interviewed him in his senior year. He had yet to receive a full scholarship.

The luxury to turn down a full ride to one school to attend another or to wait to earn a scholarship later reveals how an athletic scholarship has as much to do with money as with prestige. Sixteen participants said they wanted an athletic scholarship not because their family needed the money but because they wanted their peers and community to know they earned one. CM earned a 50 percent scholarship to attend Coastal-U. In reflecting on the process, she recognized that prestige mattered to her. "Luckily my parents [paid] for the rest of my education and I'm leaving college without any debt. . . . Thinking back on it, scholarship is just something that makes you look better when you tell people that you got it, that's how it was for me. And, I mean, it's still the case. People still ask me, 'Oh did you have a scholarship?' I'm like, 'yeah.' And they

Table 6.2
Athletic aid at Division I schools

Year	Men's	Women's	Coed[a]	Total
2003	$597,287,341	$490,962,030	$0	$1,088,249,371
2004	$649,751,302	$536,870,074	$1,265,412	$1,187,886,788
2005	$701,127,395	$581,572,264	$1,305,987	$1,284,005,646
2006	$741,262,831	$627,609,382	$1,315,293	$1,370,187,506
2007	$795,386,612	$676,330,350	$710,816	$1,472,427,778
2008	$861,869,634	$737,326,000	$1,188,488	$1,600,384,122
2009	$917,017,519	$783,067,561	$958,144	$1,701,043,224
2010	$974,384,211	$840,859,857	$948,644	$1,816,192,712
2011	$1,026,833,131	$888,568,335	$973,775	$1,916,375,241
2012	$1,084,932,000	$943,642,382	$1,005,394	$2,029,579,776
2013	$1,133,252,529	$987,407,747	$1,068,583	$2,121,728,859
2014	$1,198,783,977	$1,042,721,107	$1,122,517	$2,242,627,601
2015	$1,299,141,101	$1,125,910,841	$1,368,764	$2,426,420,706
2016	$1,360,547,514	$1,186,970,439	$1,687,776	$2,549,205,729
2017	$1,416,559,033	$1,241,647,093	$1,682,829	$2,659,888,955

SOURCE: U.S. Department of Education (2020).
[a]As discussed in chapter 3, NCAA competition remains largely gender segregated. True coed programs are rare. More common is for schools to combine resources across teams, such as having the same coach for men's and women's cross country. In these instances, schools may report their funding as "coed."

still are like, 'Wow that's so crazy. That's awesome.'" CM did not need an athletic scholarship to attend college. Her family could pay, but she sought assistance for symbolic reasons—to be admired by her peers. The monies that funded CM's scholarship came from the unpaid labor of predominately Black men's football and basketball players.

Universities spend a disproportionate amount of scarce scholarship resources on athletes over merit- or need-based scholarships (Comeaux, 2007; Smith, 2011; Sperber, 2000). Coastal-U gives 40 percent of its scholarships, close to $12 million per year, to athletes. The Equity in Athletics Disclosure Act requires institutions with intercollegiate athletics programs to report their athletic spending as part of Title IX compliance. As table 6.2 shows, in the most recent year reported Division I institutions awarded $2.66 billion in athletic scholarships (U.S. Department of Education, 2020). That is an increase of $1.6 billion since 2003, the first year of publicly available data.

As I argued in the introduction, the NCAA justifies the billions in financial aid by presenting college sports as a *pathway of opportunity*. This messaging teaches the public to conflate athletic scholarships with low-income men of color in revenue sports. Scholarships are compensation for unpaid athletic labor and a means for upward mobility. Yet the NCAA's own data dispute this narrative. The vast majority, 86 percent, of college athletes play nonrevenue sports (NCAA, 2019). These athletes are almost exclusively white middle-class and second-generation college students. Thus, billions in athletic scholarships are going to those from already-advantaged communities.

When universities award athletic scholarships, they confer symbolic and material value onto the recipients. Prestige is a cultural construct that functions as a form of power by conferring symbolic worth. In Bourdieusian terms, prestige can be transformed into economic value when it is associated with material goods such as college access. Through athletic scholarships universities legitimate the capitals accrued in white suburban communities. Universities reward the behaviors, dispositions, values, and traits displayed by white suburban athletes by giving them reduced-cost or free attendance to their institutions. Thus, athletic scholarships legitimize the capital accrued in white suburban communities, while also legitimizing the institution's right to remove and transfer rights and resources from one (predominately Black) population to another (predominately white) population.

Conclusion

Current law permits colleges to allocate special admission slots for athletes but not for racial minorities. The slots often operate outside of and in contrast to a public university's typical admission practices. Special admissions for athletes have lower academic standards and higher rates of acceptance that mostly benefit white middle-class applicants. Athletes like Captain America, who make significant athletic contributions to the university, justify special admission practices. Captain America's athletic achievements present athletic admissions as a rigorous and objective process that identifies top athletes. Instead, I argue that through the interactional effects between regulations, hopeful college athletes' actions, and confirmatory behavior by college recruiters, individuals are selected because they align with white middle-class norms. Broadly, this practice narrows the selection pool and affirms the long-standing cultural definition of amateurism, or that college sports should be restricted to elite white athletes.

The preceding chapters described the broad structural easements that algin athletic merit with white middle- and upper-class communities. Structural alignment alone will not reproduce inequality. Reproduction needs advantaged groups to enact and protect their elevated status.

The underregulated nature of athletic admission permits white middle-class individuals to activate their advantages. Study participants attended camps, took a gap year, and toured campuses on unofficial visits to secure their advantage. Universities rewarded these additional strategies with admission.

When advantaged groups activate and claim their benefits, they reinforce institutional arrangements predicated upon the exclusion of others. University admission is also premised on scarcity. When universities admit one individual, they deny someone else that same spot. College admissions encode greater symbolic and material value on those who are included. Iceman could "make up for" his educational deficits because others are not provided such a route. Consequently, when athletic admissions include and elevate some, they deny and subordinate others.

Advantaged groups' sense of entitlement is often masked through meritocratic discourse. Meritocratic beliefs pervade college admission. Universities present their processes as fair, objective, neutral routes to reward deserving applicants. The onerous requirements and hurdles built within college admission present those who successfully make it through as having earned and therefore deserving their achievement. The overrepresentation of white middle- and upper-class individuals in higher education becomes palatable because they worked for and were not handed admission (Crenshaw, 1988; Harris, 1993; Johnson, 2014; Khan, 2012; Shamash, 2018; Weis et al., 2014; Weis and Fine, 2012). Presenting admissions as such disguises the subjective, normative, and power-laden standards, measures, and evaluations, all of which are designed for white middle- and upper-class communities. The process is filled with subjective interpretations, such as whether someone "fits" within the program. By elevating interpersonal interactions, universities instill an antimeritocratic selection process in athletics. Schools prefer those who meet normative standards of acceptability, re-creating social systems of race, class, and gender.

Conclusion

Altering the Path

In 2017 I presented drafts of this book at academic conferences. Reviewers and conferencegoers often asked whether and how my findings related to the "big-time" college sports: men's football and basketball. Does upward mobility exist for football and basketball? What are those teams' recruitment and admission practices? How will the recent court cases related to football change your findings? How can your findings help us address the exploitation of football players?

These questions reflect the dominance of men's football and basketball in our society generally and in higher education specifically. Any study of sports, these questions suggest, should be tethered and filtered through the big-time programs. These questions also reflect a research prerogative in the academy: that which is most visible has the greatest impact on education. Those who study the reproduction of privilege have found that the most entrenched and nefarious forms of power are those that attract the least of our attention. Thus, a task of researchers who study power is to "make the invisible visible" in ways that question the assumed truth and logic that govern our social world (Lareau, 2011, p. 13). This book argued that big-time sports and programs are visible expressions of domination but do not represent the totality of how power within college athletic admissions functions.

I started this book with the story of Caylin Moore—a Black man who grew up in South-Central LA and used his football skills to earn a college and later Fulbright and Rhodes scholarships. Moore's exceptional story represents how narratives attached to big-time sports programs disguise the everyday realities of intercollegiate athletics. Across media, cultural, and educational institutions, we learn the commonsense account of how athletic admissions functions. Moore's story teaches the public that college sport is an upward mobility vehicle: *Athletic recruitment enables college sports to ignore one's social standing and objectively and fairly evaluate the individual. Successfully recruited athletes are those who relied upon individual-level resources such as grit, determination, and hard work. By requiring individual-level resources for ascendance, college sports is society's safety valve. For those who cannot ascend through the compulsory education system to a better life, sports offer another chance.* Repeatedly telling this story, but with new characters in each iteration, teaches the public how social systems operate and who will most likely benefit from them. The public learns that sports should be linked to our education system because this union offers double mobility opportunities: someone can receive an elite education and a chance for a professional sports career. The public ultimately sees college sports as *expanding* higher education access.

In this book, I recast the athletes in recruitment. Doing so changes the plot. College sports do not expand access; they narrow the applicant pool. College athletic recruitment requires communal, familial, and individual resources. The state has concentrated these resources in white suburban communities, giving youth in these areas an automatic advantage. White suburban communities cultivate a sense of entitlement to retain their lead. They learn how to strategically activate their privilege and prevent others from advancement. Athletes like Monique, whose race and class status already primed them to attend university, use their material and symbolic capital to pursue athletics and secure a more prestigious college spot.

This new story of athletic admission does not displace the accounts of big-time programs. Instead, I documented the interrelationship between the Olympic and revenue-generating sports within the neoliberal university. This book interrogates how one social setting—college athletic admissions—can produce multiple and competing reproductive narratives and outcomes. Athletes like Moore convince the public that athletic admissions are fair, open, and transparent. When we tune into Moore's story, we tune out Monique. We do not see athletic admissions as subjective, restrictive, and opaque. We do not hear that Moore is the exception—not the rule. We do not learn how Moore is contained in the most exploitative, revenue-generating corners of the institution to support athletes like Monique.

Special Admission: Legitimating Inequality

To link the fates of Monique and Moore, I located the state in college sports. Potential college athletes interact with the state as they develop the athletic talent universities desire. The state's presence in athletes' lives takes various forms. The state's *formal* workings include direct governorship of the public expressed through laws, military, and policing—the most visible state forms. The suburbs result from direct state action. Suburbs arose through historic laws like redlining and are maintained through contemporary laws like property taxes. These state projects concentrate resources in suburban areas—resources required to develop athletic talent. Even in the *removal* of these visible forms, state power expands. Deregulation, or the absence of the state from facets of public life, is a potent form of neoliberal power. The removal of publicly funded recreational sports activities—especially from lower-income, minority communities—increased privatized sports. Suburban residents doubly benefit from state support as they have retained publicly subsidized sports and can pay for privatized versions. When college recruiters select athletes from private clubs, they confer greater value to those teams over the public options. Here, the state's *relational* dimension is visible. The state cannot saturate every facet of American life alone. It partners with other state institutions like schools, private entities like rowing clubs, and citizens like suburban residents to enact its will. Uniting these disparate forms of the state secures its primary prerogative: domination and control (Brown, 1995).

Placing sport in the realm of the state invites inquiry into how social and cultural practices perpetuate inequality. I invoked various scholarly traditions including decolonial, whiteness, feminist, and neoliberal approaches to power to identify how the state produces disparate conditions for athletes to compete for a college roster spot. Bourdieusian approaches were particularly helpful to show how already-advantaged groups use physical activity to transfer and legitimate their privilege. Bourdieusian studies demonstrate how middle-class communities protect their class position by creating cultural sporting activities that rely upon forms of *economic capital* (like time, resources, organizational access), *social capital* (like community networks), and *cultural capital* (like dispositional orientations toward sport forms) (DeLuca and Andrews, 2016; Lee et al., 2009; Messner, 2009; Smyth et al., 2014; Stefansen et al., 2018; Stirrup et al., 2015). Much of this research focuses on the *production* of whiteness and class through controlling cultural meanings attached to sports. Yet producing culture or capital does not secure the accumulation effect needed for reproduction and intergenerational domination (Bourdieu, 2011). The value attached to white middle-class forms of capital must be validated and confirmed by dominant institutions.

The U.S. compulsory K–12 education system brings together varied individuals to evaluate their potential social contribution. Educational institutions certify the capital accrued in dominant communities. The transition from high school to college is a moment of mobility and accumulation as someone moves beyond the state-mandated K–12 curriculum toward the promise of greater educational and social rewards. College admission legitimates the capitals produced by dominant groups by rewarding them with access to a valued social good (Bourdieu and Passeron, 1977). Decades of research into the policies and practices of college admission show that the selection process favors material (economic resources) and symbolic (attitudes, behaviors, dispositions) characteristics of those from white middle-class communities (Bowen and Bok, 1998; Bowen et al., 2009; Bowles and Gintis, 1976; Davies and Guppy, 1997; Demerath, 2009; Dixon-Román, 2017; Haveman and Smeeding, 2006; Horn and Nunez, 2000; Ishitani, 2003; Jackson and Kurlaender, 2014; Kaufman, 2005; Khan, 2012; Lareau, 2011, 2015; Piketty, 2014; Rivera, 2016; Teranishi and Parker, 2010; Terenzini et al., 1996; Weis et al., 2014).

In *Special Admission*, I positioned athletic admission as a legitimating institution. The Bourdieusian approach shows that power reproduction cannot be reduced to economic capital accumulation. I discussed how white suburban communities produce varied forms of capital—economic, physical, social, and cultural—that colleges value and reward with admission. These forms are interrelated and mutually dependent. For instance, athletes with greater access to economic and social capital increased their physical capital. The state-sponsored bureaucratic admission process allows athletes to exchange certain physical capitals for college admission. By defining athletic talent through criteria linked to the capitals produced and secured by white suburbs, colleges *legitimate* these capitals as more valuable than others. The *symbolic violence*, or state authority granted to colleges to define and reward merit criteria, enables higher education to present their admission process as fair and objective. White suburbanites who are recruited as college athletes seem to deserve their spot on the team. In reality, they were recruited because colleges designed admissions in their favor.

College Access for the Gentleman Amateur

To show how college athletic admission functions as a legitimating institution, I had to first locate the varied ways the state uses athletic admissions for cultural control. I began by tracing the history of college sports' controlling cultural ideal: amateurism. Existing research into U.S. amateurism largely positions the governing principle as a tool for elites to exploit largely lower-income, racial-minority, male athletes in revenue sports (e.g., Baker and Hawkins, 2016; Grenardo, 2016; Sack and Staurowsky, 1998). By reexamining the history of amateurism and how it structured the formation of college sports, I offered a compatible narrative of how amateurism protects sport access for elite white men.

In chapter 1, I described how the origin of college sports, rooted in the ideal of the white *gentleman amateur*, still informs the practices, policies, and hierarchies present in the institution. The cultural ideal of the gentleman amateur—a wealthy white man who has the privilege to participate in sport for pleasure—was propagated by the nation's organic intellectuals including college presidents, sports leaders, and journalists and was cemented as a governing apparatus through state action. From the original support and mandate of President Theodore Roosevelt through the most recent federal court cases, the state legitimates the amateur ideal and marks college sports as inherently educational in nature and therefore entitles them to certain rights and benefits.

The gentleman amateur persists today because he was refashioned through several historic hegemonic crises. Colleges created the first amateurism crisis. University leaders believed college sports could increase their national profile, student body, and profits. Under capitalist conditions, competition among colleges produced ever larger spectator events. To provide the best show for spectators, colleges compromised their elitist values and recruited white working-class athletes who needed money to attend college. Colleges used various means—paying athletes through campus jobs or directly through tuition waivers—to recruit and retain them. The spectacle and the presence of "working-class ringers" drew much ire in the press and from sports purists. Rather than regulating away universities' right to profit from sports, the governing leagues refashioned amateurism in the 1950s. Universities could profit and athletes could receive limited compensation in the form of scholarships. Amateurism brokered this compromise by redefining tolerable compensation as educational funding. This compromise also contained the impure elements of commercialism into one or two profit-generating sports. Working-class athletes, who required a scholarship to attend university, were contained in the already-contaminated revenue-producing sports. Universities and the NCAA could then credibly claim that the remainder (and majority) of college athletes remained true gentleman amateurs. This compromise was not without costs. The NCAA has since faced legal challenges from athletes claiming rights as employees. The NCAA has thus far protected its amateur model through support from the state, which recognizes amateurism as a genuine historic principle worth preserving.

The second major hegemonic crisis originated outside the ivory tower. The cultural underpinnings of the gentleman amateur were enlivened through oppositional rhetoric. His existence was always defined as something he was not; he was *not* a savage, *not* a lady, *not* a professional. This oppositional rhetoric justified the long-standing overt exclusion of women and racial minorities from college sport participation. The 1960s civil rights and feminist movements targeted college sports as one of many terrains for national reform, and the gentleman amateur was once again reformulated. The state granted limited access to college sports to women and racial minorities so long as they adhered to the state-backed terms of the gentleman amateur. For white women this meant remaining in segregated, underfunded, and underrecognized portions of the institution. For Black men this meant entering into the highest profile but most exploitative commercial terrains. For Black women this meant remaining on the margins of college sports as they have yet to secure legal protections to grant them access. Containment did not end but instead refashioned amateurism.

Athletic Talent: More Than a Pair of Shoes

Narratives that conflate athletic talent with individual characteristics obscure the NCAA's elitist origins. Chapter 2 opened with the story of Olympic runner Jenny Simpson, who believed all it took to succeed in track and field was "a pair of shoes." Presenting sport achievement as requiring little or no infrastructure reestablishes it as a platform of opportunity. Instead, throughout the book I refocused athletic talent away from individual characteristics toward the community. Simpson's pathway to a college athletic scholarship and later the Olympics—much like my study's participants—started in a majority-white suburb with plentiful low-cost recreational sports and a highly ranked public high school with eighteen sports, including lacrosse, beach volleyball, bowling, slow-pitch softball, and water polo. Simpson's high school also has two certified athletic trainers on staff to serve the physical and health needs of the high school athletes. Needless to say, Simpson used much more than a pair of shoes to develop her athletic abilities.

Chapter 1 explored how college athletic admissions is a state-sponsored institution. Chapters 2 and 3 built upon this framework and showed how the state unites varied forms of public and private life to create disproportionate opportunities for certain communities to develop the athletic talent that aligns with the gentleman amateur ideal. During our interviews, college athletes detailed the abundant resources and support systems required to access intercollegiate athletics. Becoming a college athlete, they explained, requires community infrastructure such as access to large, safe spaces to recreate and train, a wide variety of sport options to test out and find the best fit, pay-to-play competitive club programs, coaches with certain skills and expertise, and caregivers and adults to do the volunteer labor needed to support athletic programs. These community resources are winnowing mechanisms. Access remains guarded by economic capital in the form of money and time. Once in, athletes face a barrage of internal assessments that determine if they stay in a given sport. As athletes successfully traverse the various athletic winnowing mechanisms in their communities, they accrue additional advantages like embodied skills and social connections to reputable coaches.

To contextualize study participants' narratives, I created a unique dataset using ten years of Coastal-U track and field and rowing rosters. I compared the hometown incomes of athletes to Coastal-U students and found that rowers and track and field athletes were more likely than the general student body to come from higher-income, majority-white, and high-ranking school systems.

These findings suggested a correspondence between white middle-class communities and athletic recruitment.

State action restricts access to communities with abundant athletic infrastructure. I described how direct state action such as redlining, school funding regimes, and property taxes create white suburban neighborhoods and permit these areas to secure and concentrate a disproportionate amount of state resources. These resources help youth access the gentleman amateur form of athletic talent universities value. For instance, I discussed how suburban public schools are more likely than those in urban and rural areas to host the wide variety of sports teams offered by universities. By offering more sports as well as the particular sports sponsored by universities, suburban public schools grant their students greater opportunities to test out and refine their abilities until they find their athletic fit.

Importantly, not everyone within white suburban communities has equal opportunities to develop athletic talent. In chapter 3, I discussed how the post–civil rights era prohibited *formal* state-sponsored discrimination but preserved the legal mechanisms that elevate capitalism, whiteness, and masculinity. Lingering inequality is reduced to individualized causes, such as the *choices* people make in navigating our social systems. The language of choice disguises how race, class, and gender power relations structure unequal choices for people of color, lower-income people, and women. The public narratives attached to sports—*all you need is a pair of shoes*—obscure how today's athletes cannot freely *choose* to play sports.

Instead, white suburban men have the most athletic options and prospects, while women and Black people play *certain* sports. Black athletes whose class position afforded them economic entry to suburban communities still faced racial barriers to sport participation. Black athletes recounted being the only person of their race in their community schools or sports. Malcolm became a track athlete in part because of daily racism he endured during school. Malcolm described getting through the school day as living in "enemy territory" because he felt "attacked" and misunderstood. Even though his well-resourced public school had plentiful sports opportunities, he did not want to spend his free time fraternizing with the enemy. Instead, his father put in the time and effort to research and identify a local private track club with greater racial diversity than the school teams. He enrolled his children on the team. Malcolm described how he embraced his club track team because it was a place where he could just "breathe" and let his guard down.

White athletes were largely unaware that their sports originated in racial processes. Growing up within segregated environments teaches white people that "the world belongs to them" (Leonardo, 2009, p. 112). They need not fear social isolation as they are the majority in their segregated environments. They can activate and retain their racial benefits by pursuing a wide variety of sports.

As one example, Captain America's whiteness permitted her to join any sport—and she did. "I basically played every single sport there was," she told me. She competed in sports year-round, including "swimming in the summertime, or soccer in the fall, or basketball in the winter." She even tried volleyball and golf before landing on her college sport, rowing.

Captain America's sport selection was limited in a different way. Gender also shapes athletic opportunities. Direct state action, including Title IX, segregates sports by gender. State laws like Title IX seem to eradicate discrimination. As Du Bois (1935) opined, segregation can never be equal so long as it is premised on one group controlling another group's access to symbolic and material resources. The masculine state (Brown, 1992, 1995) brokers protection for women by offering them separate-and-unequal sporting opportunities that remain largely run and operated by men (Anderson, 2008; Cahn, 1994; Coakley, 2015; Dworkin and Wachs, 2009; Eitzen, 2016; Lapchick, 2018; Messner, 2002, 2009; Milner and Braddock, 2016; Pieper, 2016; Suggs, 2005; Sullivan, 2011; Travers, 2013). The sports available to women are those designed by men and built on a male standard of athleticism (Cahn, 1994; Travers, 2013). Men remain the default norm by which women's success and achievement are evaluated. Women learn their athletic success must mirror an always out of reach male athletic standard.

The crafting and implementation of Title IX illustrates the reproduction of intersectional forms of power within the sports path to college. Elevating one social category as the primary organization of our social life—race, class, or gender—inaccurately depicts how these categories are formed and take root in our daily lives. Women of color are uniquely discriminated on the sports path to college as they face overt and covert segregation. Seeking protections from the state, like Title IX, requires groups to articulate their claims within state logic (Crenshaw, 1988). One state logic is an essentialist view of what constitutes a citizen and their corresponding rights to access (Crenshaw, 1988). Title IX grants girls and women educational access equal to their male counterparts. But youth and adults do not have equal access to education. Instead, one's race and/or class position can legally place one in drastically underfunded schools and communities (Donnor, 2011; Dumas, 2011; Green and Gooden, 2016; Harris, 1993; Knoester and Au, 2017; Nelson, 2008; Rothstein, 2017). These combined state logics allow white girls and women to become Title IX's primary beneficiaries. White girls and women are more likely to live in communities and attend schools with plentiful low-cost sport opportunities offered to boys and men. White girls and women can use the state law to seek protection from gender discrimination and access to these athletic opportunities. In contrast, girls and women of color are more likely to grow up in low-income areas with underfunded schools with few sports opportunities (Mathewson, 1995; Sabo and Veliz, 2008). White women are also more likely than women of color to live in communities that comply with the law and to have their legal complaints heard by the courts (Fields, 2008; Grant et al., 2006; Mathewson, 1995). These are just some of the reasons why three-quarters of women college athletes are white (Lapchick, 2018).

Warfare: Protecting Privilege by Playing Sports

State power extends beyond formal playing fields like Congress and public schools. The state also utilizes *relational* powers and encourages citizens to take up its will (Brown, 1992, 1995, 2019; James, 1996). In the 1960s, the state prohibited overt discrimination in college admission and supported an expansion of higher education. But this expansion did not equalize educational or economic outcomes. As access grew, so did the hierarchy within higher education (Davies and Guppy, 1997; Stuber et al., 2011; Weis et al., 2014). As Weis et al. (2014) explain, "The more selective the institution, the more short- and long-term advantages accrue to the attending population" (p. 213). Global and domestic changes in the nature of and benefits associated with work, particularly middle-class work, exacerbate competition for elite spots at universities (Piketty, 2014; Weis et al., 2014). Weis et al. (2014) documented how white middle-class communities, to retain their spot in global hierarchies, commit *warfare* to activate their privilege and gain the ever scarcer resources attached to elite universities. In my study, I observed how members of white middle-class communities learned that certain sports or events could secure those scarce spots at elite universities. Through sports they retained their class and race entitlements when they failed to gain the academic merits needed for college admission. In this sense, the benefits granted to them by the state were insufficient to reproduce their privilege. They found innovative strategies to gain college admission.

Participants learned to activate their advantages through a lifetime of socialization across varied settings. Those who can access the range of public or private sports develop a *habitus*, or the embodiment of cultural characteristics that are shaped by one's social position and access to capital (Bourdieu, 1978). Part of the habitus includes a *cultural knowledge* (Lareau, 2015), or knowing how to navigate the informal and formal rules of the college athletic admission process. Within their varied community settings athletes learned from key socializers, including their caregivers, coaches, and teammates, a set of strategies that could differentiate them in the college recruitment process. Athletes learned which sports or events had the least competition in college recruitment, which camps or private clubs could enhance their skills, which club and high school coaches had leverage with colleges, and how to network with college coaches. Pursuing these strategies reflects how privileged groups actively protect their status and by doing so reproduce inequality (Bourdieu, 2011; Bourdieu and Passeron, 1977).

As white middle-class community members activate their benefits and secure the limited number of spots at elite universities, they simultaneously prevent lower-income individuals and people of color from accruing symbolic and material assets. This entrenches the connections between white middle-class communities and the characteristics colleges value. In return, as fewer lower-income and racial minorities access higher education, the characteristics associated with these communities become disconnected from and devalued by colleges (Harris, 1993; Weis et al., 2014; Weis and Fine, 2012).

It Takes Two: Confirming White Suburbia's Capitals

The strategies I listed in this book become valuable when universities validate them through their admission process. College admission confirms the behaviors, norms, values, and strategies enacted by those from white suburban areas by predominately admitting members from these communities to their institutions. Bourdieu and Passeron (1977) positioned college admission as a *legitimating institution* for individuals to convert embodied characteristics such as behaviors into legible social goods like university degrees. In chapter 6, I documented how college athletic admission functions as a legitimating institution because it permits members of white middle-class communities to invest over their life span in accruing the embodied capital coaches value. When an athlete receives admission based upon their athletic talent, the university rewards their embodied capitals with a universally recognized social good: college access. Thus, the state assigns superior value to the capitals available within white suburban communities by rewarding their members with special admission to universities.

Additionally, the strategies and capitals necessary for athletic recruitment result from a dynamic confirmation process. As privileged groups struggle to retain their advantage, they innovate, share, and develop tactics that may or may not succeed. Over time, as members of these communities observe some success and some failure, they learn which strategies work better. The most successful strategies are those that are responsive to institutional regulations. For instance, the NCAA regulates athletes' compensation. But the organization does not restrict the money someone can spend to develop athletic talent. These differing bureaucratic regulations (a result of the history I explained in chapter 1) advantage those with embodied capital (e.g., knowledge of how the rules work) and economic capital (e.g., ability to pay for private club sports) in college recruitment. In this way, the NCAA devalues one strategy (seeking payment for athletic talent prior to college) and values another strategy (paying to improve one's athletic talent).

The regulations shaping college athletic admissions no longer ban members of historically disenfranchised communities. Yet the interplay between the regulations and actions within white suburban communities achieves the same result. Universities allow coaches to define athletic talent. Coaches use discretion to define physical capital requirements in ways that align with white middle-class communities. Simultaneously, white suburban families invest in sports to mark and protect their middle-class standing (Andrews, 1999; DeLuca and Andrews, 2016; Messner, 2009). When coaches reward athletes who used costly clubs, national team affiliations, and camps as proxies for physical capital, they confirm the capital in white suburban areas. This concentrates the opportunity structure of college sports within exclusive enclaves.

Altering the Path

Spring of 2019 introduced the potential for another hegemonic crisis in college sports. For the first time, when I presented the findings from this book, I encountered a new cultural resonance with, and understanding of, my research. Operation Varsity Blues (OVB)—the largest college admissions scandal in U.S. history—brought public and scholarly interest to how college athletic admissions function for Olympic sports. OVB showed that people within and outside of higher education could collude to admit athletes with little or no sport experience to elite universities.

OVB is a titillating news story. Celebrities, wealth, and corruption are the plotlines of blockbuster hits. OVB combined the American obsession with the state lie of freedom of opportunity for all with the worship of those at the top of the economy. The capitalist element of American culture permits the wealthy and famous to retain their material and social status and indulge in extravagant spending as an earned right. The democratic element of American culture limits this spending within public institutions. People believe the state lie because the state limits how individuals can wield political and economic influence in democratic institutions like schools. When wealthy individuals purchase privileged access to education, they become traitors of this American compact who must be punished. Once again, the state intervenes and provides a happy ending. The public turns to the state to scour, prosecute, and cleanse the corruption that tarnished the mobility engine. The Justice Department services our institutions and gets them back and running in tip-top condition.

The incessant media coverage of OVB fell into this Hollywood arc, in part because actual members of Hollywood were the main actors. Institutional crises also provide a moment for public reflection and reexamination. OVB presented a new, albeit brief, shift in the stories often recounted about college athletes. At least temporarily, wealthy white girls became the new face of college sports. Caylin Moore's upward mobility tale was replaced by that of the elite angling to do whatever it takes to place their overly entitled offspring into elite universities. If their path went through athletics, so be it. Sports became simply another terrain to exploit their advantage. But the spectacle of Singer and his clients' prosecution focused upon how their actions corrupted a fair process of college admissions. The state and corresponding media coverage framed Singer and his clients as the defective parts of an already-well-functioning machine (Hextrum, 2019b; Rosen et al., 2019a, 2019b; Smith, 2019). The state presented those involved in OVB as corrupt, not as acting in ways that closely mirrored their job duties. By charging Singer and his coconspirators with federal crimes, athletic admissions became immune to larger reforms, thereby preserving the status quo.

At the time of writing, I have seen no evidence that prosecuting and incarcerating Singer and his elite coconspirators will alter college athletic admissions. Instead, I have observed the workings of the state to reconstitute the public trust in, and therefore the success of, college athletics to function as a legitimating institution. As predicted by Bourdieu (2011), the direct forms of capital exchange exhibited in OVB are visible to public scrutiny and thereby subject to regulation and prosecution. Bourdieu (2011) warns that increased state action and regulation against the "official transmission of capital" or direct economic capital exchanges, like bribing university staff for college access, increases the value and likelihood of "clandestine circulation" of symbolic capital (p. 55). Bourdieu (2011) felt so strongly about this that he concluded that cultural capital could become *the* "determinant in the reproduction of the social structure," in effect displacing direct capital (p. 55). Symbolic forms of capital are central in schooling, which is a social "instrument of reproduction capable of disguising its own function" (p. 55). The state, in coordination with elite groups, empowers schools, as legitimating institutions, to define merit and reward said merit standards. If it is no longer in the elites' or state's interest to conflate economic capital with academic merit, they will create new definitions to retain dominance. The success of this system is that schools can "disguise" the workings of these social processes by presenting them as natural outcomes of a winnowing mechanism rather than as arbitrary expressions of power. Bourdieu (2011) concludes that changing education without modifying the underlying economic and political systems will encourage a proliferation of symbolic and covert capital conversions.

Using Bourdieusian theories to map the sports path to college, this book reveals how state-secured and -permitted capital conversion works outside, alongside, and within schools. The sports path to college necessitates traversing varied terrains of public and private life. Much of the resources required to develop the athletic talent universities desire exist outside the purview of formal schooling. The initial advantages to participants flowed not through the schools but through their communities, families, and social positions. Schools were a conduit to transform these advantages into "natural," "earned," or "legitimate" social advantages. Therefore, any work to limit the reproductive forces of this pathway must extend into these varied terrains, seeking redistributive and humanizing goals in communities, housing, recreation, and schools.

Bourdieu's theory of reproduction is deterministic. He views the social world as one in which elites will always be one step ahead. Through their influence in state institutions like education, elites wield an outsized influence over the shape and nature of our society that will be to their interests, not the majority's. How can the public even begin to change the underlying economic and political systems if "public" institutions like schools are already captured by elites?

One way through Bourdieusian logic is to reexamine how the state and elite groups coordinate their efforts. Gramsci (1971) explained that democratic societies do not have a singular "elite." Instead, numerous groups are constantly vying for their interests to be heard and taken up by the state. Through competing to control the culture, gaps and inconsistencies emerge in the reproduction process—hence his notion of hegemonic crises of the state. These crises can create public openings that create chances for greater structural change. While I have yet to see OVB creating a cultural crisis, it may have provided a structural opening to draw in much-needed public interest and fury over college admissions.

Gramsci (1971) contends that power relations change through collaboration between organic intellectuals and those harmed by power relations. Through sustained dialogue and consciousness raising, these interactions spark ideas to create more humanizing and transformative institutions and pathways to them. This book as a whole and the ideas I, as someone imbued by higher education with the privilege and status of an organic intellectual, conclude with are possible discussion topics for this collective work. I end with one way to reframe athletic admissions that should be vetted through collective movements. My suggestions assume the state will continue to back college athletics as an educational enterprise. Related work could consider if, how, why, and to what extent school and sport could be untethered.

"Confirmative Action": An Alternative to Special Admissions

Throughout this book, I argued that universities defined athletic merit to align with the capitals accrued in white middle-class communities. In some cases, I found that athletes with little or no merit were granted access. Adopting "objective" benchmarks for recruitment will not create egalitarian athletic admissions. Astute analyses of how academic merit emerged in K–12 and later college admissions have revealed how uniform, objective, and static criteria of merit are always first defined in the interests of maintaining the status quo (Guinier, 2003, 2015; Harris, 1993; Lareau, 2015; McDonough, 1997; Weis et al., 2014; Weis and Fine, 2012). I believe the same would be true for athletic admissions. Instituting more rigorous and transparent athletic admissions criteria will not disrupt the transmission of advantage so long as "merit" remains conflated with white middle-class norms. How could colleges create admission criteria that do not cater to and instead minimize the influence of elite groups?

Harvard law professor Lani Guinier (2003, 2015) proposed "confirmative action" as a solution to this question. As state institutions, universities should be accountable to reflect the core principles of democratic states, namely inclusiveness, transparency, and accountability. Confirmative action would "adopt admission criteria" that "confirm" universities' democratic missions (p. 50). Democracies are premised under inclusiveness in that all people should participate in the political process. To ensure the democratic process remains inclusive, democracies also require transparency. All decision-making processes and outcomes should be available to public scrutiny and subject to reevaluation. And finally, democracies require accountability linked to producing outcomes for public good. Bringing these democratically oriented principles into admissions reorients student selection away from static measures of merit, like how someone scored on a test at one point in time, toward dynamic measures of merit, like how someone will continue to learn and grow within and beyond the bounds of higher education. Guinier (2003) summarizes how confirmative action will transform higher education and society: "Merit becomes a function of societal needs and values rather than a fixed, quantifiable entity that, like one's blood pressure or body temperature, can be measured with the proper instruments. Merit, in other words, becomes dynamic" (p. 50). One static merit measure in athletic admissions is whether at the time of recruitment an athlete can become a viable team member of a specific sport. This selection process is one of the primary ways that athletic admissions aligns with elite communities. As chapter 2 explored, elitist athletic admission practices are premised upon the alignment between the sports available at college and those available within high schools and communities. So long as athletic admissions fill the current college roster spots, the alignment will remain.

Thus, changing athletic admissions will not alter reproduction unless the sport offerings themselves change. Guinier (2003) offered a similar observation about higher education. Confirmative action requires examining the organization and nature of colleges and universities. The current college environment does not cultivate or reward democratic engagement and service. "Embedding admissions into the institution's mission," she explains, "should prompt us to reconsider issues of curriculum, learning theory, and the ways to motivate members of diverse populations to reach his or her full potential" so the college experiences match the admissions and goals of the institution (p. 47).

Applying confirmative action to college athletics would require broad-reaching changes in at least three areas. First, as I have argued elsewhere, college sports are currently designed around imperatives of hierarchy, competition, and winner-take-all incentives that substantiate whiteness, masculinity, and neoliberalism (Hextrum, 2020b, 2020c, 2020d). Universities hire and retain athletic staff and leaders who meet these imperatives (Branch, 2011; Clotfelter, 2011; Coakley, 2011a, 2015; Eitzen, 2016; Sperber, 2000). Bringing democratic imperatives and incentives into college sports requires an institutional reorientation toward challenging the assumption that elite, hierarchical, competitive sports are superior to other forms of physical activity; incorporating a broad array of sport forms that are not inherently hierarchical, competitive, and bureaucratic; creating athletic cultures that value and reward commitments to individual and community growth and development; and building relationships with other political action groups dedicated to the radical reformation of a more inclusive and humanizing society (Coakley, 2011a; Hextrum, 2020b).

With institutional backing, college athletic admissions could adopt new selection criteria that would value the broad range of physical capital and cultures. Sport sociologists have shown that youth participate in wide forms of play, games, and physical activity, yet not all forms are recognized by elite athletic organizations like college sports (e.g., Bourdieu, 1978; Coakley, 2015; Sabo and Veliz, 2008). In creating transparent and publicly scrutinized forms of merit, universities should target a broader range of desirable qualities that do not always align with existing sport forms. For example, universities should not grant such great weight to pay-to-play sport activities and instead grant greater weight to youth who participate in low-cost or free athletics. I recommend additional research into how universities could create more holistic criteria to identify and select athletes from beyond white middle-class communities.

Another cultural and structural change that must occur within all levels of sports is de jure gender segregation. While segregation is a driver for inequality, equality cannot be reached through integrating women and/or racial minorities into the current system of white patriarchal athletics that elevates competition, violence, and individualism, each of which maintain oppressive conditions (Coakley, 2011a, 2011b; Hextrum, 2017b, 2020b, 2020c, 2020d; Messner, 2002; Travers, 2013). Instead, athletic practitioners should reconceptualize and reorganize all levels of sport, including college, to elevate collaboration, well-being, and community development (Coakley, 2011a). This reorganization effort could involve changing the rules of existing sports such as eliminating the regulatory differences between softball and baseball; incorporating existing sport forms not inherently based upon competition and hierarchy such as karate, calisthenics, surfing, skateboarding, and tai chi; and inventing new forms of athletic activity. During the transition to new sport forms, women-only sports should remain. Spaces created for marginalized groups such as students at historically Black colleges and universities and women's colleges provide important vehicles for group uplift and could be instrumental in reimagining more equitable sport forms (Milner and Braddock, 2016).

Confirmative action is one way to link college admission to social processes. Changing athletic admissions alone will not eliminate much of the social harms I described in this book. The social, cultural, and economic processes that develop, nurture, and reward certain forms of athletic talent above all others are diffuse and saturated across settings. The kinds of athletic merit currently valued by institutions crisscross social concerns such as access to affordable housing, employment, education, community recreational spaces, free time, and social connections with knowledge of certain sports. In this sense, sports traverse a wide array of state institutions accountable to democratic imperatives. Athletic admissions could confirm the democratic imperatives of higher education by attuning to the needs and reforms across these varied social planes.

The Sequel: Transmission of Privilege within the University

Democratic change requires coalition building across a range of constituents. In the introduction I explained that I did not begin this project with the intention to write about college athletic admissions. My study was organized around the in-college educational experiences of athletes outside the commercial spotlight. I wanted to break the nearly century-long criticism and focus on revenue-generating sports as professional, corrupt, and antithetical to education. I was interested in whether anyone could be a true *student athlete* and, if so, whether existing social privileges along race, class, and gender dimensions secured this fate. What I found in speaking to athletes is that access to higher education does not guarantee the transmission of privilege. Instead, the transmission process becomes even more difficult and complex once they arrive in higher education. As a result, I believe that even the beneficiaries of the sports path to college may be important allies to reforming the institution in more democratic and liberatory ways.

The sports path to college demands almost a unilateral focus of time, body, and resources toward developing athletic talent. Participants did not face the educational consequences of this unilateral focus because, as Iceman explained, he could use sports to "make up for" what he lacked in academic credentials. For those who successfully made it to college via sports, their athletic and academic worlds aligned. Any time they spent on sports and away from school did not compromise their educational access. Participants arrived in college with strong academic identities and capabilities, believing they could succeed as athletes and as students (Hextrum, 2017a, 2020b). Once in college, participants felt the institutions of sport and school turn against one another, no longer aligning in their favor. Combining highly competitive and demanding athletics and academics left participants overwhelmed by, and unable to complete, their institutional obligations.

Across the study, participants endured athletic and academic rejections. Athletically they endured repeated physical injury, loss of athletic status and playing time, and numerous personal and physical invasions by the governing bodies. Academically, they faced stigma from the academic side of campus, limited class and major selection, limited engagement with faculty, limited socialization with nonathletes, limited opportunities to pursue research or student organizations, and limited chances to develop an employment résumé for future jobs beyond athletics. Faced with sacrificing their educational, personal, and future employment goals, athletes questioned why they stayed within this system (Hextrum, 2017a).

My initial analysis revealed that athletes stayed in sport for three reasons: (1) their perceived obligation to remain a college athlete after the investment their families, coaches, teammates, and communities made in their sports path to college; (2) their lifetime of positive memories and outcomes associated with sport prior to college; and (3) their internalization of the neoliberal values of the institution, which required they sacrifice their educational, personal, and professional goals to perform their sport duties (Hextrum, 2017a, 2020b).

The challenges athletes face to activate their privilege once in college offer openings for collective action and resistance. In conversation with me, athletes questioned the nature, role, and purpose of elite sports. They were curious about whether everything they did was "worth it" and how to change sports in ways that would not require such demanding individual and collective sacrifices. I ended my study at Coastal-U on a hopeful note, one in which I observed the possibility that even the most privileged current and former college athletes who benefit from the status quo are growing weary of the nature and organization of elite sports and, if given the opportunity to participate in democratic efforts, may gladly join.

Appendix A

Study Participant Background Characteristics

I determined participants' hometown characteristics by linking their pre-college zip codes to U.S. Census Bureau Data (2016). The remaining characteristics were elicited during the interview process.

Table A.1
Participant demographics

Participant	Sport	Race	Athletic aid	Home	Median income	Hometown[a] Demographics % white	Demographics % Black	Caregivers' highest ed level
Amanda	W crew	White	Partial	WA	$99,597	77.10	13.30	Advanced
Andrew	M track	White	None	MN	$68,513	66.40	17.90	BA
Anthony	M track	Black	Partial	CA	$139,709	49.30	2.30	BA
Boris	M crew	White	Partial	Netherlands	—	—	—	Advanced
Brandon	M track	White	Partial	IL	$152,778	84.20	1.10	BA
Brittany	W track	Black	Partial	CA	$74,869	30.80	20.70	BA
Camilla	W crew	White	Partial	CA	$109,592	67.80	1.20	Professional
Captain America	W crew	White	Full	CO	$111,901	97.30	0.00	Professional
Casey	W crew	White	Partial	CA	$167,561	89.80	0.60	BA
Chantae	W track	Black	Full	CA	$60,665	67.40	8.20	HS
Chelsea	W crew	White	Full	Canada	—	—	—	BA
CM	W track	White	Partial	CA	$109,762	50.80	2.10	BA
Cooper	W crew	White	Full	WA	$91,149	92.30	0.80	BA
Duane	M track	Black	Partial	CA	$58,237	39.70	26.10	Professional
Ella	W crew	White	Full	Germany	—	—	—	Professional
Erwin	M crew	White	Partial	NJ	$132,440	64.50	25.00	BA
George	M track	White	Partial	CA	$118,658	73.50	3.10	BA
Goose	M crew	White	None	TX	$88,702	91.40	3.10	BA
Iceman	M crew	White	None	NY	$38,235	49.30	37.60	BA
Imani	W track	Black/Spanish/Japanese	None	CA	$81,498	62.10	10.80	HS
Josephine	W track	Black	None	CA	$81,498	62.10	10.80	BA
Joy	W crew	White	None	MI	$96,210	72.40	7.60	Professional
Kalie	W crew	White	Partial	WA	$99,597	77.10	13.30	BA
Kayla	W track	Chicana/White	Full	CA	$97,628	59.40	5.90	HS

Table A.1 (continued)

Participant	Sport	Race	Athletic aid	Home	Median income	Hometown[a] Demographics % white	Demographics % Black	Caregivers' highest ed level
Laura	W crew	White	Partial	CT	$211,313	93.00	0.40	BA
LeVar	M track	Black	Full	CA	$69,044	39.80	11.70	BA
Lisa	W crew	White	Full	Germany	—	—	—	BA
London	W track	White/Middle Eastern	None	CA	$136,150	85.20	0.50	Professional
Malcolm	M track	Black	Full	CA	$82,420	74.40	5.60	BA
Merlin	M track	White	Partial	CA	$108,211	67.70	2.10	BA
Monique	W crew	White	Partial	CA	$167,561	89.80	0.60	HS
Morgan	W crew	White	Partial	NY	$120,860	87.60	2.70	Advanced
Noelle	W crew	White	None	CA	$69,944	90.10	0.20	BA
Physicist	M track	White	Partial	CA	$135,578	83.80	1.00	Professional
Reggie	M crew	White	Partial	Australia	—	—	—	Advanced
Sanya	W track	White	Full	CA	$114,764	82.90	1.80	BA
Savannah	W crew	White	Partial	CA	$92,192	79.90	0.70	HS
Seamus	M track	White	Partial	CA	$87,329	49.50	5.70	HS
Sophia	W crew	White	None	NJ	$117,727	39.80	6.60	Advanced
Stella	W crew	White	Partial	HI	$85,837	21.50	2.50	Advanced
Steve	M crew	White	None	England	—	—	—	Advanced
Taylor	W track	White	Partial	CA	$109,693	81.60	1.60	BA
Terrance	M track	White	Partial	NV	$60,027	79.50	3.00	Advanced
Tyrell	M track	White	None	CA	$92,433	79.60	1.40	HS
Vera	W track	Black/Haitian/German	Full	Germany	—	—	—	HS
Victoria	W crew	White	Full	Canada	—	—	—	BA
Will	M crew	White	None	Australia	—	—	—	Advanced

[a] Data for hometown median income and racial demographics came from the U.S. Census Bureau (2016), represented in 2014 dollars. No adequate comparison exists for other countries represented in this study. As a result, no median income or demographics are listed for international study participants.

Appendix B
Participant Recruitment

Due to the high-profile nature of athletes on college campuses, I met with Coastal-U athletic leaders before initiating recruitment. I met with the faculty athletic representative, the senior women's administrator (top-ranking woman in the athletic department), the director and assistant director of the Student-Athlete Study Center, and coaches. During these meetings we discussed my research objectives and their questions or concerns. I also asked permission to attend athletic practices to present my research project and recruit potential participants.

Once my doctoral institution's Board of Human Subjects approved my research protocol, I began recruitment. At athletic practices I gave a brief five-minute overview of the project and my biography, emphasizing my experience as a college athlete and staff member. Initial responses from these meetings were minimal. I received about two to three responses after each team meeting. I then used the snowball recruitment method with these early volunteers (Biernacki and Waldorf, 1981) and asked if they felt comfortable recommending my project to their teammates or colleagues. Referrals proved to be a more successful method of recruitment. Three months later, I had twenty-eight volunteers. By the study's conclusion, forty-seven college athletes completed the interview process (see Hextrum, 2017, for copies of my recruitment emails, flyers, and interview protocols).

Appendix C

High School Sports Relative to College Sports

Table C.1 reflects the athletic opportunities across U.S. high schools compared to U.S. NCAA member institutions. A low percentage number indicates there are more opportunities to play a sport in high school than in college, whereas the reverse is true for a high percentage number.

Table C.1
High school sports relative to college sports

Sport	College to HS teams (%)		College to HS roster spots (%)	
	Men	Women	Men	Women
Baseball	1.83	0.00	2.18	0.00
Basketball	1.90	1.92	1.00	1.23
Beach volleyball	0.00	42.52	0.00	53.92
Bowling	0.00	1.18	0.00	1.10
Cross country	2.04	2.29	1.80	2.66
Fencing	17.36	21.85	16.23	20.24
Field hockey	0.00	4.42	0.00	2.98
Football	1.80	0.00	2.80	0.00
Golf	2.21	2.60	2.04	2.78
Gymnastics	14.71	3.89	18.66	5.92
Ice hockey	3.71	5.55	4.83	8.88
Lacrosse	2.40	4.14	3.01	3.77

(continued)

Table C.1 (*continued*)

Sport	College to HS teams (%)		College to HS roster spots (%)	
	Men	Women	Men	Women
Rifle	6.94	12.32	5.21	13.85
Rowing	39.73	118.92	54.73	263.90
Skiing	1.94	2.15	2.80	3.10
Soccer	1.65	2.77	1.32	2.40
Softball	0.00	1.90	0.00	1.74
Swim/dive	1.75	2.45	2.71	3.29
Tennis	2.60	3.06	1.64	1.50
Track/field (outdoor)	1.68	1.99	1.85	2.75
Volleyball	0.89	2.03	0.71	1.22
Water polo	2.98	4.03	2.72	3.58
Wrestling	0.68	0.00	1.00	0.00
Emerging sports				
Equestrian	0.00	82.61	0.00	126.53
Rugby	2.13	3.21	59.43	19.33
Triathlon	0.00	0.00	0.00	0.00

Acknowledgments

Special Admission extends my dissertation research. I am grateful to my doctoral advisor Lisa García Bedolla, who welcomed me into social and cultural studies at UC Berkeley. She encouraged an expansive intellectual and empirical approach to knowledge that enlivened this project. My committee members Zeus Leonardo and Raka Ray also gave me their invaluable time, attention, and insightful criticism. Zeus's theoretical insights on the interrelationship between race and class are the backbone of this book. I drew upon Raka's faith that an unwieldly and unfocused dissertation would someday "be a book" during my challenging writing moments. She also identified "the coup" buried within my early writings that later became my body of scholarly work.

In addition to my committee, numerous Berkeley faculty, administrators, and community members sustained me through my graduate studies. Many thanks to Jenny Simon-O'Neill, Liz Miles, and Teresa Gould for supporting my first job in college athletics. I am also indebted to Tony Mirabelli and Derek Van Rheenen for providing me a nearly decade-long home at the Athletic Study Center enriched with chances to combine scholarship and practice. Murray Sperber, thank you for encouraging me to pursue a PhD, showing me that college sports critics can still love the game, and providing countless hours of writing support. I apologize for all passive constructions in this text. John Cummins—our conversations and collaborations stimulated sage and nuanced insights into the inner workings of higher education that I carry to this day.

Several institutional funding programs contributed to this book. I thank the UC Berkeley Graduate Division, Graduate School of Education, and Center for the Studies in Higher Education for their financial grants throughout my PhD studies. I also received research assistance from students including Zachary Cameron, Stacy Doyle, and Suyang Lu. Financial support was provided from the Office of the Vice President for Research and Partnerships and the

Office of the Provost, University of Oklahoma. The Department of Educational Leadership and Policy Studies provided me a semester teaching release that freed me to write.

My editor, Lisa Banning at Rutgers University Press, was an early champion of this book and ensured I had the editorial support to move my vision to print. *Special Admission* benefited greatly from external reviewers. David L. Andrews and my blind reviewer struck the elusive balance of supportive yet critical feedback. Their insights helped me refine, renarrate, and reorganize this book so its interdisciplinary and theoretical aspects could shine.

My opportunities to present or publish progressed my analysis of college athletic admissions. I thank the peer reviewers, organizers, editors, and audiences at the American Educational Research Association, the Association for the Study of Higher Education, College Sport Research Institute, *Harvard Educational Review*, the North American Society for the Sociology of Sport, *Sport, Education, and Society*, *Teachers College Record*, and the UC Berkeley Center for Studies in Higher Education for their immeasurable insights incorporated in these pages.

My colleagues, mentors, and friends enveloped me with support, care, and wisdom throughout the cycles of intellectual development and disappointment. Siduri Haslerig and Mirelsie Velázquez, in particular, shepherded me through my transition from graduate student to faculty, intervening at key junctures to elevate and uplift my research, teaching, and activism. Mike Messner's mentorship knows no bounds. Starting with a chance meeting at Robin's art show in 2009, he has responded to every one of my queries, as small as a theoretical clarification and as large as publishing a book—even though we've never shared an institutional or disciplinary home. Additionally, I'd like to thank Curt Adams, Vicky Gomez, Sara Grummert, Angélica Guevara, Derek Houston, Patrick Johnson, Rae Langes, Dinorah Sánchez Loza, Damien Mason, Moira Ozias, Stacy Reeder, Heather Shotton, Angela Urick, Kelechi Uwaezuoke, Julie Ward, and Alison Wilson.

I also benefited from some shrewd readers of early book drafts. Jennifer Hoffman, Ell Lin, and Sabina Vaught provided feedback at an instrumental time. Sabina Vaught redefines intellectual generosity. She created departmental structures and systems to give me the time, space, and tenure support to write a book. In addition to her rigorous theoretical and philosophy insights, Sabina taught me how to write a captivating story by slowing down, highlighting the details, and embracing tangents. Evan Mandery showed me the value of commas and pushed my ideas beyond academic publishing. Barrett Briske traversed all iterations of this book—but most recently provided invaluable editing support to improve my writing.

My friends and family. Thank you for reminding me that I exist beyond my research. The yearly Goddess Retreats and Roommate Reunions provided necessary respites of love, life, and laughter. My mom, Stephanie Szmyd, raised three feminist daughters and along the way taught us the joy of reading and writing. My dad encouraged a love for all things sport, physicality, and nature. Shannon shows me who the *real* doctor is in the family. Thank you for always answering our calls—no matter the hour—and offering free medical advice. Robin—you are a compassionate competitor who pushed me to be a better athlete, scholar, and sister. Thanks, as well, for lending me "The Rower" to cover and capture this book. And to Steve, my armchair sociologist. You challenge me daily to think sharper, to be positive, and to be confident. You are a true partner.

All my former coaches, teammates, parents of teammates, and students. These pages reflect our journeys. Your support, encouragement, and mentorship shaped me into a college athlete and later a sports scholar. My positive athletic experiences allow me to reimagine college sports into enriching and away from exploitative ways.

Finally, this book exists because of my study participants. You offered your free labor through countless hours of interviews, emails, and questionaries and asked for nothing in return. Thank you for welcoming a stranger into the intimate corners of your lives. I am especially thankful to two participants, Merlin and Sophia. Your belief in the project, your help with recruitment, and your enthusiasm for my written work facilitated and inspired this project. Working for a college football program, attending graduate school, and living through one too many once-in-a-lifetime political-economic disruptions are a few of the experiences that led me to reexamine my own access to and ascendance within sport. While some of you may disagree with my scholarly interpretations, know that I did all I could to honor your experiences in this work.

Notes

Note to Preface

1 Throughout the book I use the term "they" if the person has not expressed their preferred gender pronoun.

Introduction

1 Style guides suggest that authors capitalize the racial descriptors *Black* and *White* as they signify racial-ethnic groups and are proper nouns. This stylistic suggestion wrongly places Black and white as equally positioned racial groups deserving equal treatment in writing. In reality, the white racial-ethnic group has no inherent claim to identity and culture outside of the subordination and domination of racialized minorities (Harris, 1993; Leonardo, 2009; Mills, 2003; Vaught, 2017). I chose to lowercase *white* throughout in an attempt to differently position racial groups and, in doing so, remove some of the implicit legitimacy whiteness cultivates for white identities, white groups, and white power.

2 Throughout the yearlong inquiry, I employed several qualitative processes to ensure rigor, including keeping detailed field notes, journaling on emergent themes, and discussing initial findings with participants and members of the athletic community including former athletes and athletic academic support personnel (Ravitch and Carl, 2016). After transcribing the interviews verbatim, I began open coding and read each interview, identifying possible themes, repetitions, and patterns. I then interpreted the descriptive codes to identify further patterns and discern higher order themes. I challenged my initial themes by rereading each narrative for conflicting or confirming statements for my initial claims; checking insights against the literature and studying institutional documents; and discussing initial findings with participants and members of the athletic community, including former athletes and athletic academic support personnel (Ravitch and Carl, 2016). Document analysis was particularly important in the final stages of solidifying institutional ethnographic findings (Naples, 2003; Smith, 2005). I relied on athlete narratives to enliven institutional documents from Coastal-U and the NCAA and

on the documents to understand how the institution shapes athletes' lives (for a sample of my coding process, see Hextrum, 2017a, 2019a).

3   During the study, men's rowing had no person of color. Women's rowing had one person of color. She was not recruited prior to college but instead joined the team during college—a process I will describe in more detail in chapter 6.

Chapter 2   The State Alignment

1   International students are excluded from community income calculations because no international equivalents to the U.S. census exist. This brought the total participant count to 1,035.

Chapter 3   Build a Wall

1   Olympic rowing hosts eight events for men and six for women—another instance of gender disparity. These events are divided by weight class (lightweight, which limits the maximum weight of the rowers, and open weight, which places no weight limit on rowers), rowing type (sculling, in which the rowers use two oars, and sweep rowing, in which the rowers have one oar but are paired on opposite sides of the boat), and number of participants (pair has two sweep rowers, quad has four scullers, and the eight has four sweep rowers). In the United States the predominant event is the eight-person boat race. A greater description of the intricacies of rowing and the costs associated with the variance in the sport can be found in the "Private Boat Clubs" section of chapter 4.

2   The 2K refers to the 2,000-meter test that is a common evaluative tool in rowing. Rowers complete the test on an ergometer ("erg" for short), a stationary rowing machine. (The ergometer is to rowers what a treadmill is to runners.) Coaches and athletes often use the 2K score to rank one another's performance. Most college and Olympic rowing races are two thousand meters in length.

References

Adler, P., and Adler, P. (1991). *Backboards & blackboards: College athletics and role engulfment.* New York: Columbia University Press.

Anderson, E. (2008). "I used to think women were weak": Orthodox masculinity, gender segregation, and sport. *Sociological Forum, 23*(2), 257–280.

Andrews, D. L. (1999). Contextualizing suburban soccer: Consumer culture, lifestyle differentiation and suburban America. *Culture, Sport Society, 2*(3), 31–53.

Anyon, J. (1980). Social class and the hidden curriculum of work. *Journal of Education, 162*(1), 67–92.

Apple, M. (2004). *Ideology and curriculum* (3rd ed.). New York: Routledge.

Aspen Institute. (2018). *State of play 2018: Trends and developments.* Aspen, CO: Aspen Institute.

Au, W. W. (2008). Devising inequality: A Bernsteinian analysis of high-stakes testing and social reproduction in education. *British Journal of Sociology of Education, 29*(6), 639–651.

Baker, A. R., and Hawkins, B. J. (2016). Academic and career advancement for Black male athletes at NCAA Division I Institutions. *New Directions for Adult and Continuing Education, 2016* (150), 71–82.

Baker, B. D., and Corcoran, S. P. (2012). *The stealth inequalities of school funding: How state and local finance systems perpetuate inequitable student spending.* Washington, DC: Center for American Progress.

Beamon, K. K. (2008). "Used goods": Former African-American college student-athletes' perception of exploitation by Division I universities. *Journal of Negro Education, 77*(4), 352–364.

Beamon, K. K. (2010). Are sports overemphasized in the socialization process of African American males? A qualitative analysis of former collegiate athletes' perception of sport socialization. *Journal of Black Studies, 41*(2), 281–300.

Bederman, G. (1995). *Manliness and civilization: A cultural history of gender and race in the United States, 1880–1917.* Chicago: University of Chicago Press.

Bick, J. (2007, February 25). Looking for an edge? Private coaching, by the hour. *New York Times.*

Biernacki, P., and Waldorf, D. (1981). Snowball sampling: Problems and techniques of chain referral sampling. *Sociological Methods & Research, 10*(2), 141–163.

Binder, A. J., Davis, D. B., and Bloom, N. (2016). Career funneling: How elite students learn to define and desire "prestigious" jobs. *Sociology of Education, 89*(1), 20–39.

Blumenstyk, G. (2020, January 22). The edge. *The Chronicle of Higher Education.* https://www.chronicle.com/newsletter/the-edge/2020-01-22.

Boliek, B. (2015). The potential reach of *O'Bannon v. NCAA. Mississippi Sports Law Review, 5*(1), 28–42.

Bourdieu, P. (1978). Sport and social class. *Social Science Information, 17*(6), 819–840.

Bourdieu, P. (2011). The forms of capital. In I. Szeman and T. Kaposy (Eds.), *Cultural theory: An anthology* (pp. 81–93). Malden, MA: Wiley-Blackwell.

Bourdieu, P., and Passeron, J. C. (1977). *Reproduction in education, society, and culture.* Thousand Oaks, CA: Sage.

Bowen, W. G., and Bok, D. (1998). *The shape of the river: Long-term consequences of considering race in college and university admissions.* Princeton, NJ: Princeton University Press.

Bowen, W. G., Chingos, M. M., and McPherson, M. S. (2009). *Crossing the finish line: Completing college at America's public universities.* Princeton, NJ: Princeton University Press.

Bowles, S., and Gintis, H. (1976). *Schooling in capitalist America: Educational reform and the contradictions of economic life.* New York: Basic Books.

Branch, T. (2011). The shame of college sports. *Atlantic, 308*(3), 80–110.

Brown, D. J. (2013). *The boys in the boat: Nine Americans and their epic quest for gold at the 1936 Berlin Olympics.* New York: Penguin Books.

Brown, E. S. (1907, August 11). Reformation is on in sports. *Salt Lake Tribune,* p. 4.

Brown, W. (1992). Finding the man in the state. *Feminist Studies, 18*(1), 7–34.

Brown, W. (1995). *States of injury: Power and freedom in late modernity.* Princeton, NJ: Princeton University Press.

Brown, W. (2005). Neo-liberalism and the end of liberal democracy. *Theory & Event, 7*(1), 37–59.

Brown, W. (2019). *In the ruins of neoliberalism: The rise of antidemocratic politics in the west.* New York: Columbia University Press.

Bruggeman, M. (2019, February 28). The lasting impact. *USRowing News.* http://www.usrowing.org/news/2019/02/28/the-lasting-impact-patricia-spratlen-etem/.

Buchman, C., Condron, D. J., and Roscigno, V. J. (2010). Shadow education, American style: Test preparation, the SAT and college enrollment. *Social Forces, 89*(2), 435–462.

Buck, K. (2017, April 12). The rise of athlete and Rhode's scholar Caylin Moore. *Los Angeles Sentinel.* https://lasentinel.net/the-rise-of-athlete-and-rhodes-scholar-caylin-moore.html.

Bucy, M. (2013). The costs of the pay-to-play model in high school athletics. *University of Maryland Law Journal of Race, Religion, Gender & Class, 13*(2), 278–302.

Burgess, D. J., and Naughton, G. A. (2010). Talent development in adolescent team sports: A review. *International Journal of Sports Physiology and Performance, 5*(1), 103–116.

Butler, J. (2011). *Bodies that matter: On the discursive limits of sex.* New York: Routledge.

Butler, J., and Lopiano, D. (2003). *The women's sports foundation report: Title IX and race in intercollegiate sport.* East Meadow, NY: Women's Sport Foundation.

Byers, W., and Hammer, C. (1995). *Unsportsmanlike conduct: Exploiting college athletes.* Ann Arbor: University of Michigan Press.

Cahn, S. K. (1994). *Coming on strong: Gender and sexuality in women's sport*. Champaign- Urbana: University of Illinois Press.

Calarco, J. M. (2014). Coached for the classroom: Parents' cultural transmission and children's reproduction of educational inequalities. *American Sociological Review, 79*(5), 1015–1037.

Calarco, J. M. (2018). *Negotiating opportunities: How the middle-class secures advantages in school*. New York: Oxford University Press.

Call, The (1905, November 27). Nineteen killed on gridiron—Football claims a heavy toll on lives. *The Call, 98*(180), 1.

Carrington, B. (2013). The critical sociology of race and sport: The first fifty years. *Annual Review of Sociology, 39*(1), 379–398.

Carter, P. L., Skiba, R., Arredondo, M. I., and Pollock, M. (2017). You can't fix what you don't look at: Acknowledging race in addressing racial discipline disparities. *Urban Education, 52*(2), 207–235.

Carter, W. B. (2000). Student-athlete welfare in a restructured NCAA. *Virginia Journal of Sports and the Law, 2*(1), 1–103.

Carter, W. B. (2006). The age of innocence: The first 25 years of the National Collegiate Athletic Association. *Vanderbilt Journal of Entertainment and Technology Law, 8*(2), 211–291.

Cater, F. (2020, May 2). Federal judge dismisses U.S. women's soccer team's equal pay claim. NPR. https://www.npr.org/2020/05/02/849492863/federal-judge-dismisses-u-s-womens-soccer-team-s-equal-pay-claim.

Cheslock, J. (2008). *Who's playing college sports? Money, race and gender*. Washington, DC: Women's Sport Foundation. http://www.womenssportsfoundation.org.

Chicago Tribune. (1905, December 5). Manly game, but clean: President says purify football but don't weaken it. *Chicago Tribune*. https://search.proquest.com/docview/173252825?accountid=12964.

Clayton, J. (2020). Origin & history of men's lacrosse. *World Lacrosse*. https://worldlacrosse.sport/about-world-lacrosse/origin-history/.

Clotfelter, C. T. (2011). *Big-time sports in American universities*. New York: Cambridge University Press.

Coakley, J. (2011a). Ideology doesn't just happen: Sports and neoliberalism. *ALESDE, Curitiba, 1*(1), 67–84.

Coakley, J. (2011b). Youth sports: What counts as "positive development"? *Journal of Sport and Social Issues, 35*(3), 306–324.

Coakley, J. (2015). *Sport in society: Issues and controversies* (11th ed.). New York: McGraw-Hill.

Collins, P. H. (2005). *The politics of Black feminist thought* (2nd ed.). New York: Routledge.

Colombo, J. D. (2010). The NCAA, tax exemption, and college athletics. *University of Illinois Law Review, 2010*(1), 109–164.

Comeaux, E. (2007). The student (less) athlete: Identifying the unidentified college student. *Journal for the Study of Sports and Athletes in Education, 1*(1), 37–44.

Cooky, C., and McDonald, M. G. (2005). "If you let me play": Young girls' insider-other narratives in sport. *Sociology of Sport Journal, 22*(2), 158–177.

Cooky, C., Messner, M. A., and Hextrum, R. H. (2013). Women play sport, but not on TV: A longitudinal study of televised news media. *Communication & Sport, 1*(3), 203–230.

Cooper J. N. (2012). Personal troubles and public issues: A sociological imagination of Black athletes' experiences at predominately white institutions in the United States. *Sociology Mind*, *2*(3), 261–271.

Côté, J., Fraser-Thomas, J., and Jones, E. (2005). Play, practice, and athlete development. In D. Farrow, J. Baker, and C. MacMahon (Eds.), *Developing sport expertise: Researchers and coaches put theory into practice* (pp. 17–28). London: Routledge.

Crehan, K. (2016). *Gramsci's common sense: Inequality and its narratives*. Durham, NC: Duke University Press.

Crenshaw, K. (1988). Race, reform, and retrenchment: Transformation and legitimation in antidiscrimination law. *Harvard Law Review*, *101*(7), 1331–1387.

Crenshaw, K. (1991). Mapping the margins: Intersectionality, identity politics, and violence against women of color. *Stanford Law Review*, *43*(6), 1241–1300.

Crenshaw, K. (1992). Race, gender, and sexual harassment. *Southern California Law Review*, *65*(3), 1467–1476.

Creswell, J. W. (2013). *Qualitative inquiry and research design: Choosing among five approaches* (3rd ed.). Thousand Oaks, CA: Sage.

Cummings, M. (2019, July 30). Exhibit at Sterling Library explores history of coeducation at Yale. *Yale News*. https://news.yale.edu/2019/07/30/exhibit-sterling-library-explores-history-coeducation-yale.

Curry, T. J., and Jiobu, R. M. (1984). *Sports: A social perspective*. Englewood Cliffs, NJ: Prentice Hall.

Daly, M., and Bengali, L. (2014). *Is it still worth going to college?* San Francisco: Federal Reserve Bank.

Davenport, C. B. (1911). *Heredity in relation to eugenics*. New York: Henry Holt.

Davies, S., and Guppy, N. (1997). Fields of study, college selectivity, and student inequalities in higher education. *Social Forces*, *75*(4), 1417–1438.

Davis, A. (1981). Reflections on the Black woman's role in the community of slaves. *Black Scholar*, *12*(6), 2–15.

DeFrantz, A. L., and Young, J. (2017). *My Olympic life: A memoir*. New York: Klipspringer Press.

DeLuca, J. R. (2013). Submersed in social segregation: The (re)production of social capital through swim club membership. *Journal of Sport and Social Issues*, *37*(4), 340–363.

DeLuca, J. R., and Andrews, D. L. (2016). Exercising privilege: The cyclical reproduction of capital through swim club membership. *Sociological Inquiry*, *86*(3), 301–323.

Demerath, P. (2009). *Producing success: The culture of personal advancement in an American high school*. Chicago: University of Chicago Press.

Dirlam, Z. (2011, June 1). Scandal at Ohio State (part 1 of 5): The tattooed five and Tressel's cover up. *Bleacher Report*. https://bleacherreport.com/articles/719411-scandal-at-ohio-state-part-1-of-5-the-tattooed-five-tressels-cover-up.

Dixon-Román, E. J. (2017). *Inheriting possibility: Social reproduction and quantification in education*. Minneapolis: University of Minnesota Press.

Donnor, J. K. (2011). Moving beyond *Brown*: Race and education after *Parents v. Seattle School District No. 1*. *Teachers College Record*, *113*(4), 735–754.

Du Bois, W.E.B. (1935). *Black reconstruction: An essay toward a history of the part which Black folk played in the attempt to reconstruct democracy in America, 1860–1880*. London: Forgotten Books.

Duda, J. L., and White, S. A. (1992). Goal orientations and beliefs about the causes of sport success among elite skiers. *Sport Psychologist*, *6*(4), 334–343.

Dumas, M. J. (2011). A cultural political economy of school desegregation in Seattle. *Teachers College Record, 113*(4), 703–734.

Dunkle, M. (1974). Equal opportunity for women in sports. In B. Hoepner (Ed.), *Women's athletics: Coping with controversy* (pp. 8–18). Washington, DC: AAHPER.

Durand-Bush, N., and Salmela, J. H. (2002). The development and maintenance of expert athletic performance: Perceptions of world and Olympic champions. *Journal of Applied Sport Psychology, 14*(3), 154–171.

Dworkin, S., and Wachs, F. L. (2009). *Body panic: Gender, health, and the selling of fitness*. New York: New York University Press.

Dyer, R. (1993). *The matter of images: Essays on representations*. New York: Routledge.

Eckstein, R. (2017). *How college athletics are hurting girls' sports: The pay-to-play pipeline*. Lanham, MD: Rowman & Littlefield.

Edwards, H. (1979). Sport within the veil: The triumphs, tragedies and challenges of Afro-American involvement. *Annals of the American Academy of Political and Social Science, 445*(1), 116–127.

Edwards, H. (2000). The crisis of the Black athlete on the eve of the 21st century. *Society, 37*(1), 9–13.

Eitzen, D. S. (2016). *Fair and foul: Beyond the myths and paradoxes of sport* (5th ed.). Lanham, MD: Rowman & Littlefield.

Espenshade, T. J., and Radford, A. W. (2009). *No longer separate, not yet equal: Race and class in elite college admission and campus life*. Princeton, NJ: Princeton University Press.

Evening Star. (1906, November 28). Hard blow at Harvard sports. *Evening Star*, p. 9.

Fabricant, M., and Fine, M. (2015). *Changing politics of education: Privatization and the dispossessed lives left behind*. New York: Routledge.

Farrey, T., and Schreiber, P. (2017, March 17). The gentrification of college hoops. *The Undefeated*. https://theundefeated.com/features/gentrification-of-ncaa-division-1 -college-basketball/.

Ferber, A. (2007). The construction of Black masculinity: White supremacy now and then. *Journal of Sport and Social Issues, 31*(1), 11–24.

Fields, B. (2001). Whiteness, racism, and identity. *International Labor and Working-Class History, 60*(1), 48–56.

Fields, S. (2008). Title IX and African-American female athletes. In M. Lomax and K. Shropshire (Eds.), *Sports and the racial divide: African-American and Latino experience in an era of change* (pp. 126–145). Jackson: University of Mississippi Press.

Finch, R. (1998). *The story of New York State canals*. New York: New York State Engineer and Surveyor.

Flowers, R. D. (2009). Institutionalized hypocrisy: The myth of intercollegiate athletics. *American Educational History Journal, 36*(2), 343–360.

Franklin, D. R., and Zwickel, S. W. (2018, October 18). In admissions, Harvard favors those who fund it, internal emails show. *Harvard Crimson*. https://www .thecrimson.com/article/2018/10/18/day-three-harvard-admissions-trial/.

Furrow, A. D. (2013). *Instilling a rugged manhood: The popular press coverage of college athletics and the National Collegiate Athletic Association, 1896–1916*. Doctoral dissertation, Scripps College of Communication of Ohio University.

Gane, N. (2014). Sociology and neoliberalism: A missing history. *Sociology, 48*(6), 1092–1106.

Gems, G. (2000). *For pride, profit, and patriarchy: Football and the incorporation of American cultural values.* Lanham, MD: Scarecrow Press.

Gilbert, W. D., Gilbert, J. N., and Trudel, P. (2001). Coaching strategies for youth sports: Part 1: Athlete behavior and athlete performance. *Journal of Physical Education, Recreation & Dance, 72*(4), 29–33.

Gillborn, D. (2005). Education policy as an act of white supremacy: Whiteness, critical race theory and education reform. *Journal of Education Policy, 20*(4), 485–505.

Giroux, H. A. (1981). *Ideology, culture, and the process of schooling.* Philadelphia: Temple University Press.

Giroux, H. A. (2014). *Neoliberalism's war on higher education.* New York: Haymarket Books.

Goldstein, D., and Healy, J. (2019, March 13). Inside the pricey, totally legal world of college consultants. *New York Times.*

Goldstein, S. (2018, June 5). Nine out of 10 new jobs are going to those with a college degree. *Market Watch.* https://www.marketwatch.com/story/nine-out-of-10-new -jobs-are-going-to-those-with-a-college-degree-2018-06-04.

Gould, D., Dieffenbach, K., and Moffett, A. (2002). Psychological characteristics and their development in Olympic champions. *Journal of Applied Sport Psychology, 14*(3), 172–204.

Gouthro, P. (2014). Stories of learning across the lifespan: Life-history and biographical research in adult education. *Journal of Adult and Continuing Education, 21*(1), 87–103.

Gramsci, A. (1971). *Selections from prison notebooks* (Q. Hoare and G. Smith, Eds. and Trans.). New York: International.

Grant, C. B., Roberts, D., and Rubinowitz, L. S. (2006). Race and gender in the *Law Review. Northwestern University Law Review, 100*(1), 27–70.

Green, T. L., and Gooden, M. A. (2016). The shaping of policy: Exploring the context, contradictions, and contours of privilege in *Milliken v. Bradley*, over 40 years later. *Teachers College Record, 118*(3), 1–30.

Grenardo, D. A. (2016). The continued exploitation of the college athlete: Confessions of former college athlete turned law professor. *Oregon Law Review, 95*, 223–286.

Grove, R. (2011, December 21). Top 10 lessons from Ohio State's tattoo-gate. *Forbes.* https://www.forbes.com/sites/sportsmoney/2011/12/21/top-10-lessons-from-ohio -states-tattoo-gate/#509e199c390d.

Guinier, L. (2003). Social change and democratic values: Reconceptualizing affirmative action policy. *Western Journal of Black Studies, 27*(1), 45–50.

Guinier, L. (2015). *The tyranny of the meritocracy: Democratizing higher education in America.* Boston: Beacon.

Gusa, D. L. (2010). White institutional presence: The impact of whiteness on campus climate. *Harvard Educational Review, 80*(4), 464–490.

Guttman, A. (1978). *From ritual to record: The nature of modern sports.* New York: Columbia University Press.

Hackman, R. (2015, August 4). Swimming while Black: The legacy of segregated public pools lives on. *Guardian.* https://www.theguardian.com/world/2015/aug /04/black-children-swimming-drownings-segregation.

Halberstam, D. (1985). *The amateurs: The story of four young men and their quest for an Olympic gold medal.* New York: Ballantine Books.

Halikias, D., and Reeves, R. V. (2017, July 11). *Ladders, labs, or laggards? Which public universities contribute most.* Washington, DC: Brookings Institute.

Harris, C. I. (1993). Whiteness as property. *Harvard Law Review, 106*(8), 1707–1791.

Harris, O. (1994). Race, sport, and social support. *Sociology of Sport Journal, 11*(1), 40–50.

Harrison, A. K. (2013). Black skiing, everyday racism, and the racial spatiality of whiteness. *Journal of Sport and Social Issues, 37*(4), 315–339.

Harrison, C. K. (2000, March/April). Black athletes at the millennium. *Society*, 35–39.

Harvard Crimson. (2014). Harvard-Yale Regatta—150 years of tradition. *Harvard Crimson*. https://www.gocrimson.com/sports/mcrew-hw/tradition/harvard-yale-regatta.

Harvey, D. (2005). *A brief history of neoliberalism*. New York: Oxford University Press.

Hattery, A. (2012). They play like girls: Gender and race (in)equity in NCAA sports. *Wake Forest Journal of Law & Policy, 2*(1), 247–265.

Haveman, R., and Smeeding, T. (2006). The role of higher education in social mobility. *Future of Children, 16*(2), 125–150.

Hawkins, B. (2013). *The new plantation: Black athletes, college sports, and predominately white institutions*. New York: Palgrave-MacMillan.

Haycock, K. (2004). The elephant in the living room. *Brookings Papers on Education Policy, 2004*(1), 229–247.

Heald, B. (2001). *Lake Winnipesaukee*. Chicago: Arcadia.

Hegewisch, A., Phil, M., and Hartmann, H. (2019). *The gender wage gap: 2018 earnings differences by race and ethnicity*. Institute for Women's Policy Research. https://iwpr.org/publications/gender-wage-gap-2018/.

Heilig, J., and Darling-Hammond, L. (2008). Accountability Texas-style: The progress and learning of urban minority students in a high-stakes testing environment. *Educational Evaluation and Policy Analysis, 30*(2), 75–110.

Hendrickson, R. M. (2001). Rethinking affirmative action: Redefining compelling state interest and merit in admission. *Peabody Journal of Education, 76*(1), 117–135.

Hextrum, K. (2014). A feminist perspective on the school-to-labor pipeline. *Berkeley Review of Education, 5*(1), 89–112.

Hextrum, K. (2017a). *Racing to class: School, sport, and inequality*. Doctoral dissertation, University of California, Berkeley.

Hextrum, K. (2017b). Segregated bodies: Gender reproduction within college sport. In A. Milner and J. Braddock II (Eds.), *Women in sport: Breaking barriers, facing obstacles, Vol. 2* (pp. 169–185). Santa Barbara, CA: Praeger.

Hextrum, K. (2018). The hidden curriculum of college athlete recruitment. *Harvard Educational Review, 88*(3), 355–377.

Hextrum, K. (2019a). Reproducing sports stars: How students become elite athletes. *Teachers College Record, 121*(4), 1–38.

Hextrum, K. (2019b). Operation Varsity Blues: Disguising the legal capital exchanges and white property interests in athletic admissions. *Higher Education Politics & Economics, 5*(1), 15–32.

Hextrum, K. (2020a). Amateurism revisited: How US college athletic recruitment favors middle class athletes. *Sport, Education, and Society, 25*(1), 111–123.

Hextrum, K. (2020b). Individualizing conflict: How ideology masks college athletes' educational compromises. *Studies in Higher Education, 45*(4), 755–767.

Hextrum, K. (2020c). Bigger, faster, stronger: How racist and sexist ideologies persist in college sports. *Gender and Education, 32*(8), 1053–1071.

Hextrum, K. (2020d). Segregation, innocence, and protection: The institutional conditions that maintain whiteness in college sports. *Journal of Diversity in Higher Education, 13*(4), 384–395.

Hirsch, A. R. (1983). *Making the second ghetto: Race and housing in Chicago 1940–1960.* New York: Oxford University Press.

Hoff, D. L., and Mitchell, S. N. (2006). Pay-to-play: Fair or foul? *Phi Delta Kappan, 88*(3), 230–234.

Hood-Williams, J. (1995). Sexing the athletes. *Sociology of Sport Journal, 12*(1), 290–305.

hooks, b. (1984). *Feminist theory: From margin to center.* Chicago: Pluto Press.

Horn, L., and Nunez, A. (2000). *Mapping the road to college: First-generation students' math track, planning strategies, and context of support* (NCES 2000-153). Washington, DC: National Center for Education Statistics.

Hoynes, H., Miller, D., and Schaller, J. (2012). Who suffers during recessions? *Journal of Economic Perspectives, 26*(3), 27–48.

Ingrassia, B. M. (2012). *The rise of the gridiron university: Higher education's uneasy alliance with big-time football.* Lawrence: University Press of Kansas.

International Olympic Committee. (2019). Key dates in the history of women in the Olympic movement. https://www.olympic.org/ioc/what%20we%20do/promote%20olympism/women%20in%20sport/background/key%20dates.

Ishitani, T. T. (2003). A longitudinal approach to assessing attrition behavior among first generation students: Time-varying effects of pre-college characteristics. *Research in Higher Education, 44*(4), 433–449.

Jackson, J., and Kurlaender, M. (2014). College readiness and college completion at broad access four-year institutions. *American Behavioral Scientist, 58*(8), 947–971.

Jacobs, M. (2019, September 15). Will a California bill give players a slice of college sports' $14bn pie? *Guardian.* https://www.theguardian.com/sport/2019/sep/15/sb-206-college-sports.

James, J. (1996). *Resisting state violence: Radicalism, gender, and race in U.S. culture.* Minneapolis: University of Minnesota Press.

Jaschik, S. (2018, August 6). How Harvard can legally favor alumni children and athletes. *Inside Higher Ed.* https://www.insidehighered.com/admissions/article/2018/08/06/education-department-once-investigated-harvards-preferences-alumni.

Jayakumar, U. M., and Comeaux, E. (2016). The cultural cover-up of college athletics: How organizational culture perpetuates an unrealistic and idealized balancing act. *Journal of Higher Education, 87*(4), 488–515.

Johnson, H. B. (2014). *The American dream and the power of wealth: Choosing schools and inheriting inequality in the land of opportunity.* New York: Routledge.

Jones, C. (2020, October 24). Three charts show a K-shaped recovery. *Forbes.* https://www.forbes.com/sites/chuckjones/2020/10/24/three-charts-show-a-k-shaped-recovery/?sh=2d743631305f.

Jones, S. K. (2019, March 29). Final Four a 'big-ticket' for insurers covering NCAA tournament. *Insurance Journal.* https://www.insurancejournal.com/news/national/2019/03/29/522024.htm.

Journal of Blacks in Higher Education. (2014). Key events in Black higher education: JBHE chronology of major landmarks in progress of African-Americans in higher education. *Journal of Blacks in Higher Education.* https://www.jbhe.com/chronology/.

Jury, M., Smeding, A., Stephens, N. M., Nelson, J. E., Aelenei, C., and Darnon, C. (2017). The experience of low-SES students in higher education: Psychological barriers to success and interventions to reduce social-class inequality. *Journal of Social Issues, 73*(1), 23–41.

Kaliss, G. (2013). *Men's college athletics and the politics of racial equality: Five pioneer stories of Black manliness, white citizenship, and American democracy.* Philadelphia: Temple University Press.

Katznelson, I. (2005). *When affirmative action was white: An untold history of racial inequality in twentieth-century America.* New York: Norton.

Kaufman, P. (2005). Middle-class social reproduction: The activation and negotiation of structural advantages. *Sociological Forum, 20*(2), 245–270.

Kenyon, E. A. (2017). Lived experience and the ideologies of preservice social studies teachers. *Teaching and Teacher Education, 61*(1), 94–103.

Keuk Ser, K. K. (2016, August 17). See 120 years of struggle for gender equality at the Olympics. Public Radio International. https://www.pri.org/stories/2016-08-17/see -120-years-struggle-gender-equality-olympics.

Khan, S. R. (2012). *Privilege: The making of an adolescent elite at St. Paul's School.* Princeton, NJ: Princeton University Press.

Kirby, K. M. (1996). *Indifferent boundaries: Spatial concepts of human subjectivity.* New York: Guilford.

Kirshner, A. (2018, August 30). All the things the NCAA considers unsportsmanlike conduct in college football. *SBNation.* https://www.sbnation.com/college-football /2018/8/30/17472846/ncaa-celebration-rules-unsportsmanlike-conduct.

Kleeman, G., and Ikstrums, I. (2011). *Implement inspector's handbook.* Indianapolis: USA Track & Field.

Knoester, M., and Au, W. (2017). Standardized testing and school segregation: Like tinder for fire? *Race Ethnicity and Education, 20*(1), 1–14.

Kunesh, C. E., and Noltemeyer, A. (2019). Understanding disciplinary disproportion-ality: Stereotypes shape pre-service teachers' beliefs about Black boys' behavior. *Urban Education, 54*(4), 471–498.

Kurashige, S. (2008). *The shifting grounds of race: Black and Japanese Americans in the making of multiethnic Los Angeles.* Princeton, NJ: Princeton University Press.

Ladson-Billings, G. (1994). *The dreamkeepers: Successful teachers of African-American children.* San Francisco: Jossey-Bass.

Ladson-Billings, G. (2003). *Critical race theory perspectives on the social studies: The profession, policies, and curriculum.* Greenwich, CT: Information Age.

Lansbury, J. H. (2001). "The Tuskegee Flash" and "the Slender Harlem Stroker": Black women athletes on the margin. *Journal of Sport History, 28*(2), 233–252.

Lapchick, R. (2018). *The 2017 college sport racial and gender report card: College sport.* Orlando: University of Central Florida, Institute for Diversity and Ethics in Sport. http://nebula.wsimg.com/5665825afd75728dc0c45b52ae6c412d?AccessKeyId =DAC3A56D8FB782449D2A&disposition=0&alloworigin=1.

Lareau, A. (2011). *Unequal childhoods: Class, race, & family life* (2nd ed.). Berkeley: University of California Press.

Lareau, A. (2015). Cultural knowledge and social inequality. *American Sociological Association, 80*(1), 1–27.

Larned, C. W. (1909). Athletics from a historical and educational standpoint. *American Physical Education Review, 14*(1), 1–9.

Lassiter, M. D. (2012). Schools and housing in metropolitan history: An introduction. *Journal of Urban History, 38*(2), 195–204.

Lee, J., Mcdonald, D., & Wright, J. (2009). Young men's physical activity choices: The impact of capital, masculinities, and location. *Journal of Sport and Social Issues, 33*(1), 59–77.

Lensmire, T. (2014). White men's racial others. *Teachers College Record, 116*(3), 1–32.

Leonard, D. J. (2017). *Playing while white: Privilege and power on and off the field.* Seattle: University of Washington Press.

Leonardo, Z. (2004). The color of supremacy: Beyond the discourse of "white privilege." *Educational Philosophy and Theory, 36*(2), 137–152.

Leonardo, Z. (2009). *Race, whiteness, and education.* New York: Routledge.

Llewellyn, M., and Gleaves, J. (2014). A universal dilemma: The British sporting life and the complex, contested, and contradictory state of amateurism. *Journal of Sport History, 41*(1), 95–116.

Long, M. C. (2015). Is there a "workable" race-neutral alternative to affirmative action in college admissions? *Journal of Policy Analysis and Management, 34*(1), 162–183.

Lorber, J. (1994). *Paradoxes of gender.* New Haven, CT: Yale University Press.

Lumpkin, A. (2013). Critical events: Historical overview of minorities (men and women) in college sports. In D. Brooks and R. Althouse (Eds.), *Racism in college athletics* (pp. 31–62). Morgantown, WV: Fitness Information Technology.

Maatz, L., and Graves, F. (2012). *Title IX at 40: Working to ensure gender equity in education.* Washington, DC: National Coalition for Women and Girls in Education.

Marin Waves. (2016). Club registration. https://www.marinwavestrack.com/Club_Registration.html.

Martin, C. (2010). *Benching Jim Crow: The rise and fall of the color line in southern college sports 1890–1980.* Urbana: University of Illinois Press.

Martin, M. (2017, February 5). Football played key role in Rhodes scholar's path to success. *All Things Considered.* https://www.npr.org/2017/02/05/513591468/football-played-key-role-in-rhodes-scholars-path-to-success.

Massey, D. S., and Denton, N. A. (1998). *American apartheid: Segregation and the making of the underclass.* Cambridge, MA: Harvard University Press.

Mathewson, A. D. (1995). Black women, gender equity and the function at the junction. *Marquette Sports Law Journal, 6*(1), 239–266.

McClintock, A. (1995). *Imperial leather: Race, gender, and sexuality in the colonial contest.* New York: Routledge.

McDonough, P. M. (1997). *Choosing college: How social class and schools structure opportunity.* Albany: State University of New York Press.

McLaren, P. (2014). *Life in schools: An introduction to critical pedagogy in the foundations of education* (6th ed.). Boston: Pearson.

Mendenhall, T. C. (1993). The first boat race. *Yale Alumni Magazine.* http://archives.yalealumnimagazine.com/issues/93_03/regatta.html.

Messner, M. (1992). *Power at play: Sports and the problem of masculinity.* Boston: Beacon.

Messner, M. (2002). *Taking the field: Women, men and sports.* Minneapolis: University of Minnesota Press.

Messner, M. (2004). On patriarchs and losers: Rethinking men's interests. *Berkeley Journal of Sociology, 48*(1), 74–88.

Messner, M. (2009). *All for the kids: Gender, families, and youth sports.* Berkeley: University of California Press.

Miller, P. B. (1998). The anatomy of scientific racism: Racialist responses to Black athletic achievement. *Journal of Sport History, 25*(1), 119–151.

Mills, C. W. (1997). *The racial contract.* Ithaca, NY: Cornell University Press.

Mills, C. W. (2003). *From class to race: Essays in white Marxism and Black radicalism.* Lanham, MD: Rowman & Littlefield.

Milner, A. N., and Braddock, J. H., II. (2016). *Sex segregation in sports: Why separate is not equal.* Santa Barbara, CA: ABC-CLIO.

Miracle, A., and Rees, R. (1994). *Lessons from the locker room: The myth of school sports.* Amherst, MA: Prometheus.

Moody, J. (2019, February 15). A guide to the changing number of U.S. universities. *U.S. News and World Report.* https://www.usnews.com/education/best-colleges/articles/2019-02-15/how-many-universities-are-in-the-us-and-why-that-number-is-changing.

Moran, M. (1999). Standards and assessments: The new measure of adequacy in school finance litigation. *Journal of Education Finance, 25*(1), 33–80.

Morey, M. (2014, May 14). Philanthropists and the White House: Who's the boss? *Atlantic.* https://www.theatlantic.com/business/archive/2014/05/philanthropists-and-the-white-house/370805/.

Morris, E. (2005). "Tuck in that shirt!" Race, class, gender, and discipline in an urban school. *Sociological Perspectives, 48*(1), 25–48.

Mowatt, R. A. (2009). Notes from a leisure son: Expanding an understanding of whiteness in leisure. *Journal of Leisure Research, 41*(4), 511–528.

Musto, M., Cooky, C., and Messner, M. A. (2017). "From fizzle to sizzle!" Televised sports news and the production of gender-bland sexism. *Gender & Society, 31*(5), 573–596.

Naples, N. (2003). *Feminism and method: Ethnography, discourse analysis, and activist research.* New York: Routledge.

National Center for Education Statistics (NCES). (2018). *Total fall enrollment in degree-granting postsecondary institutions, by attendance, status, sex, and age: Selected years, 1970 through 2027.* Washington, DC: NCES. https://nces.ed.gov/programs/digest/d17/tables/dt17_303.40.asp.

National Federation of State High School Associations (NFHS). (2019). *2017–2018 high school athletics participation survey results.* Indianapolis: NFHS.

National Football Foundation and College Hall of Fame. (2019, June 11). *2018–2019 report: Amazing college football popularity highlighted by impressive ratings and attendance data.* Washington, DC: National Football Foundation.

NCAA. (2011). The NCAA inclusion of transgender athletes. http://www.ncaa.org/sites/default/files/Transgender_Handbook_2011_Final.pdf.

NCAA. (2015). Who we are. http://www.ncaa.org/about/who-we-are.

NCAA. (2016). Student-athletes. http://www.ncaa.org/student-athletes.

NCAA. (2017). *Division I manual, 2017–2018.* Indianapolis: NCAA.

NCAA. (2018). NCAA recruiting facts: College sports create a pathway to opportunity for student-athletes. Indianapolis: NCAA.

NCAA. (2019). Education & research: Division I graduation success rates. http://fs.ncaa.org/Docs/newmedia/public/rates/index.html.

NCAA. (n.d.). NCAA emerging sports for women process guide. http://www.ncaa.org/about/resources/inclusion/ncaa-emerging-sports-women-process- guide.

NCAA v. Board of Regents of the University of Oklahoma, et al. 468 U.S. 85 (1984).

Needham, H. B. (1905, June). The college athlete: How commercialism is making him a professional Part I—Recruiting and subsidizing. *McClure's Magazine, 25*(2), 1–14.

Nelson, L. (2008). Racialized landscapes: Whiteness and the struggle over farmworker housing in Woodburn, Oregon. *Cultural Geographies, 15*(1), 41–62.

New York Daily Tribune. (1906, December 23). Pure sport is the aim—What the Intercollegiate Athletic Association has done. *New York Daily Tribune*, p. 8.

New York Herald. (1852, August 9). Regattas. *New York Herald*, p. 2.

Noguera, P. (2003). Schools, prisons, and the social implications of punishment: Rethinking disciplinary practices. *Theory into Practice, 42*(4), 341–350.

Norris, M. (2004, August 10). Abdullah: A first among U.S. Olympic rowers. NPR. https://www.npr.org/templates/story/story.php?storyId=3844701.

Oakes, J. (2005). *Keeping track: How schools structure inequality.* New Haven, CT: Yale University Press.

Office of Civil Rights. (1979, December 11). A policy interpretation: Title IX and Intercollegiate Athletics. *Federal Register, 44*(239). https://www2.ed.gov/about /offices/list/ocr/docs/t9interp.html.

Orfield, G., and Frankenberg, E. (2013). *Educational delusions? Why choice can deepen inequality and how to make schools fair.* Berkeley: University of California Press.

Oriard, M. (2001). *King football: Sport & spectacle in the golden age of radio & newsreels, movies and magazines, the weekly & the daily press.* Chapel Hill: University of North Carolina Press.

Osborne, R. (2016, November 12). From LA slums to TCU football team, he's now a Rhodes scholar finalist. *Star-Telegram*. http://www.star-telegram.com/news/local /community/fort-worth/article114334573.html.

Osburn, S. (2019, October 29). Board of governors starts process to enhance name, image and likeness opportunities. http://www.ncaa.org/about/resources/media -center/news/board-governors-starts-process-enhance-name-image-and-likeness -opportunities.

Ostojic, S. M., Mazic, S., and Dikic, N. (2006). Profiling in basketball: Physical and physiological characteristics of elite players. *Journal of Strength and Conditioning Research, 20*(4), 740–744.

Otterbein, J. (2014, March 27). College sports history: It starts with Yale-Harvard Regatta. *Hartford Courant*. https://www.courant.com/courant-250/moments-in -history/hc-250th-ct-college-history-0313-20140227-story.html.

Pascarella, E. T., Pierson, C. T., Wolniak, G. C., and Terenzini, P. T. (2004). First-generation college students: Additional evidence on college experiences and outcomes. *Journal of Higher Education, 75*(3), 249–284.

Patten, D. (2019, April 9). NCAA title game viewership falls from last CBS championship of 2017-update. *Deadline*. https://deadline.com/2019/04/ncaa-tournament -championship-ratings-virginia-texas-tech-cbs-the-voice-1202591765/.

Patterson, B. F., and Mattern, K. D. (2011). *Validity of the SAT for predicting first-year grades: 2008 SAT validity sample.* New York: College Board.

Patterson, B. F., and Mattern, K. D. (2012). *Validity of the SAT for predicting first-year grades: 2009 SAT validity sample.* New York: College Board.

Patterson, B. F., and Mattern, K. D. (2013). *Validity of the SAT for predicting first-year grades: 2010 SAT validity sample.* New York: College Board.

Patterson, B. F., Mattern, K. D., and Kobrin, J. L. (2009). *Validity of the SAT for predicting first-year grades: 2007 SAT validity sample.* New York: College Board.

Paxson, F. L. (1917). The rise of sport. *Mississippi Valley Historical Review, 4*, 143–168.

Perry, A., Rothwell, J., and Harshbarger, D. (2018, November). *The devaluation of assets in Black neighborhoods: The case of residential property*. Washington, DC: Metropolitan Policy Program, Brookings Institution.

Pew Research Center. (2014, February 11). *The rising cost of not going to college*. Washington, DC: Pew Research Center. http://www.pewsocialtrends.org/2014/02/11/the-rising-cost-of-not-going-to-college/.

Pickett, M., Dawkins, M., and Braddock, J. (2012). Race and gender equity in sports: Have white and African-American females benefited equally from Title IX? *American Behavioral Scientist, 56*(1), 1581–1603.

Pieper, L. (2016). *Sex testing: Gender policing in women's sports*. Chicago: University of Illinois Press.

Piketty, T. (2014). *Capital in the twenty-first century*. Cambridge, MA: Harvard University Press.

Pope, S. W. (1996). Amateurism and American sports culture: The invention of an athletic tradition in the United States, 1870–1900. *International Journal of the History of Sport, 13*(3), 290–309.

Pope, S. W. (1997). *Patriotic games: Sporting traditions in the American imagination 1876–1926*. New York: Oxford University Press.

Ravitch, S. M., and Carl, N. M. (2016). *Qualitative research: Bridging the conceptual, theoretical, and methodological*. Thousand Oaks, CA: Sage.

Ris, E. W. (2017). The education of Andrew Carnegie: Strategic philanthropy in American higher education, 1880–1919. *Journal of Higher Education, 88*(3), 401–429.

Rittenberg, A. (2016, December 30). The remarkable story of TCU's Rhodes Scholar, Cailyn Moore. *ABC News*. http://abcnews.go.com/Sports/remarkable-story-tcus-rhodes-scholar-caylin-moore/story?id=44467921.

Rivera, L. A. (2016). *Pedigree: How elite students get elite jobs*. Princeton, NJ: Princeton University Press.

Roediger, D. (2017). *Class, race and Marxism*. Brooklyn, NY: Verso.

Roosevelt, T. (1890). "Professionalism" in sports. *North American Review, 151*(405), 187–191.

Roscigno, V. J. (1998). Race and the reproduction of educational disadvantage. *Social Forces, 76*(3), 1033–1061.

Rosen, E. S., O'Connell, J. D., Kearney, K. A., and Wright, L. A. (2019a). *United States of America v. Gordon Ernst et al.* Federal Indictment Criminal Number 19-CR-10081. https://www.justice.gov/file/1142881/download.

Rosen, E. S., O'Connell, J. D., Kearney, K. A., and Wright, L. A. (2019b). *United States v. David Sidoo et al.* Case 19-10080-NMG. https://www.justice.gov/usao-ma/page/file/1152906/download.

Rothstein, R. (2017). *The color of law: A forgotten history of how our government segregated America*. New York: Liveright.

Rust, J. (2013). Examining American eugenics and Utah's sterilization laws. *Utah Historical Review, 3*, 253–268.

Ryan, C. L., and Bauman, K. (2016). *Educational attainment in the United States: 2015*. Washington, DC: U.S. Census Bureau.

Sabo, D., and Veliz, P. (2008). *Go out and play: Youth sports in America*. East Meadow, NY: Women's Sports Foundation.

Sack, A., and Staurowsky, E. (1998). *College athletes for hire: The evolution and legacy of the NCAA's amateur myth*. Westport, CT: Praeger.

Sadker, M., and Sadker, D. (1994). *Failing at fairness*. New York: Touchstone.

Said, E. (1978). *Orientalism*. New York: Vintage.

Schilt, K. (2010). *Just one of the guys? Transgender men and the persistence of gender inequality*. Chicago: University of Chicago Press.

Shabazz, R. (2015). *Spatializing Blackness: Architectures of confinement and Black masculinity in Chicago*. Urbana: University of Illinois Press.

Shamash, R. (2018). (Re)production of the contemporary elite through higher education: A review of critical scholarship. *Berkeley Review of Education, 8*(1), 5–21.

Sherman, R. (2016, April 12). The NCAA's new March Madness TV deal will make them a billion dollars a year. *SBNation*. https://www.sbnation.com/college -basketball/2016/4/12/11415764/ncaa-tournament-tv-broadcast-rights-money -payout-cbs-turner.

Shilling, C. (1991). Educating the body: Physical capital and the production of social inequalities. *Sociology, 25*(4), 653–672.

Shulman, J., and Bowen, W. (2001). *The game of life: College sports and educational values*. Princeton, NJ: Princeton University Press.

Singer, J., and May, R. (2010). The career trajectory of a Black male high school basketball player: A social reproduction perspective. *International Review for the Sociology of Sport, 46*(3), 299–314.

Skiba, R. (2012). "As nature has formed them": The history and current status of racial difference research. *Teachers College Record, 111*(1), 1–49.

Smith, D. (2005). *Institutional ethnography: A sociology for people*. Lanham, MD: Altamira Press.

Smith, J. (2012). Reflections on using life-history to investigate women teachers' aspirations and career decisions. *Qualitative Research, 12*(4), 486–503.

Smith, J. M. (2009). "It's not really my country": Lew Alcindor and the revolt of the Black athlete. *Journal of Sport History, 36*(2), 223–244.

Smith, L. (2019). *Affidavit in support of criminal complaint*. Boston: U.S. District Court of Massachusetts. https://www.justice.gov/file/1142876/download.

Smith, R. (1988). *Sports and freedom: The rise of big-time college athletics*. New York: Oxford University Press.

Smith, R. (2011). *Pay for play: A history of big-time college athletic reform*. Urbana: University of Illinois Press.

Smyth, J., Mooney, A. and Casey, M. (2014). Where has class gone? The pervasiveness of class in girls' physical activity in a rural town. *Sport, Education and Society, 19*(1), 1–18.

Southall, R. M., and Staurowsky, E. J. (2013). Cheering on the collegiate model: Creating, disseminating, and imbedding the NCAA's redefinition of amateurism. *Journal of Sport and Social Issues, 37*(4), 403–429.

Spece Jr, R. G., and Yokum, D. (2015). Scrutinizing strict scrutiny. *Vermont Law Review, 40*(2), 285–351.

Sperber, M. (2000). *Beer and circus: How big-time college sports has crippled undergraduate education*. New York: Macmillan.

Stanley, G. K. (1996). *The rise and fall of the sportswoman*. New York: Peter Lang.

Stefansen, K., Smette, I., and Strandbu, A. (2018). Understanding the increase in parents' involvement in organized youth sports. *Sport, Education and Society, 23*(2), 162–172.

Stephens, N. M., Hamedani, M. G., and Destin, M. (2014). Closing the social-class achievement gap: A difference-education intervention improves first-generation students' academic performance and all students' college transition. *Psychological Science, 25*(4), 943–953.

Stevens, M. (2009). *Creating a class: College admissions and the education of elites.* Cambridge, MA: Harvard University Press.

Stirrup, J., Duncombe, R., and Sandford, R. (2015). "Intensive mothering" in the early years: The cultivation and consolidation of (physical) capital. *Sport, Education and Society, 20*(1), 89–106.

Stuber, J. M., Klugman, J., and Daniel, C. (2011). Gender, social class, and exclusion: Collegiate peer cultures and social reproduction. *Sociological Perspectives, 54*(3), 431–451.

Suggs, W. (2005). *A place on the team: The triumph and tragedy of Title IX.* Princeton, NJ: Princeton University Press.

Sullivan, C. F. (2011). Gender verification and gender policies in elite sport: Eligibility and "fair play." *Journal of Sport and Social Issues, 35*(4), 400–419.

Sun, The (1896, April 19). Stanford's girls win—They beat Berkeley's girls at basketball. *The Sun*, p. 5.

Sun, The (1903, November 8). Roble over colored player—Charges by Dartmouth and denials by Princeton regarding Bullock. *The Sun*, p. 8.

Sut, J. (1989). Cultural studies and the sport/media complex. In L. Werner (Ed.), *Media, sports, and society* (pp. 70–97). Thousand Oaks, CA: Sage.

Swanson, R. A. (2011). "I never was a champion at anything": Theodore Roosevelt's complex and contradictory record as America's "sports president." *Journal of Sport History, 38*(3), 425–446.

Teranishi, R. T., and Parker, T. L. (2010). Social reproduction of inequality: The racial composition of feeder schools to the University of California. *Teachers College Record, 112*(6), 1575–1601.

Terenzini, P. T., Springer, L., Yaeger, P. M., Pascarella, E. T., and Nora, A. (1996). First generation college students: Characteristics, experiences, and cognitive development. *Research in Higher education, 37*(1), 1–22.

Thelin, J. (2011). *A history of American higher education* (2nd ed.). Baltimore: Johns Hopkins University Press.

Title IX of the Education Amendments of 1972, 20 U.S.C. §1681–1688.

Topeka State Journal. (1908, January 3). Gregory is stirred up—vigorously denies the story of being bribed to enter Michigan. *Topeka State Journal*, p. 12.

Travers, A. (2013). Thinking the unthinkable: Imagining an "un-American," girl-friendly, women-and trans-inclusive alternative for baseball. *Journal of Sport and Social Issues, 37*(1), 78–96.

U.S. Bureau of Labor Statistics. (2020a). Ability to work from home: Evidence from two surveys and implications for the labor market in the COVID-19 pandemic. *Monthly Labor Review.* https://www.bls.gov/opub/mlr/2020/article/ability-to-work-from-home.htm.

U.S. Bureau of Labor Statistics. (2020b). News release: The employment situation–November 2020. https://www.bls.gov/news.release/pdf/empsit.pdf.

U.S. Census Bureau. (2016). Quickfacts: Median household income (in 2014 dollars). https://www.census.gov/quickfacts/map/INC110214/00.

U.S. Department of Education. (2014). *The condition of education 2014* (NCES 2014-083). *Annual earnings of young adults.* Washington, DC: NCES.

U.S. Department of Education. (2020). Equity in athletics data analysis. https://ope.ed.gov/athletics/#/.

U.S. Equal Employment Opportunity Commission. (1964). Title VII of the Civil
 Rights Act of 1964: Definitions. SEC 2000e (Section 701). https://www.eeoc.gov
 /laws/statutes/titlevii.cfm.

USRowing. (2016). Rules of rowing. http://www.usrowing.org/docs/default-source
 /referees/2016rorfinal(web).pdf?sfvrsn=0.

USRowing. (2018). FAQ about the under-19 national team. http://www.usrowing.org
 /junior-national-team-faq/.

USRowing Juniors. (2018). HP camps junior women. http://usrowingjrs.org/usj
 /camps/hp-camp-2/junior-women/df.

Vaught, S. E. (2011). *Racism, public schooling, and the entrenchment of white supremacy:
 A critical race ethnography.* New York: State University of New York Press.

Vaught, S. E. (2017). *Compulsory: Education and the dispossession of youth in a prison
 school.* Minneapolis: University of Minnesota Press.

Washington Times. (1903, November 10). Color line drawn on the gridiron—
 Princeton charged with mistreating Bullock, Dartmouth's negro player. *Washington Times*, p. 8.

Washington Times. (1909, January 2). College athletes will meet today—Notable
 delegates attend gathering of Intercollegiate Athletic Association—Will set strict
 amateur ruling. *Washington Times*, p. 10.

Weedon, C. (1997). *Feminist practice & poststructuralist theory* (2nd ed.). Oxford: Basil
 Blackwell.

Weirs Beach. (2019). When did Native Americans inhabit Weirs Beach? *Weirs Beach,
 New Hampshire Guidebook.* http://weirsbeach.com/reasons-to-visit/history/natives/.

Weis, L., Cipollone, K., and Jenkins, H. (2014). *Class warfare: Class, race, and college
 admissions in top-tier secondary schools.* Chicago: University of Chicago Press.

Weis, L., and Fine, M. (2012). Critical bifocality and circuits of privilege: Expanding
 critical ethnographic theory and design. *Harvard Educational Review, 82*(2),
 173–201.

Weis, L., and Fine, M. (2013). A methodological response from the field to Douglas
 Foley: Critical bifocality and class cultural productions in anthropology and
 education. *Anthropology & Education Quarterly, 44*(3), 222–233.

Wessells, A. T. (2011). The ultimate team sport?: Urban waterways and youth rowing
 in Seattle. In S. Sutton and S. Kemp (Eds.), *The paradox of urban space* (pp. 53–71).
 New York: Palgrave Macmillan.

Whaples, R. (2005). Andrew Carnegie" In *Economic history encyclopedia.* http://eh.net
 /encyclopedia/carnegie-andrew/.

Wilder, C. S. (2013). *Ebony and ivy: Race, slavery, and the troubled history of America's
 universities.* New York: Bloomsbury.

Willis, P. (1977). *Learning to labor: How working class kids get working class jobs.* New
 York: Columbia University Press.

Wiltse, J. (2014). The Black-white swimming disparity in America: A deadly legacy of
 swimming pool discrimination. *Journal of Sport and Social Issues, 38*(4), 366–389.

Woelk, N. (2016, June 28). For Buffs, road to Rio runs through campions center.
 University of Colorado Athletics. https://cubuffs.com/story.aspx?filename=track
 -and-field-for-buffs-road-to-rio-runs-through-champions-center&file_date=6/28
 /2016&path=track.

Wright, B. (1997). "For the children of the infidels": American Indian education in the
 colonial colleges. In L. F. Goodchild and H. S. Wechsler (Eds.), *ASHE reader
 series: The history of higher education* (pp. 72–29). Boston: Pearson.

Wun, C. (2016). Against captivity: Black girls and school discipline policies in the afterlife of slavery. *Educational Policy, 30*(1), 171–196.

Yale Alumni Magazine. (2014, May/June). Who was the first African American student at Yale? *Yale Alumni Magazine.* https://yalealumnimagazine.com/articles/3876-who-was-the-first-african-american-student-at-yale.

Zarate, M. E., and Pachon, H. P. (2006). *Equity in offering Advanced Placement courses in California high schools, 1997–2003.* Los Angeles: Tomas Rivera Policy Institute.

Zdroik, J., and Veliz, P. (2016). The influence of pay-to-play fees on participation in interscholastic sports: A school-level analysis of Michigan's public schools. *Journal of Physical Activity and Health, 13*(12), 1317–1324.

Zonta, M. (2019, July 15). Racial disparities in home appreciation. Center for American Progress. https://www.americanprogress.org/issues/economy/reports/2019/07/15/469838/racial-disparities-home-appreciation/.

Zschoche, S. (1989). Dr. Clarke revisited: Science, true womanhood, and female collegiate education. *History of Education Quarterly, 29*(4), 545–569.

Index

About the Author

KIRSTEN HEXTRUM is a former NCAA Division I two-time national champion rower and a current national expert on college athletic admissions. Prior to joining the faculty in educational leadership and policy studies and women's and gender studies at the University of Oklahoma, she worked in academic support services for college athletes and completed her PhD at the University of California, Berkeley. Her work has appeared in top academic journals including *Harvard Educational Review, Studies in Higher Education*, and *Teachers College Record*, in journalistic outlets such as the *Atlantic, Guardian, Boston Globe, Bloomberg News*, and *NPR*, and in the documentary *The Business of Amateurs*.

Available titles in the American Campus series

Printed in the United States
by Baker & Taylor Publisher Services